The Boat People and Achievement in America

The Boat People and Achievement in America

A Study of Family Life, Hard Work, and Cultural Values

Nathan Caplan, John K. Whitmore, and Marcella H. Choy

Ann Arbor   The University of Michigan Press

1992   1991   1990   1989   4   3   2   1

Library of Congress Cataloging-in-Publication Data

Caplan, Nathan S.
   The boat people and achievement in America : a study of family
life, hard work, and cultural values / Nathan Caplan, John K.
Whitmore, and Marcella H. Choy.
      p.   cm.
   Bibliography: p.
   Includes index.
   ISBN 0-472-09397-5 (alk. paper)
   1. Indochinese Americans—Economic conditions.   2.   Indochinese
Americans—Social conditions.   3.   Refugees, Political—United
States.   I.   Whitmore, John K.   II.   Choy, Marcella H., 1940–
III.   Title.
E184.I43C37   1989
306'.0899922—dc19   89-30371
                                                                  CIP

Preface

This project started in 1981 as a large-scale survey designed to assess the economic progress of recently arrived refugees from Indochina. Although we were aware of the plight of the Boat People and concerned with the substantive issues involved, it was the methodological problems that initially consumed our attention and time. There were meetings with federal, state, and local officials to gain access to data relevant to sampling and baseline information. A host of sampling problems arose as a result of incomplete administrative lists of refugees. In the end, an area probability sampling procedure was used to select most of our respondents. The survey questionnaire, in three languages, had to be constructed and pretested. Then seventy-five bi- and trilingual native-speaking interviewers in five sites across the nation had to be hired and trained. The data collection period was hectic. Indeed, project members will not forget the many times we worked through the night in order to keep the study on schedule, handling routine problems of sampling and some not so routine problems arising from the multinational makeup of our refugees—locating a Lao typewriter; working with translators to gain agreement on interpretations in Chinese, Lao, and Vietnamese for questionnaire items; and so on.

At some point in this endeavor, we looked up from the data long enough to realize that what was really going on before us was a natural experiment. It was evident to those of us who traveled to the sites and saw the refugees at the airports arriving from half a world away, with bits of belongings, little or no knowledge of English, and, at best, minimal prior contact with Western ways. They arrived in the United States only to be scattered across the country to cities that varied in physical geography and basic demographics. The one thing common across the sites was the recession: high unemployment levels and record high poverty levels. The experiment had started, and we were a part of it.

A key link in the chain of events leading to the writing of this book was the realization that these refugees were making more progress than had been expected: they were moving out of economic dependency, finding jobs, and climbing out of poverty at a steady pace. Our measures confirmed it. At the same time, we began to take note of news articles reporting on the extraordinary academic accomplishments of the refugees' children. Although Asian scholastic achievement is almost assumed in the United States, it was not expected to occur among these particular Asian children, at least not so soon. They had lost one to three years of schooling in refugee camps, the vast majority came from homes where no one knew any English upon arrival in this country, and most had parents with little education. Moreover, they settled in low-income metropolitan areas, whose schools, while not the very worst, were definitely not the best. We set about studying a subsample of refugees and found, as with the economic achievements of the parents, that these children were indeed doing well, with outcomes that were similar across the sites, despite schools that varied in teaching methods, resources, remedial programs, and innovative reforms. Education, like economic self-sufficiency, seemed to be a normative accomplishment of the refugees, with minimal deviation among the refugees themselves, regardless of the varied circumstances across the country. Here was the challenge to unravel the reasons for their achievements and to relate them to the real world, using both phenomenological and quantitative data and drawing from an interdisciplinary approach.

A survey is of necessity a cooperative undertaking, involving many individuals over a fairly long period of time. We have had the good fortune to have worked with highly dedicated people over the years who gave more than was called for to collect and report on the data about the Boat People. At the height of activity, the project involved some seventy-five native-speaking interviewers and five research coordinators in the field. In addition, there was a permanent research staff of five full-time persons, as well as coders, keypunchers, computer programmers, research assistants, and translators at the Institute for Social Research, University of Michigan. To name them all would be impossible. And yet to each, whose names and efforts we remember still, we owe a deep debt and extend our gratitude.

Nonetheless, with such an enterprise as the one we embarked upon, there need be, and fortunately were, some key individuals without whom the project may never have been started or completed. We would like to acknowledge these individuals here, in appreciation of their help, support, and good advice. Lee Sechrest was critical to the study for his early encouragement to consider the project and, most particularly, for his help in administering and protecting the scientific integrity of the research. Gary Gregg, Janice Harrington, Alison Geist, and Quang Bui bore the day-to-day responsibilities of the study. They, along with Sarah Olson, who handled the secretarial and routine administrative responsibilities with the panache worthy of the head of IBM, made up our inner circle during the early years of the project. Marita Servais took charge of the computer responsibilities, and she, along with the members of the inner circle named above, saw many a dawn break in order to meet deadlines and keep the project together. Our site coordinators, Nancy Volk (Seattle), Zonia Tappenier (Orange County), Arlene McKay (Chicago), Lewis Dratt (Houston), and Kathleen Lique (Boston), oversaw the fieldwork, keeping track of the interviewers and interviews and keeping in touch with us in Ann Arbor. My Keomany and Lai Hong Tran, Indochinese refugees themselves, were particularly outstanding interviewers and informants, who exemplified from the beginning the characteristics that we came to recognize in our sample later. F. Thomas Juster, director of the Institute for Social Research at the time of our study, saw us through some terrible budget crunches and protected us from outside interference. James Wessel, assistant director, provided us with the resources with which to prepare the manuscript toward the end of the writing. Toyo Biddle and Alan Gall, of the Office of Refugee Resettlement (HHS), and Marion Faldet, of the Spencer Foundation, provided us with the funding, without which none of this would have taken place.

Additionally, Kenneth Latta stepped in at critical moments in the preparation of the manuscript to ensure that the word processing would continue apace. Over the years, a set of assistants helped us with the complicated tasks of collecting, structuring, preparing, or typing parts of the manuscript. Fran Eliot, Sheila Addington, Katie Wilcox, and Jill Kern, with patience and good cheer, lived through many drafts, written in different hands. To their disadvantage, we tend to be pencil nibblers rather than word-processor types, and, in consequence, they had to endure longhand copies that were as hard to decipher as the Lao, Chinese, and Vietnamese versions of the questionnaires being used in the field.

Finally, our appreciation to our families for their forbearance and support during the long spells of obsessive work.

We dedicate this book to the groups and individuals who volunteered freely of their time and resources in order to ease the burdens of these refugees during their initial phase of resettlement in the United States. The dedication of this book reflects only a fraction of what their benefaction has meant to the refugees themselves and to others, like ourselves, who support the refugees' efforts to carve out new lives for themselves in the United States.

Contents

Chapter 1
The Boat People

In 1978, hundreds of thousands of people from Vietnam, Cambodia, and Laos began a flight that has become ingrained in our minds as that of the "Boat People." Unlike those who were airlifted out of Vietnam after the fall of Saigon in April, 1975, this second wave of refugees carried much less with them by way of material resources, reflected greater ethnic diversity, was limited in education and occupational skills, and endured great hardship in their attempts to flee the area. While the large majority of these refugees left by sea, many in untrustworthy vessels, others crossed the Mekong River from Laos or made their way across Cambodia into Thailand (see map 1). All of them lived in crowded and unsanitary camps for months or years before leaving for third countries and final asylum.

This movement of the Boat People reflected the ebb and flow of international politics current at the time. The earlier flight of refugees from Vietnam, almost entirely Vietnamese, had slowed considerably by the middle of 1978. Refugees from Laos (Lao, Hmong, and other highland minorities) had been crossing the Mekong for several years, and the Thai government placed them in camps in Northeast Thailand. Cambodia lay under the control of the Khmer Rouge and Pol Pot. Few were leaving that country. In 1978, however, tensions among the Communist nations of East and Southeast Asia reached a boiling point. Already the Chinese in Peking were supporting the socially and nationalistically radical Khmer Rouge regime in Cambodia against the Vietnamese. In April, the Vietnamese regime made a drastic shift in economic policy and moved to restore the urban economy. While this affected both Vietnamese and Chinese within Vietnam, the Chinese of Haiphong in the north and Cholon (adjacent to Saigon) in the south took the brunt of this act. These Chinese were thus caught by the pincers of economic action internally and international political action externally. The Vietnamese saw them as both economic saboteurs and fifth columnists. Whether pushed out or taking the way of least resistance, thousands of Chinese left Vietnam in mid-1978, most by sea on old boats secured through the network of overseas Chinese. Many died on the way, and neighboring Southeast Asian states (Malaysia, Indonesia, and the Philippines), often unwilling to add to their already large Chinese populations, at times pulled the refugee boats back to open waters. These Sino-Vietnamese refugees had little desire to return to China, nor did Peking really want them.

Tensions continued to rise on the international scene as 1978 wore on. The Socialist Republic of Vietnam and the United States were negotiating possible relations until, in the fall, the United States broke off the talks and proceeded to recognize China in December of that year. Vietnam developed closer ties with the Soviet Union, and, seeing China on both sides of them, the Vietnamese attacked China's surrogate in Cambodia—Pol Pot and the Khmer Rouge—at the end of the year. The result was a massive flood of Cambodians (mainly Khmer but with many Chinese and some Chams) over the border into Thailand. The Thai government did not want these people declared as "refugees" in the international sense, for fear that its already overburdened resources would be required to undertake the tremendous task of caring for them. Only long-term negotiations between the United States and Thailand enabled Cambodians to leave for this country.

In the meantime, to relieve Bangkok of some of its problems in dealing with the thousands of Khmer "displaced persons," the United States began to allow more Lao and Hmong, already established in camps in Northeast Thailand, to leave for the United States. At the same time, however, more and more Vietnamese were leaving their country, mainly by sea, as

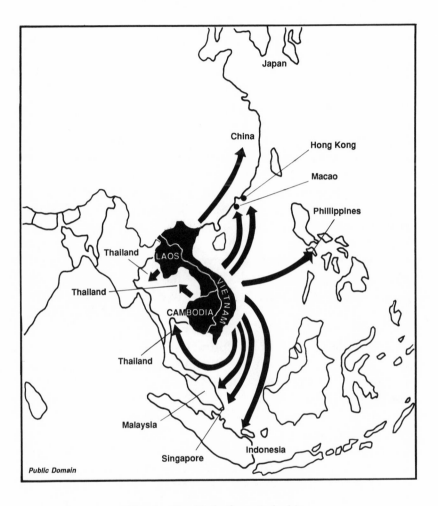

Map 1. The Flight from Indochina

the flow of Chinese from Vietnam ebbed. They, too, suffered the growing predations of pirates in the Gulf of Siam—pillage, rape, and murder.

What can we say about these new arrivals on our shores? For most of us, they appear as an insignificant segment of our population, soon to be absorbed in the melting pot. Is the study of these Indochinese only a curious examination of a tiny, if long-suffering, portion of our people? Or perhaps of an interesting, but small, number of exemplary refugees who have found a niche here? Such views are misleading; their nearly one million members make them our largest Asian minority group. Comparable figures for the other large Asian-American populations, based on the 1980 census, are Chinese, 806,040; Filipinos, 774,652; Japanese, 700,974; Asian Indians, 361,531; and Koreans, 354,593.

The refugees have now begun to share in the Asian-American success stories we have become accustomed to find reported in the news media. They have made these accomplishments despite having entered this country only with what was on their backs. In their heads, however, they brought with them the knowledge of life as they had lived it, despite the recent chaos of their home countries, as well as the desire to establish their families anew, in ways that they believed were possible in their new homeland. Their only resources were the cultural patterns of their societies. With this living framework, they were ready to pursue their lives in new circumstances.

Having survived the difficult, indeed at times horrible, flight from Indochina, these survivors have demonstrated the capacity not to forget it but to go beyond it. Having arrived with little or no English but with a sense of how life ought to be lived, these refugees, especially the children, have rapidly forged ahead in the early stages of resettlement in their new homeland. In later chapters, we will present the results of our large-scale survey, conducted in five sites across the United States, and explore the means by which the refugees have wrought their niche in American society. But for now, let us have them tell how they came to be here.

Few Americans seem to know who these refugees are and what drove them to flee their homelands, risking their lives and those of their children. And even fewer know what their experiences were on the boats, in the refugee camps, and in America, their new home. Here we present several of our respondents from Indochina who are willing to share the stories of their lives and their experiences in Southeast Asia and in the United States.

Life in Indochina

I was born and raised in a middle-class family in Nha Trang, a beautiful city along the central coast of Vietnam, torn by thirty years of war. (Vietnamese)

I was born on April 17, 1951, in a village of ninety houses twenty-five kilometers from Thakhek. My parents were rice farmers, and I had two brothers and a sister. I helped my father by taking care of the buffalos (feeding them after they pulled the plow), and sometimes I also went fishing. I went to the village school, and by the time I was seven years old I had completed the third grade, which was the highest grade taught in my village in 1962. (Lao)

My parents originally came from China. I was born and grew up in Bac-Lieu, a province south of Saigon. I went to Chinese school there.

I am the second son of my parents. My parents had four children, all boys. In Bac-Lieu the highest Chinese education was up to junior high level. When I graduated from junior high, my grandfather did not want me to leave Bac-Lieu and study in Cholon [Saigon's Chinatown]. He wanted me to stay at Bac-Lieu to help the family's business so that my older brother could continue his education in Saigon.

My family's business, which was wholesale and retail sale of agricultural products such as rice, grains, . . . was created by my grandfather. He owned two businesses, one in Cholon and one in Bac-Lieu. He was quite well

known and active in Bac-Lieu's Tsao-Chau community.
He let my father manage the business in Bac-Lieu. In my
family they wanted each son responsible for a different
matter. When I turned twenty years old, all my family
members moved to Cholon and took care of my grandfather's business. The store in Bac-Lieu was handed over
to my uncle. At Saigon, after business hours I studied
and improved my Vietnamese.

I married my wife thirteen years ago. We have two
children, one thirteen-year-old son and one eight-year-
old daughter. My wife's family is also Tsao-Chau. They
owned a retail store; they sold soft drinks and ice. My
wife also went to the Chinese school, but she only finished sixth grade, and she stayed home doing housework. We got married through a matchmaker.

My father died before I got married, so before 1975 my
older brother and I inherited and ran the business. We
lived in a big and old-fashioned family. My grandmother,
my mother, my older brother's family, and my two younger brothers and my family all lived together in a three-
story building in Phung-Hung Street. The ground floor
was for business. We had our meals together. (Chinese)

Escape

In 1975 we thought that if Saigon would fall into the
Communists' hands we would leave, but we stayed instead.

At the end of 1977 my family's business was registered
by the government; we were not allowed to do business
anymore. We understood that we could not live under
that regime; we had no future at all. We especially wanted
a future for our children, so we decided to search for ways
to escape. (Chinese)

In Vietnam there was a modern saying: "If the electric
light poles had feet, they would try to leave." Under the

*Communist regime life was hell, and there was no free-
dom. We couldn't live without freedom. We decided to
escape.* (Vietnamese)

*Former soldiers [Royal Lao army] were assigned to re-
move mines and unexploded bombs dropped by the
American B-52s. They also refilled enormous holes
caused by the bombs and other explosives over the thirty
years of war. Fearing this fate, I was pushed to risk my life
and my children's lives to escape rather than submit to a
future as hopeless as the one I faced in Laos.* (Lao)

*People are unfairly treated there and do not get enough
food and no medical care. I do not like a government that
treats people like machines. So I escaped with my wife
and two children.* (Lao)

*The decision to leave [Vietnam] was one of the most
painful ones in my life. I had to leave everything behind
and face so many uncertainties, being caught and jailed,
storms at sea, starvation and pirates . . . furthermore, I
didn't know what was awaiting me when I got to the new
country. But the Communists were more than I could
handle. Now I am homeless without a real nationality.*
(Vietnamese)

Flight

*When I escaped, I encountered many problems because
Laos and Thailand are separated by the Mekong River. I
had to use a wooden log to swim across the river at night.
I had to swim as quietly as possible. I was very afraid that
I would get caught by the Communists while trying to get
across the river. All I could bring along with me was 600
Baht [Thai money, which was equal to $30 at that time].
What I left behind in Laos were a wooden house, house-*

hold supplies, and other belongings, which were confis-
cated by the Communists. (Lao)

I got permission to go back to my hometown for my
sister's wedding celebration. During the party, at about
8:00 P.M. when everybody was enjoying the drinking,
including the soldiers and police, we left home, went to
the Mekong River (a little over an hour away from the
village), and floated on a wooden post across the Mekong
to the Thai border. That was May 31, 1979. We got to
Moukdahan, Thailand, at 11:00 P.M. I left behind my
parents, sister, brother, three buffalos, and the rice fields.
The rice fields had already been nationalized by the government, but I was worried that they would confiscate
the three buffalos because we escaped. (Lao)

In 1978, I had a friend who lived in a small town of Bac-
Lieu close to the sea and owned a boat. He planned to
escape by this boat with twenty other people. I joined his
plan and stayed in Bac-Lieu for one month to wait for the
departure. When the time was right, I would go home
and take my wife and my children to join them. However,
our plan fell through. We were followed, and his neighbors started to pay attention to his activities, so we scattered. I went back to Saigon. I had no other choice but to
wait for my friend's next plan because I had already paid
him 18 taels of gold for my family. I waited for one year.
In 1979, in Bac-Lieu, the government let people leave
"half-officially." My friend took his boat to Bac-Lieu and
repaired it so that he could carry 220 people. The local
people had to pay him 8 taels of gold for each person; the
people from Saigon had to pay him 9 taels for each. The
gold was paid to him, and it was his responsibility to talk
and arrange with the authority so our names could be on
the list allowed to leave. To leave "half-officially" meant
that the Communists agreed to let us go. Perhaps the
Chinese were not useful to them; they did not want us, so
they let us go. When we left, there were five other boats
leaving at the same time, but three boats returned be-

cause the winds and the storm scared them. My boat kept on going.

On the eighth day we saw a ship. We thought we had arrived at Thailand Bay, so we signaled for help. When we got closer, we knew this was not a foreign ship but a pirate boat. We increased the speed and turned away from them, but they chased us. We stopped. They took my friend, the boat owner, to their boat, and they asked us to go to their boat so that they could give us food and water. We followed their instructions. After we were full, they surrounded us and asked us to hand out every valuable thing we owned. People took out rings, gold. . . . They were not satisfied and said those were not enough. They began checking all over our bodies. They took men to a different place to check—my son fainted; my wife embraced our daughter, who cried without stopping. The pirates checked us one after another. When they were sure that we had nothing left, they let us go back to our boat.

Our boat had just departed for a short distance when another pirate boat attacked. The owner did not stop. They hit and destroyed the edge of one side of our boat. We were very scared. We forced the owner to stop. Not very long after, more pirate boats arrived and surrounded us. This time they could not find anything, so they wanted women and children to go to their boat. No one made a move. At the same time, they found gold hidden by the owner at the chimney of the engine. They were satisfied.

We were lucky. Because the pirates got gold, girls and women were not raped. After we arrived in camp we learned that those on almost every boat that arrived after us were raped and robbed. Each pirate boat had about ten people. They painted their faces; their skins were dark like the Thais. They spoke the Thai language. I also heard one leader of the pirates who spoke Tsao-Chau; it was he who told the pirates to let us go after they found the gold.

In this boat, besides my family, there were also three

members of my third brother's family. My mother and the fourth brother fled first. They also left from Bac-Lieu. Before this, my fourth brother was put in jail for nine months and ten days for trying to escape. After he was released from prison, he escaped the country. My first brother's family left next at Vung-Tau. Then there were seven of us. When we left we carried some clothes, pictures, papers, rings, and money enough for temporary living in camp. But we lost everything except my wife's ID card. The pirates who checked our things threw everything into the sea.

Not very long after that, we got into Malaysian territory. They let us stay there for one night and gave us water. But the next morning they pulled our boat to the middle of the sea and deserted us.

By then we had already lost our compass. We did not know where we were going. We just let the boat go without knowing the direction. But it was not too long until we saw an Indonesian fishing boat, and soon after we were rescued by their coast guard.

The coast guard took us to their fleet. They gave us food and water, then they sent us to Kuku Island.

There were sixty men, ninety women, and a number of children who escaped on the three-by-eighteen-meter boat. We were at sea for nine days. There was one woman just out of the hospital with her newborn child who also left on this boat. Though a lot of people were faint and vomited, all of us survived even from gale-force storms. When we landed there was an old woman age eighty who died. Her family members did not want to take her out because she was too old to travel, but she begged them to take her so that she could see with her own eyes that they landed safely. (Chinese)

Together with some very close friends who had also served in the former South Vietnamese Army, I planned the way to freedom. Unfortunately, on the day of departure the man in charge of the food and navigation equip-

ment couldn't come because the rendezvous area was covered by the Communist coast guard to investigate the drowning of a body that was found on the beach. We couldn't wait. We were well aware of the risk involved, but "either we perish in the sea or we go to prison or we get to freedom." We decided to go on, hoping that if everything was all right, if we could get to the open sea within a day, we could be rescued by an international vessel.

Our boat was eighteen meters in length and two and a half meters in width and carried twenty children and forty-five adults. We left Cam Ranh Bay on the eve of September 16, 1977, without any provisions. There were storms on the high seas. Without the navigation equipment we could not manage the tiny boat. We threw away all five of our fuel-filled tanks and all our possessions to lighten the boat.

We starved for fourteen days. My mother-in-law was the first one who died, then all four of my children and other children, too. Altogether we lost eighteen children and two adults. In those fourteen incredible days, several ships passed by. None of them responded to our cry for help. We were once given some food by a passing Taiwanese merchant ship.

On the eve of the fourteenth day a ship came. This was not a big ship, and we could climb or jump onto it in the dim light of the day. After getting onto the deck, we finally realized that it was a Russian ship. Too late to withdraw! The Russians isolated us and didn't give us anything to eat or drink. The second day aboard we saw land. I asked a sailor in English where we were, and he replied: "Shanghai!" But that was not true. Coming closer, I recognized the port of Da Nang! Ten minutes later the Vietnamese Communist coast guard locked us in jail.

The women and children were released after forty-five days in prison, but all of the men had to remain. I was released after almost three years, thanks to the corruption and solicitation of bribes at many levels of Communist officialdom. I was released under a special condition: the whole family was to go to a "new economic zone." That meant going to an uncertain future, no education for the children, just an exile for the rest of our lives.

My wife asked me to leave the country alone. We were broke. Everything was gone. I stayed with her for two weeks, lived our last days together, and then I escaped to Saigon.

From Saigon I took a bus to the border and walked across the border into Cambodian territory. I walked, rode a bike, buffalo cart, train, truck, or any means of transportation for days and nights. One week later I arrived at the Khmer-Thai border. There troops took me to the Mac Muon camp with other Vietnamese. Thanks to the intervention of the International Red Cross, we were released and transferred to Camp 007 in Thailand and then to Khao I Dang refugee camp. That was at the end of March, 1980. I was there until October. (Vietnamese)

Life in the Camps

While I was in a refugee camp in Thailand, I had the most difficult time. Specifically, the room was so narrow. Lack of food and water. The ration distributed by Thai authorities was so limited. It was necessary for me to sneak outside the camp, which was prohibited, to look for work to earn extra money. I worked very hard to earn a little money to meet my daily needs. If I got caught by the Thai officer, I would be punished for doing so. The Thai officer insulted and mistreated us like animals.

While waiting to come to the United States, I imagined that life in the United States must be hard for us, because of the language barrier and different culture as well as climate. But in my thoughts, I was willing to struggle with all the problems that I might encounter. (Lao)

My life in the refugee camp in Thailand was terrible. They treated us like animals. They were inhuman. (Vietnamese)

In the camp in Thailand life was very hard. They had the power to take care of us but treated us like we were not human. In the United States it is different; things are good, and we have freedom. (Lao)

Khao I Dang, a refugee camp in Thai territory, was little more than a prison camp, crowded with more than one hundred thousand people living in terrible conditions with minimal food, medical services, and shelter and no recreational or educational activities. Also, the Thai government was always saying that Thailand would force us back to our homeland because we were a very heavy burden on them.

After eight months living in Khao I Dang, I was transferred to Chan Bu Ri camp to be interviewed for resettlement. Then came the day they announced the decision. Some were eligible to go directly to the United States because they had relatives there. The rest would be transferred again to Galang in Indonesia for training during the transition period. I was in the latter group.

Galang was really a refugee camp, where the refugees were well prepared to get ready for the adjustments to the new culture, the new way of life in America. There were cultural orientation classes, work experience classes, short-term vocational training classes, and English-as-a-second-language [ESL] classes which used audiovisual methods. I took the ESL classes and tried hard for days and nights to study and practice the new language with some other refugees. (Vietnamese)

Six months after I escaped to Thailand, my wife and children escaped to Thailand, too. At that time it was the dry season; the Mekong River was dry in places. My wife and children walked across the Mekong River, and I went to pick them up at the border.

We had a complete family in the camp. We had a small room. We got food from the United Nations. The food wasn't good but was enough for us to survive. I had to find a job. I got a job outside of the camp. At that time it was easy to go out of the camp or come back. My job was cutting wood. Sometimes the Thai bosses cheated the Laotian workers. They didn't want to pay us. If they paid, they paid a very low salary because we were Laotian refugees. My three children went to school in the camp offered by the United Nations. They studied English. It was very hard for me and my family in the camp. I worried about my parents, children, life. I didn't know how I could raise my children. I didn't know what was going to happen to us next.

The situation in the camp was very bad. There was a lot of robbery, even killings. A lot of Lao Hmong were killed in camp because the Lao Hmong had silver that they used for making jewelry. There wasn't enough food. My wife stayed home and took care of the children. We waited for our parents to escape for about two years, but they didn't. Then we decided to register to go to another country. My friends told us not to stay in Thailand. We applied to go to France, Argentina, and the United States. I wanted to come to the United States, but if one of those countries had called me first, I would have gone. (Lao)

Expectations

[While in the camp] we received information from relatives or friends in the United States advising us to learn English and get ready to make a big change in our lives. We were also told that to survive in the United States was not easy; there were other ethnic groups from Asia and Europe who had been in America for decades, there was competition in the job market, and there were prejudices, tension, and discrimination. Most of us believed

that we could overcome all obstacles to survive. Any country in the free world should be better than Communist Vietnam. (Vietnamese)

When I lived in the camp, many people received letters from friends and relatives that told them not to be afraid to go to the United States. The government would help them until they were able to stand on their feet. The government would let them study English and a skill, send children to school, and give them free lunch and food stamps. If you could work, the future was there to build. The majority of people worried because they did not know what kind of job they could do if they did not speak English.

As for me, I just was afraid of not knowing the language, but then I thought of the government's resettlement program—and that there would be someone to meet me at the airport and take me into a house with furniture and plenty of food in the refrigerator. I was half convinced and half suspicious but, even so, very excited about our new life ahead. (Chinese)

I want the magnificent "American Dream": a wife, a dog, a house, a bathroom. (Lao)

Arrival

All we brought with us was mosquito nets, blankets, rice baskets, and five Lao national skirts.

We arrived on Friday, January 14, 1980, at 2:00 P.M. A Laotian friend met us at the airport, and an agency arranged an apartment for us for the first month. We slept during the day and felt drowsy until the following Monday. A friend of mine, who had been here longer, took me to the agency, where we got information about how to use the stove and oven, catch the bus (paying when you get on when on the way to town and when you get off when coming from town). We were told that for security reasons we should look through the hole in the door when someone knocked at the door and not to open it if we didn't know them, especially at night. A neighbor said I should have something to spray in the face of people who might try to break into my apartment. (Lao)

We got to the United States in December, 1979. The sponsor and the caseworker were waiting for us when we got out of the plane. We were happy to be in the United States, but we were anxious, not knowing what life would really be like. We didn't know the sponsor or how they would take care of us. We had heard in letters from our friends that the sponsor would take good care of us. We stayed with the sponsor the first night. Our sponsor was an American family. We were surprised at their nice house, good food. I could not speak English. I had to open the dictionary every time I wanted to say something to the sponsor.

We were very tired when we first arrived. After one night we moved to our own apartment. For four days after we moved, we just stayed home. We slept during the day and watched TV during the night. We were very surprised to see snow. Our sponsor really took good care of us. He bought food and sticky rice for us. He took us to apply for public aid and to see the doctor. He gave us a weekly allowance. He bought boots and coats for my family and took my children to register for English classes at the community college. (Lao)

When we arrived at the airport, my mother, my older brother, his American friend, my mother's sponsor who is American, and a representative of the agency met us. It was so good to see each other again. Then my mother's sponsor took us to her home; served us refreshments; gave us blankets, cookware, and household items; and sent us to this apartment.

When we first stepped into this apartment, we were

quite surprised because it was empty. We thought we had to sleep on the floor again. My brother had rented this apartment two days before. That night we stayed at my mother's house. The next morning, we went back to clean the apartment and moved in right away. Then my brother and mother took us to the supermarket. My wife and I were very surprised and felt awkward because people just picked goods from the shelf and put them into their carts without bargaining, as in Vietnam. It was so easy to shop here. No one had told me about this.

The subway was different from trains in Vietnam. We found the Americans very well groomed and well dressed. We arrived in August, so we did not feel cold.

When we first arrived, the agency gave my family $1,000. We paid the rent and the deposit for the apartment. The remaining was enough for that month's living expenses. Several days later, my brother made an appointment with the department of public aid and went with us to apply for assistance. While waiting for the approval from public aid, we were worried about the rent because we had to pay soon. My wife went to the agency to ask for help. They gave us another month's rent. Then we got our public aid, so our living was temporarily settled.

My wife was sad because she did not know if she would see her family again. They were still in Vietnam. No one was able to escape. She had two brothers who tried to escape once, but they did not succeed and were put in jail. They were released, but they did not have money to escape again. Hopefully, ODP [Orderly Departure Program] would eventually bring them here. Her family thought we had died at sea because they had no news from us six months after we escaped. They later learned we were alive.

One week after we arrived, my brother told me that the community college had opened new ESL classes. He asked us whether we wanted to study or not. My wife and I immediately went there to register. For the first four months, we did not have bus fare assistance, so we walked to classes every day. The ESL class in the United States was good because the teacher was American, so we got to speak English with her. My English improved a lot.

At the beginning we bought and tried a lot of American foods. We bought some hot dogs, cheeses, pickles, Jell-O, potato chips. . . . It tasted delicious when we first tried it. Now we do not like them anymore. For the first two months we did not drink milk. Then we heard that our bodies needed milk, especially for the cold weather, so we started to buy milk, and I heated the milk before I drank it. I did this only once or twice; after that we just drank milk right out of the refrigerator. After we were here for one month, my brother's American friend invited us to the restaurant to try hamburger and pizza. At that time it was delicious; now we do not like it anymore.

Some of the furniture we had was picked up by me from the street. Some was given by my mother's sponsor and friends. After I was employed, I had money to buy new things and replaced the very old and torn ones.

At the community college we made friends with a Vietnamese lady. She had lived here for many years and sometimes took my family to her house in the suburbs and showed us a lot of scenery. Sometimes I took my wife and the children to a museum and downtown by subway.

After I finished the Indochinese program at the community college (nine months), I applied for vocational training in auto-body repair. I wanted to learn this skill because I thought it was good for my career. In the United States, there were a lot of cars, and surely the repair services would always be in demand. I am happy that I chose the right skill to learn. Without this training, I would not have been hired for my present job. In the auto-body training class, there were five Chinese-Vietnamese students. After the training, we went to this company to apply for a job; two weeks later all of us were hired.

I felt bitter when I got here, because in Vietnam our

business had been established for three generations. We worked hard to build our lives again from zero. As refugees, we accepted starting all over again. I got much assistance. When I just arrived here, I got public aid. Then I got the vocational training, and I was employed after that. I feel happy and consoled with my present situation. (Chinese)

The most distressful fact is the brutal and radical change in the moral code. We Asians think differently. I understand that I have to readjust myself to the new society in order not to be rejected. So I try to reach a harmony between occidental and oriental cultures.

Right now I am doing well. I have a job, my wife is about to graduate in computer science, and so our future seems pretty much assured.

Though I am faithful to my country and cultural values, I am grateful to this nation and its people for granting me liberty and security. (Vietnamese)

Overview

The refugees from the countries of Indochina who came to the United States have two aspects of their lives that we must remember. The first is what they inherited from their parents—their ideas of how life should be lived. The second is their experiences in homelands whose histories in the twentieth century have been marked by political, social, and cultural struggles that have continued to the present day. The ever-evolving traditions of these varied peoples have received rough treatment, particularly in recent years. Many of the refugees have come out of situations very different from those in which the ideals of their societies were rooted. The wars, the mass movements of populations, the great explosion of urban dwellers, and the desperate struggle for survival in chaotic times all have shaken the relationships between past and present.

Nevertheless, experiences and ideals of past life and the values of social relations and family remain and are being utilized to adjust to life in this country. The struggle to determine what of the past is of value and what may be abandoned continues. Though it is taking place in a different country and a different culture, in many respects this reformulation of cultural and social values is still a part of previous dilemmas. The twentieth century has seen, particularly in Vietnam, the need to mesh indigenous patterns with the modern world. Indeed, the story of the modern history of the region has been cultural and social chaos as well as war and political struggle. The problem of how to handle "the modern" is thus a dilemma brought to this country and intensified here. Even though they now find themselves amid different hills and rivers and even though a different history sits upon the land, few among them will abandon completely the place whence they came.

In our research on the Indochinese refugees, we have attempted to assess their level of economic self-sufficiency and scholastic achievement since arriving in the United States. In this work, we will present our findings and attempt to explain the basis for their achievements. Chapter 2 presents a detailed picture of the refugees, their native countries, and the relevant historical backdrop and demographics, with some detail on the characteristics of the three ethnic groups studied— Vietnamese, Chinese, and Lao. Also described are features of the escape from Indochina, the stay in refugee camps, arrival in the United States, and the organizational efforts and programs to assist them during the early stages of resettlement. Finally, the household and value patterns of the refugees are examined in some detail.

Chapter 3 presents the economic and educational achievements of the refugees. With respect to economic status, data are presented on employment, characteristics of the jobs held, income sources, and poverty-level standing. Particular emphasis is given to the changes in these variables over time and significant directions in their trajectories. The academic achievements of the children in the refugee households

are presented in terms of grade point average (GPA) by subject area across the five sites and standardized achievement
test results, namely the California Achievement Test (CAT)
scores. The latter are presented to give a sense of the relative
standing of these children in terms of national norms. The
meaning of the results, in both an absolute and a relative
sense, is discussed.

Chapter 4 presents an explanation for the Indochinese
refugees' economic and educational achievements. Here we
explore the role of their cultural values and family life in
effecting these outcomes. Key predictor variables, identified
as a result of a variety of statistical analyses of the data base,
represent our effort to configurate a sense of the achieving (or
nonachieving) family. Finally, we note the importance of an
opportunity structure, without which all efforts at economic
and educational success are for naught.

Chapter 5 presents a recapitulation of the influences on
economic and educational outcomes and discusses the meaning of the research results and their implications in terms of
larger societal and national issues. In this chapter, we focus
chiefly on the educational crisis in America; we look at the
basis for a negative perception of our school system and relate
our findings on educational achievement, cultural values, and
family interaction to the problem.

Chapter 2
Profile of the Refugees

I still have what is needed to start over: willpower, patience, and hard work. (Vietnamese)

Our study examines what is, in a sense, a natural experiment, because the unforeseen and contingent historical circumstances under which the refugees arrived in the United States provided the opportunity for study of their progress under conditions very much like those of a true experiment. When the refugees arrived, they landed with a clean slate and started from scratch. Their material possessions were virtually identical: little more than the clothes on their backs. Thus, when we speak of what they brought with them, the referent is not their material possessions but their cultural heritage. Once here, the refugees were scattered across the continent, to sites that differed in geography, economy, and demographic makeup. From the standpoint of social science methodology, these conditions are close to ideal for drawing conclusions with confidence and inferential clarity from communitywide "open air" research.

A special problem, however, associated with the study of any refugee group in their host country is whether or not those who left differ in important ways from those who remained behind. This selection process may result in a creaming off of those who are, in fact, more likely to succeed, compared to those who remained. In the case of the Boat People, there may also be an issue of selective survival. It is reported that about 50 percent of the boats that left Vietnam with refugees experienced deaths of family members because of the viciousness of Thai pirates or the exigencies of the migration. Possibly one-half or more of the boats and passengers that reached the open seas perished. Those who escaped by land probably had a high percentage of survivors, but the conditions in the refugee camps were abysmal, and near-starvation and diseases took their toll. Thus, it is possible that preselection in conjunction with survival factors may have resulted in bias toward resettlement success for those who made it to the United States. We can only speculate about the character and extent of such bias. It is a fact of life to be taken into consideration in conducting and interpreting such research.

We can say, however, that the refugees included in the present study—those who left Southeast Asia in 1978 or later—differ demographically from those who came out at the fall of Saigon in 1975 (Montero 1979). The more recent refugees arrived with fewer material resources, personal contacts in the United States, education, job skills, English language skills, and westernization experience in general. In every sense, therefore, they are more like "ordinary" Indochinese than those who preceded them to the United States.

The main source of data for this study derives from two rounds of survey interviews with refugee samples in five sites across the nation: Seattle, Orange County (California), Chicago, Houston, and Boston. The first round was conducted in 1981, on 1,384 households comprised of 6,775 individuals. The second took place in 1984, using a subsample of the first study. Three ethnic groups—Vietnamese, Chinese-Vietnamese, and Lao—which made up the major ethnic components of the Boat People at the time of our first survey, were included in the study. Interviews were conducted in the respondents' native languages by native-speaking interviewers.

Demographic patterns for nonrefugee neighbors across the five sites are similar. The nonrefugees residing in areas from which we drew our samples are mainly white. The site that differs most from the others with respect to the white/ nonwhite ratio for residential integration is Boston, where blacks make up approximately 10 percent of the inhabitants in our sampling areas. The principal difference among the whites residing in these neighborhoods pertains to the Anglo/ Hispanic balance. The whites in Boston, Chicago, and Seattle sampling areas are almost exclusively from Anglo backgrounds, whereas roughly 30 percent of the whites in Orange County and Houston are Mexican-American and Chicano. Further details on design, sampling, site selection, data base, and statistical analyses done are included in the Appendix (pp. 181–204).

In this chapter, we provide empirical data on the Boat People included in our study. We include information on where they came from and their backgrounds, their length of stay in the camps, their status upon arrival in the United States, and the supportive services available to them. Finally, we look at two important resources within the people themselves: the organization of their families and households and their cultural values, the patterns and ideals of which are rooted in their native cultures. Yet, despite the transplantation, these cultural "vestiges" have proven robust and have much significance for an understanding of their progress in resettling in America.

In Southeast Asia

About half of the households in this study are ethnic Vietnamese, 20 percent are ethnic Chinese from Vietnam, and 30 percent are ethnic Lao. All came from lowland civilizations and participated in the major religions of these countries. Half the Vietnamese and Chinese households identify themselves as Mahayana Buddhist, following that form of salvationist Buddhism common to East Asia. A fifth are Roman Catholic, double their representation in Vietnam's population, and a sixth may be seen as Confucian, following ancestral rituals and precepts of the Chinese sage. The Lao households are almost all Theravada Buddhist, holding the merit-oriented belief system of mainland Southeast Asia. Several households of all three ethnic groups are Protestant, reflecting American influences, and 10 percent declare that they hold no religious preference.

The flow of people during the war years in Vietnam and Laos was toward the capital cities of Saigon and Vientiane and the regions south of them, areas away from most of the fighting. The heavy majority of the refugees from Vietnam, both Vietnamese and Chinese, came from the southern third of the country, known in colonial times as Cochinchina. Half the respondents from Vietnam were born and raised in this area and were joined by the third of the respondents who had left southeastern China, the northern segment of Vietnam (Tonkin), or its central area (Annam) to come south. In Laos, more than a third of the respondents were born and raised around Vientiane, where another sixth joined them from other parts of the country. Almost all the rest (about 40 percent) lived in the provinces of the south (Khammouane, Savannakhet, Sedone, and Champassak), areas under Royal Lao Government control and close to Thailand.

The devastation of the war years led to a great increase in the number of urban residents, and more than three-quarters of the respondents had lived in the cities for at least some portion of their lives; less than a quarter lived exclusively in the countryside. Almost all the Chinese (87 percent) and Vietnamese (83 percent) came from the cities; only 62 percent of the Lao were urban. It is no surprise, then, that the Lao respondents had the greatest number of farmers and that the Chinese consistently held urban occupations (shopkeepers, clerks, assistants, construction workers, auto mechanics, machine operators, and factory workers). Professionals and fishermen were most likely to have been Vietnamese.

The levels of education among the three groups also reflect what the occupational patterns tell us. The Vietnamese had a much greater interest in higher education than did the Chinese or the Lao. The major focus of the Chinese had been on secondary education. For most of the Lao, primary education had been the main form available to them. Thus, 79 percent of Lao adults, 57 percent of Chinese adults, and 36 percent of Vietnamese adults had not gone beyond elementary school; almost two-thirds of the Vietnamese, less than half of the Chinese, and less than a quarter of the Lao had attended high school; and 14 percent of the Vietnamese, 4 percent of the Chinese, and 5 percent of the Lao had gone to college.

Males were more likely than females to have gone farther in school. Only a third of the adult women had gone beyond elementary school, whereas more than half of the men had. Males were predominant at all levels of advanced education. The women who worked outside the home were just as likely as men to have been farmers, shopkeepers, or factory workers.

A comparison of the refugees in the study and their compatriots who stayed at home shows that the Chinese in our sample are closest to being representative of their home society. Their highly urban background, medium educational levels, and urban skills are undoubtedly not too different from those of their community in Vietnam. In that the Lao refugees are more rural, less educated, and more agriculturally oriented than the Chinese and the Vietnamese, they, too, have a similarity to the society they left behind. Nevertheless, Lao society is even more heavily rural and agricultural than is represented by the Lao refugees, who are about six times more likely to be urban than those found in Lao society. Accordingly, their educational level is on the average higher, and their occupations in Laos were considerably more often nonagricultural than is true for Lao society at large. The Vietnamese refugees, with the exception of those in fishing, are almost entirely urban, yet in their society Vietnamese are most often rural. Only 3 percent of the Vietnamese refugees identified themselves as farmers, many times lower than what we would expect in an occupational census of Vietnam.

The refugees as a whole, then, are much more urban, more highly educated, and skilled in jobs more related to the urban environment than the majority in the societies they left behind. Nevertheless, in comparison to the first wave of Indochinese refugees who left in 1975, those who fled in 1978 and later are much more diverse ethnically and have less education, poorer English proficiency, and lower job skills. The 1975 group of Vietnamese tended to have higher status in their home society (i.e., better education and higher-status occupations) and to have had much more contact with the Americans in Vietnam (Dunning 1982; Montero 1979). The later refugees represent a much broader spectrum of Indo-chinese society than those who came after the fall of Saigon in 1975.

From the Camps to America

The details of the movement of these refugees from their homelands onto the international scene is best left to their own narratives, which we sampled in chapter 1. We feel that their perilous escapes and their desperate lives in the camps of first asylum should not be probed for statistical use. We shall attempt instead only a general outline of the time in the camps of Southeast Asia and the movement from the camps to this country.

The refugees spent varying lengths of time in these camps before their departure for the United States. The Southeast Asian camps in which the refugees sought safety and waited for placement in the United States were basically of two types: those of first asylum in Thailand and Malaysia and those established by the United States for the refugees already guaranteed entry to this country. The main U.S. camp is on the Bata-an peninsula on Luzon in the Philippines. Almost two-thirds of our respondents spent as long as a year of total camp time awaiting their move to the United States. The remaining third waited as long as three years or more.

Breaking these figures down by ethnicity, the Lao were in the camps for the longest time. On the average, they spent more than a year and a half (almost twenty months), mostly in the first-asylum camps of Northeast Thailand. The Chinese were in the first-asylum camps around the South China Sea and spent an average of a year in both first-asylum and Ameri-can camps; the Vietnamese were in those same camps for a somewhat shorter period, an average of nine months. Indeed, 81 percent of the Vietnamese were in the camps for a year or less, compared to 62 percent of the Chinese and only 47 percent of the Lao. Twenty-three percent of the Lao spent more than two years in the camps, compared to less than 3 percent of the Chinese and just over 1 percent of the Vietnamese.

While in the American camps, the refugees had the opportunity to study English and to take part in a variety of counseling and training sessions. Almost a quarter of the refugees reported that they took English classes there. A quarter of the Lao and the Vietnamese were able to take advantage of these classes, but only 14 percent of the Chinese did, probably reflecting the early arrival of the latter.

The movement of the refugees from the camps in Southeast Asia to the United States took place in three well-defined periods. The first began in October, 1978, and ended by the summer of 1980. (With the large number of Cuban and Haitian entrants that June, all refugee quotas seemed to shift to the Caribbean.) The second period, from July, 1980, through September, 1981, saw the pace increase. Although the rates of immigration throughout this period were more consistent, there was more diversity with regard to the countries of origin of the immigrants. In this phase, there were more Cambodians and Laotians than in the first period, but Vietnamese remained the majority in both phases. The third period, beginning in October, 1981, witnessed a significant decline in the numbers of Indochinese refugees coming into the United States, with, at least initially, a much higher proportion of refugees from Cambodia and a decline in the percentage from Laos.

In terms of ethnicity, the Chinese tended to arrive earliest. Almost two-thirds were in the country by late 1980. The Lao have been here the next longest, with more than half having arrived by that date. Less than half of the Vietnamese have been here that long.

Arrival and Assistance

Members of this second wave of Indochinese refugees arrived on American shores with almost no material possessions, their only riches being what they carried in their heads: their cultural background and their experiences. Their health was generally good. Only 22 percent of the respondents (21 percent of the men and 29 percent of the women) reported health problems on arrival. A strong correlation existed between age and health: only 10 percent of those in their teens had health problems when they came here, but 37 percent of those in their fifties and more than half of those sixty or older reported some health concerns.

Because competence in English is a key factor in the adjustment and resettlement of immigrants and refugees in the United States, we inquired into proficiency in English at the point of entry into the United States. Three measures of English competence were employed. The first two are based on five-point scales indicating arrival-level proficiency in reading and speaking. Based on these self-assessments of their competence in English, we found that almost 66 percent professed no proficiency in the language at all, 20 percent had the barest proficiency, 10 percent knew some English but not well, and only 6 percent possessed what might be called a reasonable grasp of the language.

The third measure, similarly scaled from 1 to 5 in proficiency, is related to seven specific tasks in which English is necessary. Here, one in three of the refugees reported that they could shop for food or get around in the city; one in five said that they could call the police or fire department; and one in nine said that they could apply for aid, talk to a doctor about a health problem, or read a newspaper. Only one in twenty believed that they could hold a job as a salesperson in terms of the language skills demanded.

Interesting as these individual-level proficiency measures are, a more comprehensive sense of the average English proficiency of the refugees when they first arrived in the United States may be gained by using the household as the unit of analysis. Our findings in general support the view that the refugees' households represent a collection of resources upon which the individuals in them may draw. Initially, at least, during the period of dependency on cash assistance, a household will survive if it includes only one person whose English ability enables him or her to shop for food or to interact with agency personnel, landlords, and so on. (To a lesser degree, this is also true of job skills.) This situation is hardly ideal, but it does incorporate the practical realities of the transition the refugees have been undergoing. Using a combination of reading, speaking, and behavioral indices, we found that in nearly three out of four (73 percent) of the households, the majority of adults, by their own reports, did not have any English ability when they arrived. A comparison of the three ethnic groups on these measures shows that the Vietnamese have consistently higher scores than the two other groups. In more than a third of the Vietnamese households, the majority of adults knew at least some English when they arrived.

Overall, then, few households had much command of English when they arrived, and in the overwhelming majority most adults had none. This deficiency proved to be a major problem for the refugees as they attempted to make their way in the labor markets of America. In summary, we may say that the Vietnamese arrived with greater English skills than the Chinese or Lao; men reported higher fluency than women; former urban dwellers had more than rural residents; those in their thirties and forties had more than either older or younger refugees; and those with higher levels of education and occupational status had much greater fluency on arrival than those with lower educational and occupational backgrounds.

Service Agencies

The development of services specifically for these refugees paralleled the growth of the refugee communities themselves. Initial efforts made to accommodate the refugees (i.e., those who fled Vietnam in 1975) laid the foundation for expanded services when the surge of second-wave, post-1978 refugees arrived. The Interagency Task Force for Indochinese Refugees (IATF), composed of eighteen federal departments and agencies, was responsible for the evacuation and resettlement of the first-wave refugees. However, the massive influx of second-wave refugees required a greater federal effort. In response, the Refugee Act of 1980 was enacted to set up a permanent mechanism for the admission of refugees to the United States, while providing for a comprehensive and uniform program of assistance and services to facilitate their resettlement. It established the Office of Refugee Resettlement (ORR) within the Department of Health and Human Services to administer the domestic resettlement program.

The role of IATF and ORR in refugee resettlement has been to allocate funds, keep track of the refugees, and organize resettlement strategies. The basic effort for refugee resettlement, however, comes from private nonprofit agencies, which are generally local affiliates of national voluntary agencies (Volags). Volags involved in Southeast Asian refugee resettlement include U.S. Catholic Conference (USCC), Lutheran Immigration and Resettlement Service (LIRS), Church World Services, International Rescue Committee, United Hebrew Immigration and Assistance Service, and American Council of Nationality Services. These agencies supply initial resettlment services (housing, food, utensils), orientation, counseling, and referral services. At the time of the study, Volags were granted $500 for each Southeast Asian resettled, to cover the expenses incurred in the process.

Individual agencies at particular sites may also offer services such as English classes, job development programs, or programs for women or the elderly. Additionally, each of the five sites had its own system to provide English language training (ESL) and employment services.

Sponsorship

All refugees or refugee families entering the United States are required to have a local sponsor who is responsible for their initial economic and social support. Sponsors of the refugees could be related or unrelated individuals, churches, or, when no other sponsor was available, a Volag. In fact, sponsorship of refugees became the primary activity of the latter. The American Council of Voluntary Agencies (ACVA), the Volags' umbrella organization, reviewed the files of refugees residing in the first-asylum camps and secured Volag sponsorship for those in need, who then moved into the American camps.

On arrival, the refugee families have either been scattered across the country according to the availability of local sponsors, placed with local branches of the Volags, or, through family reunification, located with close relatives. At the local level, 38 percent of our respondents were sponsored by relatives, 29 percent by local branches of the voluntary agencies, 16 percent by local churches, and 8 percent each by individual Americans or by unrelated Southeast Asians. The pattern of sponsorship suggests that the earlier arrivals tended to have more individual, local sponsors (churches, American families), much like the pattern that pertained in 1975. As the influx grew, however, the burden of sponsorship shifted more directly to local offices of the voluntary agencies and to previously settled refugee families. This pattern may be seen in the fact that 46 percent of the earliest arrivals, the Chinese, were sponsored by local American individuals and churches (as opposed to 20 percent of the Lao and 16 percent of the Vietnamese), whereas 46 percent of the Vietnamese were sponsored by relatives and 29 percent by local offices of the voluntary agencies. Among the Lao, the second of the three groups to arrive, 42 percent were settled by local voluntary agencies and 30 percent by relatives (in contrast to the Chinese, among whom 33 percent were sponsored by relatives and only 12 percent by the local voluntary agencies).

Thus, as the refugees continued to pour into this country from 1978 on (eventually reaching more than half a million for the second wave alone), sponsorship tended to shift away from local individuals and churches, those sponsors with relatively limited access to resources. Over time, resettlement, on the one hand, became a more institutionalized effort with better organization and access to resources, while, on the other hand, it became more the responsibility of local Indochinese communities and families.

Secondary Migration

Once the refugees were placed with a local sponsor, there was little to prevent secondary migration to another city within the state or another part of the country. An unknown number of refugees have migrated since their arrival, with the majority tending to go south and west. In our survey, 15 percent had moved from their initial placement site. The main reasons given for movement were family reunification and job opportunities. Cash assistance and other programs seem to have provided little incentive to move. Of those who had migrated in our study, one-sixth had gone from one site to another within the same state, and five-sixths had resettled from a different state. The above figures on secondary migration came from direct questioning of the refugees regarding their movements in the United States.

Another source of information on secondary migration derives from our examination of data collected from former neighbors of respondents in our sampling frame whom our interviewers could not locate. Among the nonlocatable respondents who had moved, California was the main destination. Three of the five states in our study—Texas, Washington, and California (and, to a lesser degree, Illinois as well)—had movement within them; Massachusetts appears to have been the exception. In the early 1980s, there was movement into the Texas-Oklahoma-Louisiana region and a general scattering of moves to a variety of other states. This pattern is also reflected in our data on those who had moved by site—29 percent of the respondents in Orange County had moved, whereas the percentages for Houston (14 percent), Chicago and Seattle (13 percent), and Boston (8 percent) are, at most, not even half as high.

Cash Assistance

Public assistance programs vary somewhat from site to site, a fact partly reflective of differences in state philosophies on social welfare. The primary public assistance program, however, is a joint federal-state program, Aid to Families with Dependent Children (AFDC), which provides assistance to single-parent families or families in which the second parent is "unemployable." At the time of the study, monthly payment levels for a family of four on AFDC in the five sites varied from approximately $601 in California to $118 in Texas, with Washington ($541), Massachusetts ($445), and Illinois ($368) falling between these two extremes. Massachusetts, Illinois, and California also had the "unemployed parent" (UP) option in AFDC, which allows eligibility for families with both parents living in the household if the parent designated as primary wage earner meets a criterion demonstrating temporary unemployed status.

Refugee Cash Assistance (RCA) is a federal program administered through each state to refugees who do not meet the family composition requirement of AFDC or AFDC-UP but who otherwise meet all of the income and resource eligibility criteria for AFDC and AFDC-UP. RCA is available to eligible refugees during the first eighteen months after their arrival in the United States.

The greatest variation among sites with regard to assistance exists in the area of state or local General Assistance (GA) programs. Whereas AFDC and RCA are of federal origin and involve federal funds, GA programs originate in state or local laws and therefore provide for the needs of poor residents in differing ways and degrees.

All five sites require some form of registration for those receiving cash assistance. Furthermore, in mid-1982, the federal government began to require everyone on AFDC and RCA to submit monthly reports on their eligibility. Only the state of Washington had implemented this requirement by the time of the study. The complexity of the form resulted in a good deal of confusion among the refugees, and, in one instance, some one hundred fifty families lost their eligibility because they did not submit the proper forms (*Seattle Times*, October 4, 1982, and October 19, 1982).

Household Composition

The three ethnic groups in our sample come from societies whose patterns of social organization differ. The Lao lived in a bilateral society that did not stress either the paternal or maternal lines; they counted as kin those related to them on both sides and did not have rigidly organized clans. The Vietnamese, particularly among the elite, had normative rules stressing the father-son relationship in a society that had many elements similar to the Lao; a clan form might be the ideal for the Vietnamese, but it had not reached a high level of development in that society. For the Chinese, on the other hand, the patrilineal, father-son relationship is at the core of the culture, and the rigid clan form reached its highest development in southeastern China, the original home of the overseas Chinese. In addition, once they had left China and settled overseas, these Chinese formed associations based on dialect and provincial or local origin.

The rules of immigration into the United States, however, do not allow any but the immediate family to enter together. Thus, on initial arrival, the households tend to be made up of just such nuclear families. With the passage of time, secondary migration and successful efforts at family reunification brought diverse members of the large family organizations together. The resulting structures of the refugees' households in this country reflect the extended families of earlier native forms, with a decided American influence toward nuclear organization. The forms taken by the refugee households in this country and seen in our study are defined as follows:

- Single(s): unrelated single individual(s).
- Nuclear family: husband and wife or parent(s) and child(ren) and possibly one grandparent.
- Extended family: combination of nuclear family and others related by blood or marriage *or* a household of relatives without a nuclear family being present.

- Multiple families: any combination of two or more family units unrelated to each other.

Of the adults in the respondents' households, 1,730 are immediate family members (spouses, children, siblings, parents, and grandparents), 187 are relatives outside the nuclear family (aunts, cousins, nieces, etc.), and 158 are in-laws. In addition, 698 in our sample are unrelated to the other household members with whom they share quarters.

The overwhelming majority of the adults in our sample live in or with either nuclear families (45.5 percent) or extended families (38.6 percent). Table 1 displays this information for all adults and all households. The proportion of households is higher for nuclear (53.2 percent) and lower for extended (32 percent). When we look at the total proportion of households that include a single or singles, it is 22 percent—nearly a quarter of the households in the sample. In addition, virtually all the households we surveyed include two or more adults (persons aged sixteen or older and thus potentially employable): only 8 percent of the households have one adult, 40 percent have two, and the remaining majority have at least three adults.

While we are interested in the number of adults per household, for their economic potential as wage earners, we

TABLE 1.　Household Composition for All Adults and All Households

	All Adults ($N = 4{,}160$)	All Households ($N = 1{,}384$)
Single (one)	1.7%	4.7%
Unrelated singles	6.4	5.5
Nuclear family	39.0	48.2
Nuclear family plus single(s)	6.5	5.1
Extended family	31.2	27.2
Extended family plus single(s)	7.4	4.8
Multiple families	3.9	2.6
Multiple families plus single(s)	3.8	1.9

are also interested in the number of children and their ages, because of their potential to affect the economy of the family. Without much earning power, the refugees will have difficulty keeping their children fed, clothed, and warm. But the *ages* of the children in our sample, not their presence alone, can be crucial to the refugees' current or potential self-sufficiency; young children may preclude the opportunity for adults (especially women) to prepare themselves for or to take jobs.

In terms of household composition and children, we found that about 70 percent of the households included one or more children less than sixteen years old. Among the entire sample, 17 percent of the households have one child, 20 percent have two, 14 percent have three, and another 14 percent have four or five; 5 percent of the households include between six and nine children. Of those households with children, nearly two-thirds needed someone, presumably an adult member, to care for preschoolers. Conversely, if we assume that children six years of age and older do not need full-time adult supervision and add the number of childless households to the total, using this crude measure we find that in 58 percent of the households the need to care for children should not, in theory, be a hindrance to labor-force participation by the interested and able-bodied adults in the household who are not in retirement.

Another way of considering how household composition may influence employment is by calculating the percentage of employable household members. We counted any household member between ages sixteen and sixty as employable, unless he or she were retired or disabled. Furthermore, if there were preschool children aged five or younger in the household, we assigned one adult per household as a child caretaker rather than considering that adult as a potential worker. Using this measure, we found that in the average household in our sample slightly more than half (52 percent) of its members were employable.

We now turn to a discussion of the differences that emerge when we examine household composition by ethnicity. Table 2 shows the distribution of household composition for each of the three groups. On this dimension, the Vietnamese refugees are most likely to have households in which at least one unrelated single person lives—more than one in four Vietnamese households (28 percent) include such a single (compared with 19 percent for the Chinese households and 15 percent for the Lao). The Vietnamese are consequently least likely of the three ethnic groups to live in a single nuclear family (44 percent), while the Lao are the most likely (54 percent).

Table 3 shows the specifics of household composition for each group. The Vietnamese households are indistinguishable from those of the Chinese on variables such as household size and the ratio of adults to children and, therefore, on variables such as percentage of employable adults. Among the three groups, the Chinese households are smallest, the number of youngsters aged one to five the lowest, and the youngest child in the average household is more than six years old. They include relatively more adults and fewer children. Conversely, the Lao tend to have larger households, with an average of 5.5 members. Therefore, the Lao households have slightly more adults per household (2.9), but the adults comprise only 60 percent of the households. They have more children (2.5) and the most children in the critical ages of one to five (0.93). Indeed, in every age category the Lao have more children, and their children tend to be younger. Consistent

TABLE 2. Household Composition by Ethnicity ($N = 1,384$ households)

	Vietnamese ($N = 690$)	Chinese ($N = 294$)	Lao ($N = 400$)
Single (one)	5%	7%	3%
Unrelated singles	7	5	3
Nuclear family	44	50	54
Nuclear family plus single(s)	6	4	5
Extended family	26	29	28
Extended family plus single(s)	7	3	2
Multiple families	2	1	4
Multiple families plus single(s)	3	0	2

TABLE 3. Characteristics of Household Composition by Ethnicity ($N = 1{,}384$ households; 6,775 individuals)

| | | | Average Number per Household | | | | | | |
| | | | | Children | | | | | |
	Persons*	Adults†	Under 16*	Ages 1–5*	Ages 6–11*	Ages 12–15*	Average Age of Youngest Child*	Percentage of Adults*	Percentage of "Employable" Household Members*
Vietnamese	4.7	2.8	1.7	.63	.65	.42	5.0	70%	56%
Chinese	4.5	2.7	1.6	.44	.65	.45	6.2	71%	57%
Lao	5.5	2.9	2.5	.93	.85	.65	4.8	60%	43%

* = $p < .01$
† = NS

with these observations, there are statistically significant differences (p = < .01) among the three ethnic groups in terms of the percentage of household members who are employable. In the Vietnamese households, 56 percent are employable, with about an equal percentage in Chinese households. The Lao tend to have the lowest percentage, with 43 percent. This means that the Lao have fewer people available to get jobs, and, if and when they do find work, they must support more people.

The social structures of their homelands may be seen to some degree in the composition of the refugee households. The Lao, with their more flexible kin relationships, have the highest percentage of adults in nuclear families, the most adults in their households, and the lowest percentage in nonnuclear extended-family combinations. The Vietnamese and the Chinese, with their ideals of patrilineal relationships, have almost equal percentages of adults in the nonnuclear extended-family situations. The Vietnamese, however, have a much higher percentage of single adults living alone or with unrelated individuals or families.

Cultural Values

The refugees brought with them not only their ideas of social units but, more importantly, their thoughts on how life in general should be approached. To gain an understanding of their goals and the guidelines by which they direct their lives, we looked to their values.

In the process of constructing the questionnaire to measure the cultural values of the refugees, we were faced with the problem of having little empirically based social science research to guide us. What was available for our use, though, was the extensive body of Southeast Asian literary and historical works, reports by American anthropologists studying the area, and descriptive accounts by Indochinese scholars currently living in America. These we mined for representative values of the Indochinese region, which made up the final list of twenty-six value stems included in the questionnaire.

This list of values was meant to tap several key dimensions. The first was a culturewide, Confucian-Buddhist set of values (e.g., "Perpetuate the Ancestral Line," "Seek Salvation"). A second set of values was intended to measure a family-based orientation characterized by reciprocal support and respect (e.g., "Family Loyalty," "Respect Family Members"). A third set of values attempted to identify more individual-based goals and preferences (e.g., "Carry Out Obligations," "Restraint and Discipline"). Two other dimensions were also hypothesized. A "basic needs" set may have been made more significant and salient as a result of the refugees' perilous migration to the United States (e.g., "Freedom," "Security and Comfort"). And an "American" set of values came into play (e.g., "Seek Fun and Excitement," "Balance of Work and Play"). We first asked each respondent to rate each value on a five-point scale ranging from "Very Important" to "Not at all Important." We then had the respondents indicate which three of these values they considered most important. The following, "core" values constitute the bedrock of the refugees' culturally derived beliefs.

- Education and Achievement
- A Cohesive Family
- Hard Work

Either singly or in combination, these value items were cited most often among the three most important. In addition, 98 percent or more of the respondents rated these same items at the highest levels on the scale measuring perceived importance. This near-total agreement on the importance of these three values has led us to place them at the core of the refugees' belief system.

Certainly, the central importance of the family in Asian cultures is generally recognized. Finding success through learning is another major theme. Hard work as a means for achieving life's goals may also seem obvious, but more than the will to work hard is connoted in this value. Its significance is best understood in context with a set of additional items that reveal its underlying dimensions and will be discussed later. But what should not be lost sight of is the extremely high level of consensual validation attributed to these three items. Despite their diversity in religious background, ethnicity, and country of origin, there is almost no disagreement among the refugees regarding what is of utmost importance to them.

The "normative" values, identified as follows, are titled as such because they, too, show small variation with respect to perceived importance. Consensus, however, was less than that found for the core values, with nine out of ten respondents viewing these items as "Important" or "Very Important."

- Family Loyalty
- Freedom
- Morality and Ethics
- Carry Out Obligations
- Restraint and Discipline
- Perpetuate Ancestral Lineage
- Respect for Elders
- Cooperative and Harmonious Family

The values included here encompass a number of elements we would associate with Asian beliefs concerning the family and standards of behavior. Thus, we see "Cooperative and Harmonious Family" and "Family Loyalty," "Respect for Elders," and "Morality and Ethics." In addition, the two individual-based values, "Carry Out Obligations" and "Restraint and Discipline," take their places in this generally held body of values. Another value, "Patience," was not included among the twenty-six but cropped up often in the refugees' own comments.

At the other extreme are two values listed *least* often in importance and cited most frequently as not at all important: "Fun and Excitement" and "Material Possessions." Ninety-five percent of the respondents placed these two items at the bottom in importance. But when asked to review the list of values and to indicate the preferences they considered *most* important to their *nonrefugee* neighbors, these were the two items cited most often, the very two items cited by the refugees as *least* important among their own value preferences. Given the fact that most refugees were residing in low-income neighborhoods at the time of the study, this contrast in perceived importance of values between themselves and their nonrefugee neighbors may possibly reinforce the refugees' beliefs and notions about what works and what does not work to get ahead in America. Finally, it would appear that both older and younger generations share these values. We found a correlation of .83 between samples of parents and high school children on measures of importance attributed to the value items, indicating a high level of agreement.

When exploring the connotative significance of the value items and the derivations that may be made from them, it would be misleading to use the items as individual values strung out in laundry-list fashion. This approach carries with it the implication that each value is independently and uniquely meaningful in its message. The listing of value items in this way fails to take into consideration the underlying dimensions they share in common. Consequently, we submitted these data to a factor analysis in order to gain an understanding of what these values mean, beyond the most obvious interpretation. Rating scores for each of the twenty-six value items were submitted to a series of principal-components factor analyses. Six factors or groups of values resulted from the procedure. (See the App., p. 204, for details on how the factor analyses were achieved.) The clusters of values that formed the factors show that these statistically formed groups are very similar to what could have been determined from the great Confucian and Buddhist traditions of the area. Thus, in a sense, contemporary social science methodology confirms the scholarly discussions of these traditions, illustrates the intermixture of the traditions in the lives of the Indochinese, and demonstrates the living nature of the values for the refugees. The resulting factors and discussion follow.

Factor 1: Cultural Foundation
• Respect Authority

- Perpetuate Ancestral Lineage
- Seek Salvation
- Harmony with the Land
- Traditional Customs

In the first factor, we have a set of givens, an approbation of past spiritual and cultural values with roots primarily along Confucian and Buddhist lines. The emphasis on respect, genealogical family, and kinship are strongly Confucian in origin; seeking salvation and conformity with nature are more in accord with Buddhist tenets. The emergence of this factor comes as no surprise and confirms the supposition that the values embedded in the cultural past of the Indochinese are intact and that the perspective and values in which they were reared have been carried with them to the United States. These values continue to constitute a source of motivation and guidance in dealing with contemporary problems set in a land vastly different from that in which these values originated. This factor also shows that Confucian and Buddhist values are compatible, even blended into the same cultural heritage.

Factor 2: Family-Based Achievement
- Education and Achievement
- A Cohesive Family
- Respect for Family Members
- Cooperative and Harmonious Family
- Family Loyalty

The second factor emphasizes the family as a central institution in Asian culture, within and through which achievement and knowledge are accomplished. These factor loadings point to the mutual, collective obligation among family members, plus the subordination of individual needs and desires to those of the larger family unit. Finally, cohesiveness, cooperation, and harmony characterize the quality of the working milieu required for the family if it is to accomplish its goals.

Factor 3: Hard Work
- Hard Work
- Sacrifice Present for Future
- Carry Out Obligations
- Restraint and Discipline

This clustering of values points up items that are instrumentally important to the accomplishment of achievement goals. The work ethic is as critical an underpinning to the Indochinese way of life as it is to American life. By itself, however, it may not be sufficient. Additional items included in this cluster imply modest behavior and needs and a willingness to delay present gratification for future reward. As two respondents, one Vietnamese and one Lao, noted, "I still have what is needed to start over: willpower, patience, and hard work" (after fire destroyed his possessions in the United States), and, "Without hard work and patience, your thoughts and goals would be nothing." Craving is to be overcome, and one is not to be a slave to instant gratification. In addition, there must be an acceptance of obligations and a recognition that sacrifice is the means to virtue in one's life. This combination of impulse control and discipline add up to the need for patience, perseverance, steadfast purpose, and long-range perspective. Whereas factor 2 is directed at the family, the underlying theme here is a set of imperatives for the individual.

Factor 4: The Family in Society
- Family Status in Community
- Seek New Experience
- Morality and Ethics

This set of values links the family to the realities of the past, present, and future. It portrays an optimistic, risk-taking orientation, saying that the family can reestablish itself by reconciling and balancing the cultural guidelines for moral order with the new realities in which it finds itself. This factor appeals to the need to restore balance and stability by reconciling and integrating the past with the present, thereby maintaining a living tradition in the modern world. The tie to the past and family does not shut down their minds; the refugees are not hidebound traditionalists in the face of Western culture but are looking forward to the promise it holds.

Factor 5: Self-reliance and Pride
- Respect for Elders
- Ashamed of Welfare

This factor reflects the present and gives us the culturally based context for understanding the refugee attitude toward cash assistance and self-sufficiency. Financial dependency appears not as a matter of personal shame but, as with academic achievement, a matter of family pride and respect for one's seniors in the family. Also, it concerns the level of esteem and personal worthiness attached to these relationships. Both items involve respect, bringing to mind the notion of "face" and its importance to the determination of one's sense of self-worth based on the opinion of others.

Factor 6: Coping and Integration
- Past Is as Important as Present
- Balance of Work and Play
- Seek Fun and Excitement

This set of items is similar to factor 4 in that it ties the past to the future, yet it goes farther in this area. It reveals a coming to grips with the possibilities of assimilation, without giving up what is important from the past. It is a factor that is more active than factor 4 and reveals mental apprehension associated with coping and preserving, as well as the risk in attempting to moderate cultural differences in order to get ahead. This factor may voice what the refugees explicitly tell us in other parts of the survey. They share an apprehension over the possible power and consequences of American cultural influences on the lives of the refugees, and in particular the effects on their children. These concerns and uncertainties are illustrated by the following citations.

> *I want my children to know Laotian culture. But it is very hard to teach it to them. We don't have any temple to show them our religion and culture. They go to school; they are going to learn more and more about American culture.* (Lao)

> *Children are expected to obey and respect their parents and older people. They are strictly disciplined and behave themselves according to traditional moral standards. However, this is changing now in America.* (Chinese)

But, as implied by factor 6, most refugees believe that a selective blend of Indochinese and American cultures is possible and are willing to accept its inevitability, at least in regard to their children's future, as illustrated by these comments.

> *We worry for our children. But we hope that with the kind of education they receive at home they would only Americanize in certain respects.* (Chinese)

> *My wife and I would like to return to Laos. But I want my children to live here because in Laos they could not go to college. In Laos there is no government support. Here they can go to college.* (Lao)

> *I am used to Americans, learn about their way of working, and try my best to socialize. In the meantime I still maintain the moral values inside my small family and plan to teach my children that they have to get Americanized while still being Vietnamese. It's hard, but I have no choice.* (Vietnamese)

Concerning the possibility of the Americanization of my children, I think that's just a normal thing. The kids are growing up with the environment. They are associating with their American friends more than their family at home, so they must be more Americanized, which I cannot do anything about. I don't mind it at all. It would be good for them in the future. (Vietnamese)

My children will surely be influenced by their scholastic environment and be Americanized very fast. I can't and don't intend to stop this natural process. I just want them not to forget their own culture. The ideal is the combination of the positive traits of the two cultures. (Lao)

One importance of this analysis is to stress the need to think in terms of the *clusters* of values and their combined significance in relation to the refugees' past, to the tasks at hand, and to the future. As noted, simply to say that hard work is important for success is not enough and is even misleading. Along with it must go a willingness to forgo the desire for instant gratification, to be modest in behavior and needs, and to be planful. From this more global perspective, the six factors that best characterize the value system of the refugees pertain to cultural foundation, family-based achievement, hard work, the family in society, self-reliance and pride, and coping and integration. In their broadest sense, they are a combination of Confucian and Buddhist beliefs.

Summary

When we studied the second-wave Indochinese refugees in this country, we found them in a state of transition from the life they had known in Southeast Asia to the life they hoped for in the United States. They are three quite distinct ethnic groups that have chosen to put war and politics behind them and to seek new possibilities for their families. Differences show up among the three groups. The Chinese from Vietnam, earliest to arrive, have the smallest households with older children, more adults, and medium levels of English, education, and occupation in Southeast Asia. The Lao, second to come here, live in larger households with more young children and low levels of English, education, and occupation in Laos. Latest to arrive, the Vietnamese households are middling in size and in numbers of young and adults and had the highest levels of English, education, and occupation in their homeland. Yet, despite these demographic differences, the three groups show remarkable similarities in the values they hold. The national, ethnic, cultural, and religious diversity seen here does not prevent agreement among these refugees on what is important in life. The six factor groupings of values reflect the consensus of all three groups. Thus, we see the Vietnamese, the Chinese, and the Lao with much in common as they face their circumstances in the American system.

Chapter 3

Economic and Scholastic Achievement

> *I believe that we have potential and self-confidence and will succeed step by step to achieve a respectable and responsible position in society.* (Vietnamese)

The refugees have been conspicuously successful in both economic and educational pursuits. Our interest is to present their accomplishments for what they are, to lay the groundwork for understanding how and why they occurred in the two areas under study, and to attempt a general explanation for each. Excluded from consideration are measures of success or failure in other areas of adaptive behavior, such as social skills, mental health, and acculturation. We focus on economic and educational achievements because they are of paramount importance as public policy issues and are at the very core of the material and social well-being of any society. Fortunately, it is in these areas that we have solid measures of refugee achievement.

Only the most telling evidence of economic and educational success will be discussed here. Economic self-sufficiency of the refugees was measured by (1) their labor-force participation: how many are working and in what jobs; and (2) their income: how much they bring home and from what sources, and (3) poverty-level standing. Scholastic achievement of the refugee children was assessed at the local level by grade point average and at the national level by standardized achievement test results. The test scores are particularly important in that they permit us to make national comparisons in achievement. In this chapter we will document and describe these accomplishments. Later, we will explore what may account for their occurrence.

Economic Achievement

Respondent [Chinese male] showed me a medal he received from his company. He was chosen among three hundred employees as the hardest worker of the company [$4.37 an hour, assistant cook]. (Interviewer note)

The economy determines everything. It determines the government policy toward us, and it determines the possibility or impossibility for us to find a job. That is the fate of the refugees. (Chinese)

Labor-Force Status

Employment Rate

We will be discussing labor-force status of the refugees from two perspectives: (1) the percentage of the sample participating in the work force and (2) their job status and pay. At the time of the study, 44 percent of the adults in the sample were in the labor force—1,050 who were working and 773 who were unemployed but seeking work. Thus, more than half (58 percent) of all adults in the labor force were employed. Although the unemployment rate (i.e., those who were involuntarily unemployed and seeking work) of 42 percent appears to be high, it must be recognized that it is an aggregate figure that includes all refugees seeking work, some of whom had just entered the United States. Not surprisingly, the recent arrivals were least employed and contributed most to the high unemployment aggregate among the refugees. Their presence paints a more negative picture of the unemployment rate than is true for all of the refugees in the study. The best understand-

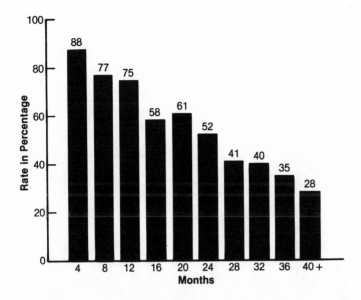

Fig. 1. Unemployment rate by length of residence in the United States

ing of the unemployment rate, therefore, is gained by looking at work-force participation by arrival time in the United States. Figure 1 shows that unemployment dropped sharply from almost 90 percent during the first months of resettlement to about one-third of that for those in the United States three years or more. Thus, the employment status of the refugees is not a steady-state condition but a constantly improving state of affairs closely associated with length of residency in the United States.

The work histories of the employed refugees were scrutinized for their length and the number and types of jobs held, to see if any improvements in job quality or pay accrued as a function of time or because of job changes. We found that regardless of the length of employment or the number of job shifts, neither the quality of the job held nor the level of pay improved. Those employed for one year, usually at their initial job, earned an average of $5.20 per hour. Those employed

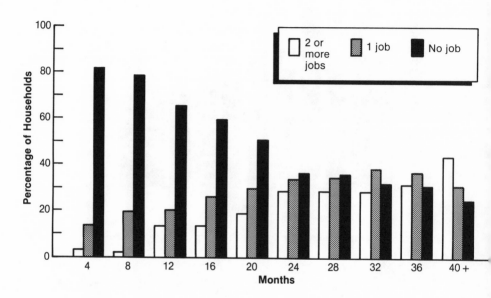

Fig. 2. Number of persons employed per household by length of residence in the United States

for two or more years, and averaging about two changes in jobs, earned only slightly higher wages, at $5.35 per hour. Thus, in general, the refugees were not moving out from poor-paying to better-paying jobs by shifting employment; nor were they significantly increasing their income through longevity in the work force.

When the unit of analysis is the household instead of the individual, a very different and more encouraging picture emerges with respect to labor-force participation and economic gain. This is because the number of jobs held in a household increased the longer the household was in the United States. Figure 2 shows changes in the percentage of the household sample with no job, one job, or two or more jobs arrayed over four-month intervals. The steady, almost monotonic increase in the percentage of multiple-job households is one of the more significant findings of our entire data set. Clearly, no adequate understanding of labor-force participation and economic advancement among the Indochinese refugees can be achieved by viewing jobs held by individuals alone. The latter data would reveal only limited progress in economic position, because the earning power of the jobs held and the potential for advancement are so restricted. In such a limited job market as that in which the refugees found themselves, individual initiative to advance could not move the household ahead economically, in either a comparative or an absolute sense. But what is impressive is the improvement in the economic position by the effort of more than one person per household entering the labor force, that is, by the pooling of human capital within the household. Among the nuclear families, this usually occurred at the time when the youngest child reached school age, thereby freeing both parents to enter the labor force.

Job Status and Pay

In order to estimate the refugees' prospects for stable employment and advancement, two indices of occupational status and economic sectors were applied to the data. The first, the Socio-Economic Index (SEI) (Duncan 1961), is based on educational and income characteristics and assigns job prestige scores to each job by occupational category. The second index of job status derives from recent work by "dual labor market" economists (see Cain 1976), who hold that the American economic system is split into two sectors: a core sector of stable or rising industries in which employment tends to be full-time, stable, and with ample opportunities for promotion; and a peripheral sector of less stable or declining industries in which work tends to be irregular, seasonal, and often part-time. The industries in which refugees worked were thus coded as core or periphery.

As defined by the SEI scores, the overwhelming majority

(71 percent) of those refugees in the labor force held low-status jobs. Slightly more than one-half (55 percent) were also employed in the periphery of the economy rather than in the core economic sector (45 percent). Thus, in the main, the refugees also tended to hold low-level, low-paying, dead-end jobs. Tables A-1 and A-2 in the Appendix (pp. 205–6) show the types of jobs held by the refugees, according to our two job-evaluation criteria, and the hourly wages associated with each.

In summary, it is essential to note and bears repeating that the labor-force participation of the refugees is not stagnant but, rather, is constantly changing so as to present an improving picture over time. This positive direction holds whether we look at the individual or the household level. Moreover, and particularly with regard to nuclear families, greater improvements can be expected as the youngest child enters school, enabling the caretaking parent to enter the labor world.

In the following section, questions concerning the refugees' income sources will be addressed. Specifically, we examine the combinations and amounts of assistance the refugees receive, the characteristics of three income source groups (cash assistance, combined, and earned), and the relationship between income patterns and length of residency.

Income Source

> *The bad feeling of depending on welfare makes me try harder to be self-sufficient.* (Chinese)

Cash Assistance

Virtually all Indochinese refugees in our sample began their American lives on welfare. For individuals unused to receiving such help, it is a reality that must be faced but not accepted for long, as one Lao states: "We don't want to receive welfare. We are not happy to receive it. But we want a job and to live a normal life. When we have enough money, we will return the cash assistance and food stamp money to the government."

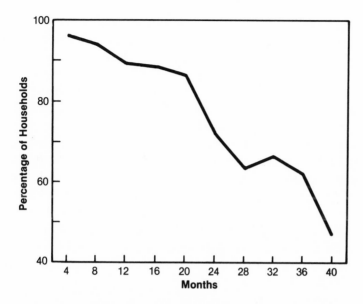

Fig. 3. Percentage of households receiving cash assistance by length of residence in the United States

For most, getting off welfare was a gradual process that was greatly dependent on the general state of the economy into which they had been thrust. Most households (65 percent) were receiving some kind of cash assistance at the time of the interview. Sources of aid were Refugee Cash Assistance, Aid to Families with Dependent Children, and Supplemental Security Income. Dependent as the majority of families were, however, being on cash assistance did change with the length of time the refugees had been in the United States. As figure 3 shows, the percentage of the households on cash assistance at four-month intervals drops rather sharply from more than 90 percent during the first four months to roughly 45 percent for those here forty months or more.

It is important to note that the receipt of assistance is not always an all-or-nothing situation. One-third of the households in the sample relied on both earnings and transfer sources of income. Allotment levels were reduced as individuals entered the labor force and decreased over time as part-time jobs expanded to full-time jobs. Of greater significance is the fact that households relied on combinations of income sources. For instance, households including elderly and disabled persons were likely to get Supplemental Security Income and continue to receive it as long as such persons remained with them. But these same households often included newer arrivals, often young singles, who were initially eligible for Refugee Cash Assistance and likely to find and hold jobs later. Thus, the makeup of the household determined whether it received cash assistance, the level of such dependency, and the length of time on it. Table A-3 in the Appendix (p. 206) shows the percentage of households reporting different combinations of assistance.

The Three Income Source Groups:
A Dependency Continuum

The refugee households may be divided into three income source groups: (1) those who received only cash assistance, (2) those who had earned income supplemented with cash assistance (combined), and (3) those who had earnings alone. While 43 percent of the households studied subsisted solely on aid, 32 percent had both assistance and earned income. The remaining 25 percent of the households depended on labor-market earnings alone.

Not unexpectedly, the refugees who were living on earned income alone were among the earliest arrivals. On the average, they had been in the United States for thirty-two months. The mean number of months in the United States for those receiving both assistance and earnings was just over two years (twenty-six months); for those who relied on assistance alone, the mean length of residency in the United States was twenty months.

An examination of earnings trends over time (fig. 4) shows that the proportion of earned income contributing to total income increased in a linear fashion. Those households with combined income and comprised of refugees who had

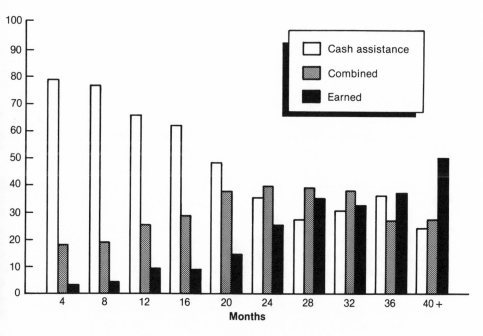

Fig. 4. Income source by length of residence in the United
States

been in the United States for more than three years depended
on earnings for 50 percent of their total income. This con-
trasts with the relative contribution made by earned income
among those in the United States a year or less, where earnings comprised from 5 to 10 percent of the households' total
income. For those households with refugees who had been in
the United States between one and three years, the proportion of earned income increased steadily with increments consistent with the length of residency in the United States.

Figure 4 serves to demonstrate a dependency/indepen-
dency continuum, with an ever-increasing reliance on labor-
market earnings and a decline of refugee households on cash
assistance over time. By focusing on household income source

over time, instead of individual income, the movement toward economic independence becomes much more apparent. The data in the figure show a steady change, particularly in the first two years, for all three groups. Households on cash assistance income alone dropped from about 80 percent in the first four months to about 25 percent after three years. The percentage of households with combined income went up from almost 20 percent in the first four months to double that for those in the United States sixteen to thirty-two months before falling off to less than 30 percent thereafer. The percentage of those living on earned income alone rose fairly steadily from 3 percent in the first four months to almost 50 percent after three years.

These data on the three income source groups indicate that government financial assistance is an important part of the economic transition process that many refugee households undergo from governmental dependence to financial independence. Moreover, the income trends in households that relied on a combination of aid and earned income lend support to the theory that financial assistance is the critical initial help refugees need to enable them eventually to stand on their own. That is, in households relying on combined incomes, earned income makes up a larger and larger proportion of total income over time. And it may be conjectured that in time the households that rely on a combined income will become financially independent. However, it is misleading to view those who support themselves with earned income alone as economically well positioned. Although they are self-sufficient and definitely financially independent, not all are out of poverty: of those households supported on earnings alone, 12 percent are still below the poverty line. Their economic position changed from being economically dependent to being "officially" nonpoor; they are now the economically self-sufficient "working poor."

Finally, changes in household composition may confound the relationship between dependency and earnings. Anecdotal data collected during the study suggest that employed singles may have joined some households, bringing their income with them to provide economic and other help to families with children. By so doing, these single individuals were helping the nuclear families and themselves in the transition from dependency to self-sufficiency, by contributing their human capital, knowledge of experiences, and other forms of personal assistance.

Poverty-Level Standing

To get a job is to survive. (Vietnamese)

An important indicator of the economic status of the refugees is change over time in the degree to which household income meets needs in relation to the official poverty level. See the Appendix for details on definitions of terms and procedures for calculating poverty level for households.

The official poverty rate for the total U.S. population in 1982, the time of this survey, was 15 percent. The Census Bureau data on poverty rate for specific segments of the population were white, 12.0 percent; black, 35.6 percent; and Hispanic, 29.9 percent. By comparison, the poverty rates for those refugee households ranged from 80 percent for those in the United States for four months or less to 30 percent for those here for three and one-half years. Thus, although there was steady improvement in economic standing over time, the poverty rate for refugees in our sample at any point in time is high, compared with the total U.S. population. However, those refugees in the United States just under four years showed rates that are not greatly different from those for blacks and Hispanics. Also, the economic status among the refugees showed changes in a positive direction. That is, if the refugees' climb out of poverty continued, even at a slower pace than that achieved during early resettlement, it could be expected that the gap between the poverty rate for the refugees and that for the population as a whole would steadily decrease. More important, the poverty rate for the United States actually rose rather dramatically from 11.4 percent to 15 percent for the years 1979 and 1982. Thus, the refugees

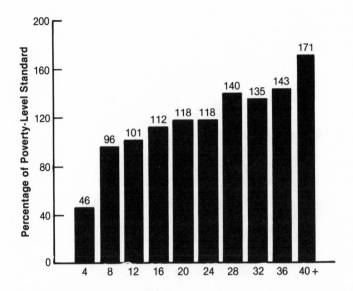

Fig. 5. Percentage of poverty-level standard of total household income by length of residence in the United States

were climbing out of poverty during a period of dramatic increase in the percentage falling below poverty for the nation as a whole.

Changes in poverty-level standing over time are shown in figure 5. It presents a rather optimistic picture. The refugees in the United States for four months or less met their needs at only 46 percent of the poverty-level standard. Yet after the fourth month, the level of needs met rose rather steadily to 171 percent of the poverty level for those who had been in the country for forty or more months. That amount of money is insufficient to guarantee a comfortable life, but it is adequate to meet basic needs and attain a reasonable life standard.

Figure 5 carries with it the promise of steady improvement at the rate of about ten percentage points over the poverty level every few months. The extremes here are in the direction of economic improvement, which typifies the aggregate economic condition. But it is impossible to bolster such faith with sound argument, because the jobs held by the refugees are not typically those that hold out much hope for economic or occupational advancement.

Climbing Out of Poverty

The source of household income—cash assistance, combined or earned—is a major determinant of economic status whether judged by poverty-level standing or self-sufficiency. Table 4 shows the mean percentage poverty level met for the three income groups. Two out of three of households on cash assistance fall below the poverty level. Households with combined income (cash assistance and earned) do better: about one-quarter live in poverty. And for those households that receive earned income alone, one out of eight fall below the poverty line. But approximately half of the households in the earned income group had earnings at 200 percent or more of the poverty standard, compared to only 16 percent of the households with combined income. The average household on cash assistance alone has income at 79 percent of the poverty level. The comparable figures for the combined and earned income houses are 146 and 218 percent, respectively. Thus, to be assured of sufficient income to achieve the poverty-level standing or beyond, a household must have acquired some earned income.

Not represented in the preceding discussion is the 10 percent of our household sample who reported having no source of income. These consisted about evenly of newly arrived households without employment who had yet to receive

TABLE 4.   Poverty Level by Household Income Source (N = 1,243)

Income Source	Percentage of Sample	Mean Percentage of Poverty Level Met	Percentage below Poverty Level	Percentage at 200% or More of Poverty Standard
Cash assistance	43.5	79	64	0
Combined	32.0	146	28	16
Earned	24.5	218	12	48

Note: Not shown is the 10 percent of the sample that had no source of income at the time of the study.

cash assistance and households in which the employed person(s) had been laid off and had yet to find other employment or income sources. Ten percent is a sizable fraction of any population segment to be without income, especially in the absence of savings or other economic resources upon which to draw. As best we could determine through our interviews, households in such circumstances relied on help from relatives, friends, and sponsors.

Jobs per Household and Poverty

Earlier, we discussed the importance to their economic advancement of the refugees' strategy of securing more than one job per household. The relationship of the number of jobs per household to poverty-level standing illustrates the significance of this point. Table 5 shows that eight out of ten households (83 percent) having no persons employed live below the poverty level, eking out existences in which only three-quarters of their needs were being met (77 percent of poverty level).

In contrast, the living standard almost doubled as measured by the poverty level (150 percent) in households in which one person was working, and the living standard nearly tripled in households with two or more persons working (215 percent). But, as mentioned earlier, it should also be noted that not all households on subsistence alone live below the poverty level, and not all households with two or more employed persons rise out of poverty. Approximately one in six households (17 percent) with no one in employment was living above the poverty line, and 7 percent remained below the

TABLE 5.   Poverty Level by Jobs per Household
($N = 1,384$)

Number of Jobs	Percentage of Poverty Level Met	Percentage below Poverty Level
0	77	83
1	150	32
2 or more	215	7

poverty line even with two or more persons in the work force. Thus, there is no hard and fast relationship between the level of work-force participation and the alleviation of poverty. In general, however, the economic standing of the household improved as more members entered the work force.

In conclusion, an examination of the economic status of the refugees with respect to their labor-force status, income sources, and poverty-level standing reveals many interesting points. Both receipt of cash assistance and poverty-level measures show the refugees' steady progress in climbing out of dependency and up to an increasingly higher standard of living. It would be misleading to quote a single rate of dependency or a single figure for the percentage living above the poverty line without considering the effect of time in the United States, since all of these economic outcome measures show steady progress over time. Starting with high rates of dependency, unemployment, and those living below the poverty line in the early months of resettlement, the refugees in the United States for two and three years show figures on these same measures that approach those for the U.S. minority groups—but with trajectories that indicate the likelihood of continued economic independence and improvement in economic status. For the same time period, the percentage of households above the poverty line fell for the U.S. population in general, and other minority groups in particular, while the country sank deeper into a period of major economic recession. The Indochinese refugees not only survived these hard times but steadily improved their economic status. Their climb out of poverty is indeed a major accomplishment.

Scholastic Achievement

An uneducated person is like unpolished jade.

A knife gets sharp through honing; a man gets
    smart through study.
                        —Vietnamese proverbs

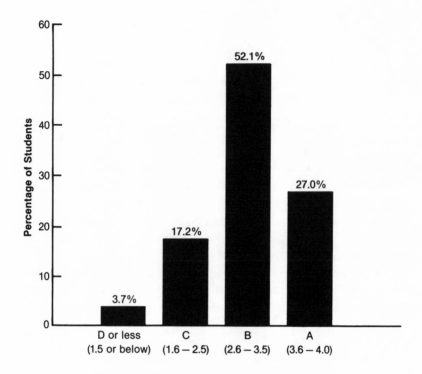

Fig. 6. Overall grade point average

Here we discuss the refugee students' educational performance, based on their 1984 grade point averages and California Achievement Test scores. The data are from actual school transcripts. In the main, the educational achievements of these children are outstanding.

Grade Point Average

Twenty-seven percent of the children had an overall GPA in the A grade range, 52 percent in the B range, 17 percent in the C range; only 4 percent had GPAs below a C. The mean numerical GPA is 3.05, a B average. These GPA results are shown in figure 6.

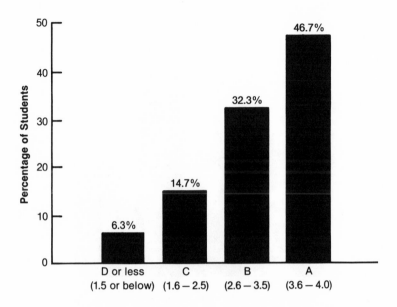

Fig. 7. Math grade point average

Of all the grades earned by the children in our sample, the most striking are the math grades. These results are shown in figure 7. Almost half (47 percent) of the schoolchildren earned an A in math. Another 32 percent earned a B, 15 percent received a C, and 6 percent fell below a C. The mean GPA for math is 3.18, a B. These grades indicate the greater facility with which these children, in general, handle courses that require a minimum of English. Here, where English competence is least required, they do better; in GPAs, by subject, math scores are the highest for the refugee children. Were they to be removed from the overall GPA, the average would drop to 2.64.

For a science GPA measure, we used a mean grade for all science courses taken by a student—biology, physics, chemistry, and "science"—or the single grade for a student who took only one such course. As shown in figure 8, 26 percent were in

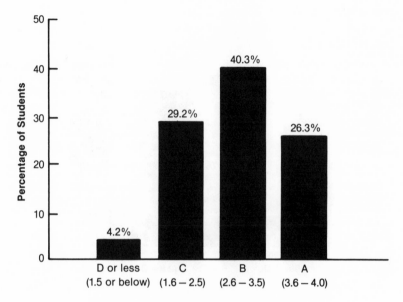

Fig. 8. Science grade point average

the A grade range for their science courses, 40 percent received a B, 29 percent had a C, and 4 percent had a D or less. The mean science GPA is 2.97, also a B but lower than that for math. Were the math and science GPA removed from the overall GPA, the average would drop to 2.46, the remaining courses being those involving more language components, such as English, history, or social studies.

We did not interview nonrefugee families in the neighborhoods occupied by the refugees, nor did we obtain parental permission from them to gain access to school transcripts for their children. And even though some school administrators were willing to send us comparative data, ethnic identity was so ambiguous as to make interpretation highly equivocal. However, we did speak with school administrators across the five sites about the progress of the Indochinese children, and, with little need for qualification, administrators reported that the refugee children excelled in their schoolwork and often referred to their overrepresentation among valedictorians in order to underscore the point. For example, in Garden Grove, a section of Orange County, the refugee community made up less than 20 percent of the school population at the time of our data collection. Yet twelve of fourteen valedictorians had Indochinese backgrounds (*Los Angeles Times,* December 19, 1985). Finally, conversations with administrators and an examination of transcripts revealed virtually no suspensions, drug use, or other forms of serious misconduct. Frequently, written comments found on the transcripts were positive remarks and most often pertained to the children's eagerness to learn, especially for children in kindergarten and the lower elementary school grades.

We were also concerned with the possibility that the GPAs were inflated by higher grades among the children in the lower grade levels, if for no more reason than that they would have suffered fewer of the exigencies associated with migration and resettlement and had not lost one to three years of schooling while in refugee camps. The school performance data, however, showed only minor differences by age and grade level. The distribution of GPAs for children in grade levels seven through nine was as follows: A, 61 percent; B, 32 percent; C, 6 percent; and D or less, 1 percent. Those in the higher grades (ten through twelve) did equally well, with 58 percent having a GPA in the A range; B, 35 percent; C, 5 percent; and D or less, 2 percent.

Finally, there is the possibility of differences in age and maturity. Were refugee children older than their nonrefugee cohorts, and, if so, might that not explain why they do so well in school? Given the disruption of life and the time spent in refugee camps, the typical Indochinese refugee child lost at least one year of formal schooling. Possibly, once in the United States, they were placed among nonrefugee children equal in schooling but chronologically younger and less mature. Comparisons of the mean age by grade level, however, revealed no substantive age differences. The average age of the refugee children at the completion of the first grade was exactly seven years; for those graduating from high school, it was eighteen years, four months. Thus, the refugee children were a few months older than the nonrefugees at the upper grade levels, but the difference is not sizable enough to be of substantive importance.

Standardized Achievement Test Results

Because the children resided in traditionally low-income, metropolitan areas, questions might unavoidably be raised concerning their school performance vis-à-vis children at the same class level nationally. Thus, we looked to standardized test scores, particularly the CAT data, to determine if their distinction in academics was the result of attending schools where good grades were easily achieved (possibly the result of less competition from their classmates or the halo effect of their eagerness to learn and quiet deportment) or the result of hard work and true learning. The data based on the California Achievement Test allow us to go beyond the limits of the GPA and gain a sense of how well these refugee children are doing in comparison to children at the same grade levels across the United States.

Most children in our sample were administered some form of standardized achievement test, such as the Texas Achievement Test or the Iowa Achievement Test. Because not all school systems administer the CAT, we have data on fewer children than those for whom we have grades at the local level. Regardless of what achievement test was used, however, the results are similar. We report here the CAT results because it was the most widely used of such tests across the five sites.

These scores show that the refugee children not only excelled in local schools but performed as well as or better than the national average on standardized achievement tests. The CAT data (arranged by quartiles) for the overall scores and for the math, language and reading, and spelling scores are presented in figures 9 through 12. At the national level, the range of scores is statistically adjusted so that one-quarter

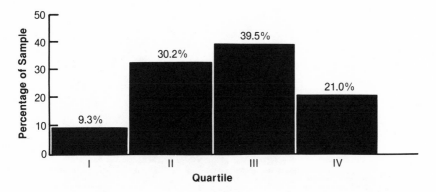

Fig. 9. Overall CAT scores

of all students taking the CAT would be expected to fall within each quartile range, extending from the lowest to the highest 25 percent. If the refugee schoolchildren were a normally distributed sample from the larger population, then, by definition, we would expect one-fourth to be in the lowest quartile, one-fourth in the second quartile, and so on. But there are some noteworthy discrepancies between the expected and the observed proportions in the spread of the refugee children's scores.

When compared on the basis of the overall CAT scores (fig. 9), the refugee children tend to be underrepresented at the extremes and somewhat overrepresented in the middle. Most obvious is their 9.3 percent in the lower or first quartile, versus the expected 25 percent. The mean score for the refugees on overall CAT performance is at the 54th percentile, or just above average. But, as seen in the figure, the scores tend to cluster toward the middle, with disproportionately fewer than expected in the lowest and highest quartiles. Thus, although the refugee children do not differ significantly from the national sample in their mean combined score, they do differ in that they show a more narrow range of individual differences.

Based on what we know from their math GPAs, we are

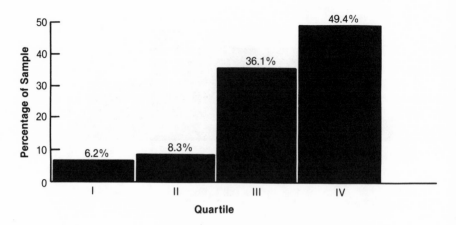

Fig. 10. Math CAT scores

not surprised to find that the refugee children are doubly overrepresented at the upper end on CAT math scores, shown in figure 10. Half of the children, or twice the expected number, scored in the top quartile range (49.4 percent versus the expected 25 percent), with a 4:1 *under*representation (6.2 percent) in the lowest quartile. More than 85 percent scored beyond the 50th percentile, with half scoring higher than 75 percent of those taking the test nationally. As with the math GPA results, these data are impressive because of the pile-up with increasing frequency toward the upper end. This trend is even more dramatic if the data are organized by deciles rather than quartiles: 27 percent of the refugee schoolchildren scored in the 10th, or highest, *decile* on math—that is, four in ten of the students were among the top 10 percent versus the expected one in ten based on national norms. The mean percentile score for the refugee group in math is 72, indicating that as a group they did better than more than 70 percent of the population of schoolchildren taking the exams at comparable grade levels nationally.

The distribution of CAT scores on spelling is skewed in

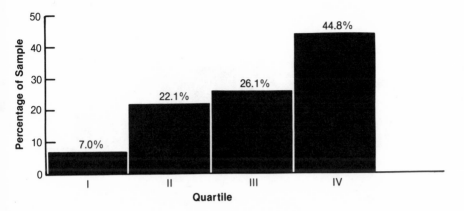

Fig. 11. Spelling CAT scores

the same direction as the math scores, but the slope is less dramatic. Figure 11 shows that 7.0 percent scored in the lowest or first quartile, 22.1 percent in the second, 26.1 percent in the third, and, 44.8 percent, or nearly twice the expected number, in the highest quartile. The mean percentile score for spelling is 59.6; they did better than six out of ten students in the nation who took the test.

The lowest test scores of the refugee children, or really those closest to national norms, are in language and reading, where the percentages in quartiles I through IV were 24.2, 30.7, 29.3, and 15.8, respectively (see fig. 12). The refugee children's scores are underrepresented at the top quartile on this subtest, contrary to their results on math and spelling. The mean score is at the 46th percentile, or slightly below the national average.

These comparatively low scores on reading and language subtests are not unexpected, given the fact that these children had been in the United States for an average of only about three and a half years and that most came from homes where no one in the household was able to speak *any* English upon arrival in the United States. Yet almost twice the expected

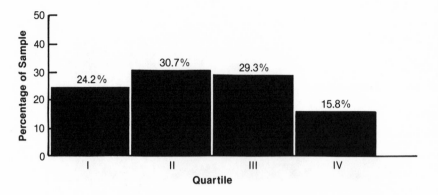

Fig. 12. Language and reading CAT scores

number scored in the top quartile in spelling, and, although not shown, a full 20 percent attained scores above the 90th percentile range.

We can only speculate about why these children excel in spelling, a task one would normally expect to be closely correlated with other language skills—the area of greatest weakness in school performance among the refugee children. There may be components involved in learning to spell, such as rote memory skills or idetic memory, that are independent of those required to perform well in the language and reading subtests of the CAT and may correlate with factors associated with ability in math.

A celebrated example of the refugee children's ability in spelling gained national attention while we were conducting the study. On April 30, 1983, the *New York Times* carried a front-page item with the headline "Mexican Food Trips Asian Refugee in Spelling Bee." The story was about Linn Yann, a twelve-year-old fifth grader from Cambodia who had been in the United States for four years, who knew virtually no English upon arrival, and who was tripped up on her way to a National Spelling Bee championship because she misspelled *enchilada.* The item drew special attention not only because of Linn's rather remarkable accomplishment in view of her limited exposure to the English language but also because she may have been eliminated unfairly: *enchilada* is not an English word. In addition, it was allegedly mispronounced when presented. Like most good spellers, Linn, having never heard the word before, spelled phonetically, in accord with the pronunciation of the presenter, and was wrong. She was quoted as saying, "I do not eat Mexican food. Maybe that was the problem. . . . I am going to study harder for next year's Spelling Bee and win." Linn's background as reported in the article was not substantially different from that of many in our sample. After her father was killed by the Khmer Rouge, she, her mother, and five brothers and sisters walked one hundred miles, hiding during the day and walking at night, before arriving at a refugee camp in Thailand, sick and malnourished. As a result of the spelling bee notoriety, she received a phone call from President Ronald Reagan, who praised her for doing so well after such a short time in the United States. A videotape of Linn's experience at the spelling bee, titled "The Girl Who Spelled Freedom," is available (Disney Productions).

Initial Efforts at Explanation

We have found the economic and educational achievements of the Indochinese refugees to be stunning in both quantity and quality. These refugees came here with almost no material goods. They arrived with very little English or transferable job skills just as the United States was entering its worst recession since the Great Depression more than four decades earlier. The refugee children spoke almost no English when they came, and they attend predominantly inner-city schools whose reputations for good education are poor. Yet by 1982, we find that the Indochinese had already begun to move ahead of other minorities on a national basis, and, two years later, their children are already doing very well on national tests. Little in their backgrounds prepared us to anticipate the great leaps in achievement that have given them parity or better with American children in such a brief period.

Our search for the bases of the extraordinary progress of the Indochinese Boat People in this country began with standard demographics and programmatic variables applied to both the economic and the scholastic outcomes. Yet this approach proved incomplete and unsatisfactory. Neither the basic demographic facts concerning the refugees nor the programmatic service efforts fully account for the effectiveness of the refugees in achieving success in the first years of their resettlement. Here we look at those variables that make some difference in the two realms of achievement.

Demographic Factors Associated with Economic Self-Sufficiency

In our search for the demographic and programmatic variables that could explain the refugees' progress, we looked at ethnicity, religion, sex, past socioeconomic standing, and other factors. Details of these analyses are presented in the Appendix (pp. 208–14). At this point, we wish to highlight only two background variables related to the economic well-being of the refugees. The explanation offered for economic achievement by our variables has to do with language and with the composition of the household. The level of proficiency in English is important to all refugees in their efforts to establish themselves in the United States. It is the main means by which refugees gain access to outside help in their new homeland and to the opportunity structure. Its importance was patently clear to the Indochinese refugees from the moment they arrived in their new country. One respondent summarizes the significance of English competence for all his fellow refugees:

> *Language is a long and dark tunnel, and the future of their new life will be found at its end. For the refugees, English is the only way to be totally free. If we couldn't pass through that tunnel after fleeing from the persecution and the oppression of the Communist regimes, we would be caught in another trap: to be isolated from the*

new environment. I took classes and tried hard for days and nights to study and practice the new language with some other refugees. (Vietnamese)

Arrival English

Using a variety of statistical approaches and the English competence scales discussed in chapter 2, we found repeatedly that among the variables in the entire data set, "Arrival English" had the greatest consequence for economic progress. This relationship is most easily demonstrated by data for nuclear families. Thirty-one percent of refugee households that average 0 ("None") to 3 ("Read street signs") in English ability lived above the poverty line, versus 63 percent for those that average 4 ("Shop for food") or better. Households with at least one person whose English upon arrival was better than the ability to read street signs were twice as likely to achieve self-sufficiency at the time of our study than households with members less proficient in English upon arrival.

Eighty-five percent of our sample would fall in the 0-to-3 category in English proficiency, and the remaining 15 percent would be in the 4-to-10 category, mainly at the 4 "end" of the scale. For more details on proficiency in English and how it was measured, see the Appendix (pp. 212–13, 218–22), but suffice it to add that this initial advantage upon arrival in the United States had a lasting effect. In all our multivariate analyses, arrival English remained a better predictor of economic station than did current English, independent of length of residency. Those with better English upon arrival got ahead earlier and stayed ahead in both English proficiency and economic well-being.

Household Composition

Refugee households in the United States were composed of a large number of nuclear or extended families, with sets of unrelated individuals in temporary or transitional arrangements, either living alone, banding together, or joining existing families. For an analysis of unemployment, household composition was measured in two ways. First, a variable was used to classify households as consisting of a single respondent; a group of unrelated singles; a nuclear family; a nuclear family plus unrelated single(s); an extended family (a combination of nuclear family plus others related by blood or marriage or a household of relatives without a nuclear family being present); an extended family plus unrelated single(s); multiple families (any combination of nuclear and/or extended families); or multiple families with unrelated single(s). Second, a variable was used to represent the percentage of employable adults—that is, the ratio of potential or current work-force participants to all household members, including dependents. In effect, this measure of percentage of adults employable was a function of the presence or absence of preschool children in the household.

The unemployment rate varied, but not greatly, with household compositions. It was lowest among those living alone (31 percent) and highest for households consisting of unrelated singles, many of whom were full- or part-time students, and for nuclear families (44 percent). Table 6 permits a summary glance at the unemployment rate and poverty-level standing by household classification. The variation by house-

TABLE 6.   Household Composition by Poverty-Level Standing and Unemployment Rate

Household Composition	Percentage of Household Sample ($N = 1,384$)	Percentage of Households below Poverty Level ($N = 1,384$)	Percentage of Individuals Unemployed ($N = 4,160$)
Unrelated singles	5.5	9	45
Extended family with singles(s)	4.8	20	40
Multiple family with single(s)	1.9	27	38
Nuclear family with single(s)	5.1	29	42
Single, living alone	4.7	29	31
Multiple family	2.6	40	37
Extended family	27.2	43	43
Nuclear family	48.2	61	44
Mean		51	42

hold composition is greater for poverty standing than for employment. Nuclear families, the household group that constitutes the largest proportion of the total sample (virtually half, or 48 percent), also comprise the largest percentage of households below the official poverty standard. Sixty-one percent of the nuclear families failed to receive the minimal income necessary to meet needs at the poverty level. The household unit making up the next largest proportion of the sample is the extended family. This group, which constitutes 27.2 percent of the total sample, is second only to nuclear family units in its failure to reach the poverty standard: 43 percent of these households fall below the poverty standard. These two groups, which together account for three out of four households (75.4 percent) in the entire sample, represent the only two classifications in the table in which only related members of the same family live under a single roof. In other words, they come closest to meeting what is routinely meant by "family" and are where most of the children, and poverty as well, are found.

Households in which families double up do about as well as extended families. Forty percent of the multiple-family households live below the poverty standard, which is quite a bit better than they would do if they lived separately. The percentage of nuclear families with single(s) below the poverty level is 29, or half that for nuclear households alone. Equally significant reductions occur for the multiple families plus single(s) (40 percent versus 27 percent) and extended family plus single(s) (43 percent versus 20 percent). In our whole data set, few attributes will be found to produce a substantive effect on economic status equal to that of the presence of unrelated, presumably employed, singles in a family-based household. Although probably a temporary arrangement tied to practical expediency, it is a real boon to the immediate economic well-being of the household and is the major reason for the combined income source described earlier.

Finally, only 9 percent of the households, consisting

solely of unrelated singles, live below the poverty level—the smallest percentage in poverty for all household groups. This is not unexpected; these households consist largely of collections of potential wage earners with fewer elderly, children, or other types of dependent persons.

Although the above household characteristics are described in terms of relationships among their members, the major effects on employment and economic standing are, in fact, not caused by these sociological arrangements but arise as a function of the number of adults in relation to the presence of preschool children. The consequence of household composition as a factor in resettlement is best understood by comparing the number of adults in relation to the number of preschool children in a household. "Adults employable," used as a variable in various statistical approaches to the data, accounted for the same amount of variation in income as did "household composition." But, exploring this further, we found that the number of employable adults in any given household was mainly a function of the number of children requiring supervision during school hours. Thus, it is not unexpected to find nuclear families at the bottom of the ladder in terms of percentage living in poverty (61 percent) and unemployment (44 percent). Once the youngest child reaches school age, both spouses in a nuclear family usually entered the work force, resulting in a dramatic improvement in the economic position of the family. This within-family multiple-job strategy, a variation of the nuclear-plus-singles strategy discussed above, is the major avenue for economic advancement for nuclear families during resettlement.

Related to this strategy is the important role of women in the economic success of the household. Indochinese women are quite willing to participate in the labor force. Opportunity for the employment of women in the United States, together with the multiple-job strategy as a means to meet the needs of the household, appear to have contributed successfully to the rise in the number of women working and the consequent achievement of economic self-sufficiency for their households. The following comment illustrates the point:

> *Respondent's [Chinese] wife will have operation next week [tubal ligation], so she can be ready for work in the near future. They have two sons.* (Interviewer note)

Other demographic variables, such as ethnicity, religion, and past education or occupation, shed little light on this achievement. Nor does program involvement indicate any better chance for success than noninvolvement. For a fuller discussion of these variables, see the Appendix.

Background Variables Associated with Scholastic Achievement

The educational achievements of the children in refugee households are even more striking than the economic accomplishments of the adults. Although they lost one to three years of formal education while in refugee camps in Southeast Asia, and despite the lack of English skills and a basic knowledge of American history and culture, they have done exceptionally well in the schools across our five sites, whether this progress is measured by standing at the local level (GPA) or on the basis of nationally standardized achievement test results. In terms of GPA, eight out of ten students had a B average or better, with almost half getting A's in mathematics. Their overall scores on the California Achievement Test were better than average, with their highest scores on the math and spelling subtests; in math, almost 30 percent placed in the top decile, three times the expected representation based on national norms.

High achievement is evident at the very outset of formal education and remains high throughout. Anecdotal comments written on transcripts by kindergarten teachers indicate that these children exhibit an eagerness and pleasure in learning, even before entering the first grade. The high results on standardized tests show no significant variation across the different school systems. It is important to note that these students attained high academic marks in schools that are in traditionally low-income or inner-city areas. That is, they succeeded in schools generally considered to be both less fortunate in terms of resources and associated with less motivated or more disruptive student bodies.

Factors within the Schools

We sought alternative ways to account for the refugee children's educational achievements, some of which we share here. First, we looked at factors within the school system. We thought that the months and, in most cases, years of lost education had been taken into account and that the refugee children had been appropriately placed in grades commensurate with their level of schooling once in the United States regardless of their chronological ages. Thus, we looked at the average ages of the children in the different grades. Although the average age of those graduating from high school is eighteen years, three months, or slightly higher than their non-refugee cohort members, the chronological age comparisons for refugee and nonrefugee students in grades one through eleven were virtually identical. Thus, physical and social maturity was ruled out as a factor in their achievements.

Also, as indicated earlier, we examined the data to determine if grades for the younger children were disproportionately higher than for their older cohorts in the higher grades. The possibility existed that such a disparity could occur because a larger fraction of the total educational experience of the younger children would have been in American schools. Judging from the comments on the transcripts, there was reason to believe that those in grade school may have benefited by a halo effect favoring those in the lower grades teaching vis-à-vis the older children subjected to a more structured educational environment with respect to student-teacher interactions and curricula content. Also there was the possibility that the younger children were less likely to have been hobbled psychologically by the trauma associated with escape and migration from Southeast Asia. But, as reported earlier, the GPA's across the grade levels revealed only modest differences.

Finally, we examined CAT results for age-level differences among the refugee schoolchildren and found that the

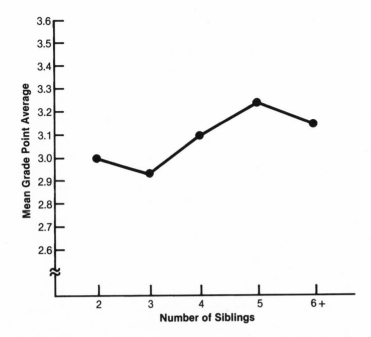

Fig. 13. Grade point average by number of children in the family in families with two or more children

younger children did better on the overall CAT results. Eight out of ten of those in elementary school scored in the 50th percentile or higher overall versus four in ten for those at the secondary school level. This overrepresentation of the younger refugee children at the upper levels of the overall CAT percentiles probably reflects better facility in English, since there is very little variation on math GPAs for grades one through twelve: about four out of ten obtained an A on math regardless of grade level. Finding little here to explain the extraordinary progress of the students, we next moved to factors within the families to see what could be gained there that would help to explain their progress.

Factors within the Family

Of special interest here is the relationship of the number of children in a family to GPA. Figure 13 gives the GPA by number of siblings in a family.

Studies on the effects of family size and birth order on school achievement have shown a strong negative relationship: the greater the number of children, the lower the level of academic achievement, with the later born doing less well than their older siblings. Researchers have found that the aggregate "intelligence" for schoolchildren, as measured by academic aptitude tests, drops about 15 percent with the addition of each child to the family. There is little argument about the direction and strength of this negative relationship between family size and academic performance, but lively debate has raged over interpretation. Some argue that the social network of the family within which parents and children form relationships accounts for the results (e.g., Zajonc 1986). Others (e.g., Rodgers 1984) hold that family size is simply a proxy for socioeconomic standing, attributing poor performance of children from large families to crowded living conditions, limited resources for learning in the home, and the host of impediments to learning associated with poverty. They argue that the larger the family, the more likely it is that they are found in poorer residential areas, impoverished of educational and economic opportunities and resources.

Among these refugees, however, families with four, five, and six or more children do as well as or better than those with fewer children. In fact, there is a positive and statistically reliable relationship between the number of children in a household and GPA if one-child families are removed from the data set. Thus, for the refugee families in which a sibship exists, the relationship between academic achievement and family size runs exactly opposite to the expected. Also, we tested for birth-order effects and sibship composition in terms of gender differences and found none.

Initially, we attempted to account for this finding on family size and GPA by looking to past socioeconomic standing. Possibly higher SES status in Indochina could carry with it the privilege and wherewithal to have larger families and the means to afford education for them. We ran statistical tests of SES measures for parents against family size and found that, as with the rest of the world's population, Southeast

Asia's family size and SES were negatively correlated. Refugee parents with higher SES standing in Indochina did, in fact, have fewer children; but once in the United States, their children performed in school no better than those from lower-SES families, even though the lower-SES children were in households with greater poverty, fewer of life's amenities and conveniences, less educated parents, and, of course, more crowding because of larger family size.

One final comment on family size and the liberalizing effect of education needs to be added. With respect to economic measures, we found that the more children in the family (i.e., the fewer adults employable), the worse off economically was that family. That finding, however, may apply only to the family's more immediate financial situation. Assuming a positive relationship between academic performance and one's future fortunes, and assuming that family loyalty holds steady, in the long run those families with more children (lower past SES) will be economically better off than those with fewer children (higher past SES) because of the larger and at least equally if not higher-achieving human capital pool from which to draw.

Some differences in GPA may be seen in ethnicity (see the App., pp. 208–9), but the differences do not hold for the CAT scores. There is also no statistically reliable difference between the sexes on either the GPA or the CAT data. This was true even when compared by subject, such as mathematics, a field traditionally dominated by males. In addition, contrary to economic achievement, English proficiency among the Indochinese adults had no impact on the scholastic achievement of their children.

Thus, we began our analyses of the data by systematically deleting sets of variables on the basis of their relationship to the economic and educational outcomes. We focused initially on the standard "knockout" items, those demographic variables that social scientists look to first for explanation, such as ethnicity, religion, gender, and past socioeconomic status, even going as far back as the French colonial period in Indochina, prior to the disruption of the years of political upheaval and war. These findings are also presented in the Appendix. But, for two important exceptions, once we went beyond the narrow provinces of simple bivariate statistical comparisons, few factors could be found to make independent statistical contributions to economic or educational progress. The two significant findings are, again, (1) the level of English proficiency upon arrival in the United States has a major and long-lasting impact on economic progress, and (2) educational performance is positively related to family size: the larger the size of the sibship, the higher the aggregate GPA.

We examined for the effects of programmatic services designed specifically to facilitate resettlement, particularly employment services and training programs and ESL. A detailed discussion of the utilization and impact of these efforts is provided in the Appendix (pp. 214–33). As with all after-the-fact assessments of ameliorative programs, a high level of equivocality is associated with estimating their effects. The refugees viewed these efforts favorably, and whereas the programs may have played important social and emotional roles in facilitating resettlement, their direct contribution to the outcome measures described here appears to have been of limited importance.

As our learning increased with the experience of examining the hundreds of variables in the data set for measurable effects on achievement, our approach became more conceptually guided. We found that we need to look elsewhere if we wish to unravel the causal threads leading to the progress made in resettlement. In consequence, we have used a wide variety of statistical techniques to search for empirical regularity and to allow the data to speak for themselves. In addition, we relied on qualitative life-history data to pull together an understanding of the important influences on the achievements of the refugees. Our analyses to this point suggest that the one element that binds economic and educational success together is the household and, more specifically, the family. We will investigate this area in the following chapter.

Chapter 4
Cultural Values, Family Life, and Opportunity

Even though not every refugee family climbed out of poverty in rapid fashion and not every refugee child was doing well in school, the amount of variation for the sample as a whole on the economic and educational outcome measures is really not great. Thus, we looked to the data and the emerging empirical regularities with a view to understanding achievement from the perspective of the Indochinese refugees as a group, rather than basing an explanation primarily on individual differences. The success of the Boat People as a group and the characteristics they share in common draws our attention more than individual differences in achievement among members of the group founded on idiosyncratic factors. Not the achievements of independent individuals but the achievements of a set of individuals with widely shared characteristics—that is, achievement in a normative sense—need to be addressed here.

Looking at the data set and employing qualitative approaches to examine the rich phenomenological material in the life-history data, we have tried to understand how this group of refugees made such progress so quickly. We try hard to avoid giving a false sense of precision by an overreliance on quantifiably treated empirical data alone and not to make a Procrustean bed of the findings by simply lopping off whatever did not meet the canons of stringent statistical proof. Thus, throughout the presentation of data, we use anecdotal comments recorded during the interviews and life-history material to lend coherence and richness to the body of empirical results. After examining the data in this way, we conclude that there are three principal components to the refugees' success: culturally based values, family life-style, and opportunity. These three domains and their roles in the etiology of achievement will be the primary focus of the following discussion.

Cultural Values and Achievement

I feel better and proud when I buy food and pay in cash. Once I went to Dominick's to buy food; at the cash register I held the food-stamp book in my hand. When the cashier told me the amount, I tore out the food stamps to pay her. She was angry and talked loudly about why hadn't I told her in advance that I was using food stamps. I told her I was sorry, I did not understand. At that time there was a line of Americans standing behind me. I felt ashamed. I just wanted to get a job as soon as possible. (Chinese)

My sponsor learned that my wife has experience in cleaning jobs and wanted to refer her to work in a hotel that opened recently. She told my wife this was a good place to work. My wife discussed this with me. We decided not to accept because, as Asians, when we heard of working in a hotel, we did not like it at all. The sponsor felt this was strange and asked my wife the reason. My wife explained to her that it was not appropriate for women to work in a hotel. They might encounter men who were drunk. . . . As for Americans, they think this is a good place to work. As for us, we do not like it. (Chinese)

Without hard work and patience, your thoughts and goals would be nothing. (Lao)

Cultural values tell a great deal about a people; they illuminate and summarize what is of significance within that society.

A cursory glance over our data on Indochinese values is enough to leave one impressed with their importance in overcoming obstacles during early resettlement; these items are at the very heart of the refugees' later successes. The shared cultural values and practices have provided these refugees with the means by which to direct the course of their lives successfully through these early stages of resettlement.

Virtually all the value items cited as core or normative in chapter 2 were positively associated with measures of economic and educational outcome. The mean household GPA for households in which the respondent rated these items as very important or important (i.e., 1 or 2 on the five-point scale) is 3.13 versus 2.78 for those who rated the items less important. The corresponding percentages for poverty-level standings are 112 and 88, respectively. Because there was so little variation among the refugees on these items, with 90 percent or more of the sample rating these items as 1 or 2, these values are best viewed as necessary but not sufficient for success in resettlement.

Instrumental Values

Some value items emerged repeatedly as predictors of achievement outcomes, even when the data set was submitted to a variety of multivariate statistical procedures. We view these as instrumentally important to achievement, because each made sizable, independent, and unique statistical contributions in accounting for differences in poverty standing, GPA, or both when pitted against all other items in the data set. These instrumental values are as follows:

- Past Is as Important as the Present
- Seek New Experience
- Security and Comfort
- Community Respect for Family
- Ashamed to Be on Welfare
- Sacrifice Present for the Future
- Balance of Work and Play
- Cooperative and Harmonious Family

- Perpetuate Ancestral Lineage
- Morality and Ethics
- − Material Possessions
- − Fun and Excitement

Of these values, three repeatedly discriminated among refugees on both economic and scholastic measures. Respondents who rated "Past is as Important as the Present" high in perceived importance lived in households with an average income level at 123 percent of poverty versus those who rated the item lower in importance, with a living standard at 69 percent of the poverty level. The difference in GPA standing is 3.14 versus 2.66, a solid B versus a B minus. Those who rated "Seek New Experiences" high in importance had a household poverty-level average of 110 percent versus those who rated the item less important, who resided in households averaging 82 percent of the poverty level. The corresponding GPAs for the children in these households are 3.09 and 2.92. The other value associated with both outcome measures is "Security and Comfort." Respondents who rated this item highest in importance came from households with a poverty-level standing of 123 percent versus 68 percent of poverty level for those who rated it lower. The corresponding differences in GPA are 3.11 versus 2.90. Only these three values repeatedly discriminated among refugees on both economic and scholastic measures, suggesting that the refugees most likely to have the broadest successes are those who (1) have the strongest respect for their past and its relevance to the present, that is, their cultural heritage; (2) are most willing to face the formidable challenge of seeking out new paths and means of adapting to the demands of different settings; and, having arrived stripped of belongings and lucky to be alive, now (3) are most desirous of physical well-being and freedom from danger.

The remaining instrumental items listed above predicted GPA, the difference being about half a grade point between the higher and lower ratings on importance by parents. They did not predict economic outcomes at statistically better than

chance levels, although some differences approached significance. With "Community Respect for the Family," we can see
that educational achievement is undergirded by strong familial identity and sustained communitywide support and respect. Interpretation of the item "Ashamed to Be on Welfare"
is problematic. As the Chinese respondent in our study quoted
earlier indicates, most refugees stated that they were uncom-
fortable being on welfare but believed that there really was not
much they could do about it at this early point in their stay in
America. Such a subjective assessment of their probability of
moving ahead economically could explain the absence of a
relationship of this item with measures of economic standing.
Even for those off cash assistance, that is, those who have
secured jobs and are moving best toward economic self-sufficiency, their ability to meet an average of 125 percent of the
poverty standard may be a sign of economic progress but is
certainly not one of economic well-being or rising affluence.
Most probably, those parents who felt most keenly about their
economic situation look to their children as the most realistic
avenue to economic security in the long run. In consequence,
the parents may have committed a higher level of effort and
support to their children's schooling, which, in turn, resulted
in higher GPAs.

"Sacrifice the Present for the Future" points up the importance of impulse control and the willingness to delay gratification in favor of school learning and its promise of long-
term gain. The presence of "Balance of Work and Play" also
indicates that this commitment is not a slavish one: although
serious about achievement, these families are not producing
overachieving neurotics who abandon the joy of life at the
expense of good grades. Being a "Cooperative and Harmonious Family" rather than one driven by internal strife and
unbridled ambition keeps them together and enables them to
pool their human capital most effectively. "Perpetuate Ancestral Lineage" and "Morality and Ethics" speak to more
basic dedication and beliefs, pertaining to continuity with the
past and the principles of good conduct. Although less obvious in their importance to educational achievment, these

items have practical consequences that probably relate to motivation and expectations regarding family support, stability, and standards.

All the items except "Material Possessions" and "Fun and Excitement" show positive relationships between perceived importance and outcome measures: the greater the level of perceived importance, the higher the measures on achievement. These latter two items, on the other hand, are shown with a negative sign to indicate that for these the ratings on perceived importance and educational outcome are related inversely: children of parents who attributed greater importance to these value items had lower GPAs. It is noteworthy that parents who attributed the highest levels of importance to "Material Possessions" were not economically better off than others in the sample, and their children did less well in school. The negative effect of "Fun and Excitement" points up the importance of moderation. Both items were discussed briefly in chapter 2 because they were perceived by the refugees to be the two values most important among their non-refugee neighbors. Given the fact that most refugees were residing in impoverished neighborhoods at the time of the study and were no better off economically than their non-refugee neighbors, this contrast in perceived importance of values between themselves and their neighbors probably served to reinforce the refugees' notions about what works and what does not work for getting ahead in America.

Values in Context

One importance of the factor analysis shown in chapter 2 is to stress the need to think in terms of the clusters of values and their underlying dimensions when combined. From this perspective, the six factors that best characterize the value system of the refugees pertain to cultural foundation, family-based achievement, hard work, resettlement and commonality of the family, self-reliance and family pride, and coping and integration. Having used a statistical approach that allows us to detect the underlying value structure of the refugees, what else may be said about these main themes? We would like now to explore the possible relationships they may have to one another and the role they may play in the resettlement process for the refugees. The following discussion is a heuristic attempt to place these value clusters in the context of resettlement and the realities in which the Indochinese find themselves during the early stages of adaptation to life in the United States.

Figure 14 summarizes the set of six factors that emerged in the factor analysis and relates them to resettlement. We have organized these along a procedural time frame, connecting the value clusters to the resettlement process at points where they may be most required for successful adaptation, as well as on an "agentic" level, relating those at the family or individual level where we believed them to be most meaningful. This family/individual dichotomy, however, should not be viewed as a hard division whereby "Hard Work" does not apply to families or "Education and Achievement" to individuals. Nor would we want to suggest that "Traditional Customs" have no place in the present as the refugees attempt to cope and integrate with life in the United States. Throughout this work we have argued for the exact opposite: it is because they have skillfully used their cultural heritage that they have made such progress in this country. The heuristic nature of the figure, then, should be kept in mind in the ensuing discussion. As a result of the discussion, though, one may get a clearer sense of not only how the values relate to one another but that there are some that, because they provide answers to the refugees at critical points in the process, may have facilitated their resettlement.

Factor 1 (Cultural Foundation) represents the set of cultural givens, the most basic attributes the refugees brought with them from Indochina. Suggested here are a pattern of living and a worldview richly and vitally connected to their cultural background. Included also is a sense of continuity with ancestral wisdom, a knowledge of rituals and ceremony that lends a coherent meaning to the mutually shared goals that bind them to others in the refugee community. These

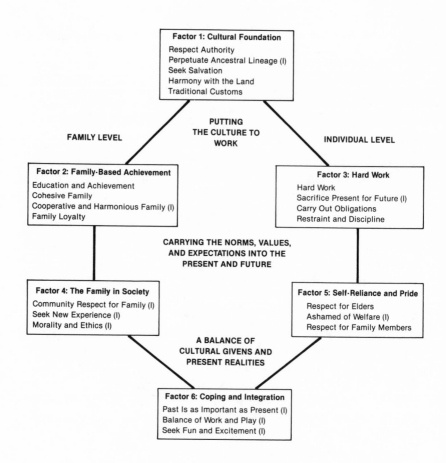

Fig. 14. Cultural values and adaptation (I = instrumental scale)

cultural forces are alive, a source of drive and motivation, with uplifting and edifying effects.

How they are put to work is reflected in factors 2 (Family-Based Achievement) and 3 (Hard Work), referring to imperatives at the family and individual levels. Factor 2 places the responsibility for self-improvement and achievement squarely in the context of the family. The parents are the teachers of cultural literacy, being responsible for inculcating and implementing the cultural values. They are the role models, as were their parents before them, and their stewardship will be judged by the success of their children in bringing honor and respectability to the family name.

Factor 3 is addressed at the individual level and what must be done at that level for the cultural givens to take hold and work. It calls for setting aside self-interest and self-indulgence in the interest of the common good. It calls for reason over instinct and, of course, hard work, patience, and a long-term perspective.

Factors 4 (The Family in Society) and 5 (Self-Reliance and Pride) parallel the previous two but carry them farther into the present. Factor 4 presents the notion of a better life for the family and the possibility that people need to be adventuresome to achieve it. This life is woven out of a fabric of social connections that go beyond blood relations and into the community and is premised on a social contract derived from shared moral standards and a common vision. The individual does not have primacy over family life or community norms, but this is not a dehumanizing experience because of the vital connection of all individuals to the broader identities, to family and community. Factor 5 reflects this better life at the individual level with emphasis on self-reliance in the context of family pride and concern for the condition and care, as well as respect for the wisdom, of those older members of the family.

Finally, factor 6 (Coping and Integration) represents awareness that the world is shared with people of other cultures, with possibly divergent values that may put cherished beliefs and ways of life at risk. But life is full of compromises, and the willingness to embrace such risks is the price paid to restore balance to life during periods of political and economic upheaval. This factor seems to say that postarrival adaptive adjustments must be made in order to accommodate to American ways if the refugees wish to advance beyond peripheral functions at the fringes of the larger society. The conflicting demands of their situation in the United States are captured by this Vietnamese respondent, who states: "I wish to dissolve into American life but still remain culturally attached to Vietnam." They are adventuresome and forward-looking but not without some apprehension.

In figure 14, we have highlighted the values of instrumental import. It can be seen that the instrumental values, those with the most immediate pragmatic relevance, are associated with the family's efforts to deal with the realities of the moment. They predominate at those points in the adaptational process where families are needing to reestablish themselves in the new society, to reaffirm who and what they are and what they will become. These are matters not only of achievement but also of maintaining the integrity of their heritage.

Parents as Carriers of the Culture

The relationship of values to achievement here is evidence that the cultural values the refugees brought with them are important tools of adaptation; they are of significance in acquiring a livelihood and, perhaps of even greater importance, in promoting school learning among the children. Children, of course, are not born with a sense of their heritage already in their heads; culture is acquired as a result of deliberate and concentrated parental effort. This inculcation of values across succeeding generations is a universal feature of the transmission of culture, and the high correlation ($r = .83$) in the value ratings of parents and children cited earlier in chapter 2 is quantitative testimony that the parents have served their stewardship well in this regard. For a closer examination of these sets of ratings and their implications, a rank ordering of the

ten most important and two least important values, as perceived by parents and children, is as follows:

Parents	*Children*
1. Education and Achievement	Respect for Family Members
2. Cooperative and Harmonious Family	Education and Achievement
3. Hard Work	Freedom
4. Respect for Family Members	Family Loyalty
5. Carry out Obligations	Hard Work
6. Freedom	Cooperative and Harmonious Family
7. Family Loyalty	Morality and Ethics
8. Restraint and Discipline	A Secure and Comfortable Life
9. Morality and Ethics	Sacrifice the Present for the Future
10. Sacrifice the Present for the Future	Carry Out Obligations
. . . .	. . . .
25. Desire for Material Possessions	Seek Fun and Excitement
26. Seek Fun and Excitement	Desire for Material Possessions

Both groups rank achievement, family-related items,
and hard work near the very top. It appears, then, that both
parents and children are committed to educational goals and
are willing to expend the effort needed to achieve them. Even
though the correlation between the rankings is high, some
discrepancies in value ratings between parents and children
are worth pointing out. A major discrepancy concerns "Carry
Out Obligations." Ninety-five percent of the parents rated this
item as 1 or 2 in importance, which put it fifth in the hierarchical standing. Seventy-one percent of the children rated it 1 or
2, placing it tenth in the ranking order of importance. That

the children in the family have less enthusiasm about obedience and carrying out chores than do the parents is to be expected, as is the difference on "A Balance of Work and Play" (not shown above), to which the children attributed greater importance (ranked fourteenth) than did the parents (ranked twenty-fourth). More serious, however, with respect to the Americanization of the children were parent-child differences with regard to "Material Possessions" and "Fun and Excitement." Although these ranked last based on ratings by both parents and children, only 20 percent of the parents viewed them at levels of 1 to 3 on the five-point scale of importance, whereas almost a third (31 percent) of the children ranked the items at similar levels. Whether this difference signifies a generation gap or possibly a sign of difference in assimilation into American culture cannot be determined. Nevertheless, the differing views may be the source of developing parental apprehension regarding the children's lack of adherence to their cultural heritage.

These data provide strong evidence that the refugees live by and transmit the cultural givens to their children, thereby linking them to a way of life and a worldview that are deeply rooted in their cultural background and that act as a source of motivation and the basis for efficient functioning in their new homeland. To be sure, there are differences between parents and children on the importance of some of the values: the two items the refugees value least but perceive their nonrefugee neighbors as valuing most, both of which are negatively correlated with GPA, are also the very items that represent the major parent-child difference. But, for the moment, this intergenerational difference is a matter of degree, not kind. The responsibility and commitment to self-improvement and achievement rests squarely in the family, and with such salience that it penetrates all levels of family life. The values, which are the subjective side of the culture, have been passed on successfully from the parents to the children, and, as we will see in the section to follow, both use them seriously, consistently, and imaginatively to practical advantage. We now turn to the refugee family to learn something of its key properties and how it goes about putting these values to work.

Family Life-style

I had the opportunity to go to California to talk to the Vietnamese League of Orange County. The audience I spoke with was made up entirely of Indochinese, new Indochinese American citizens. These were the Boat People, not the first wave but the second wave; these were people who were poor, fishermen and tailors and tanners who left in those boats, crowded in those boats, and came to the United States. They are not native English speakers. . . . When I gave the talk, the hostess for the evening apologized to me for some empty chairs. She said, "I'm sorry, Mr. Secretary, but there are some parents who work with their children every night on homework and thus could not come to hear you." I said the secretary of education grants excused absences for those parents, that's OK. (From a speech by William J. Bennett, Secretary of Education, to the Cleveland City Club, January 10, 1986, used with permission)

I wish my children would graduate [from high school] and could have further education and have a good job. For me, I have no hope; my hope is my children. (Vietnamese)

When a father and a mother look away, the child becomes foolish; when father and mother look toward him, the child becomes smart. (Vietnamese proverb)

First you learn to respect, then you learn literature. (Vietnamese proverb)

The family is a central institution in Asian life, and our findings indicate that of all its activities and functions during resettlement, there may be nothing more important than its role in instilling, transmitting, and implementing cultural values. The Indochinese family connects its cultural heritage to the new environment and opportunity structure in two ways: first, by the development of a life-style to cope effectively with the exigencies of resettlement and, second, by the allocation of its human resources that will most effectively gain it access to the available opportunities. Thus, we deliberately place the section on family life between that on cultural values, which precedes it, and the one on opportunity structure, which follows. The data on values go far to explain the normative character of the resettlement achievements of the Indochinese families, that is, the homogeneity in the level and quality of their response to the new homeland. We now look to the data to identify those attributes of the families that enabled them to give rein to their cultural background. In so doing, they crystallize available means-ends connections to resettle successfully in America.

Key Family Characteristics

> *The family tie is very tight, and the sense of family is very strong. Members of three, sometimes four generations lived under the same roof. But not here.* (Lao)

One advantage of complex statistics is that they can detect, in a straightforward and unambiguous way, factors that in bivariate comparisons appear to be producing independent and unique effects but which are, in fact, factors masquerading as effects of other variables. After all our complex statistical scrubbing and polishing of the information in the data set, three sets of items emerge to explain the refugees' success. They represent three areas of family relationships and expectations and account for almost 50 percent of the variation in outcome measures. The domains and the cumulative amounts of explanatory variance (given in parentheses) contributed by each are as follows:

- Family Sex-Role Equality (.24)
- Parent-Child Involvement (.40)
- Efficacy (.47)

We now look to these sets of variables with a view to understanding the properties of family life, its rhythm and flow, its organization, and its methods of control and regulation of labor and adaptation strategies.

Equality in the Home: Decision Making and Role Sharing

A predominant characteristic in high-achiever households in our study is an egalitarian, rather democratic definition of sex roles in the family. Equality between the sexes, particularly with regard to spousal decision making, participation in the labor force, and parental involvement in school-related activities, appears to be a key factor in postarrival adaptation. As two male respondents note:

> *I discovered that my wife is intelligent. She has learned English faster than I did, and she seems to know a lot. She used to work, but then she quit because she was pregnant. I felt happy that she could contribute to helping the family financially. In Laos it was only the husband who had financial responsibility.* (Lao)

> *In general, there is a long way ahead of us, but my wife and I will rebuild it together. She now works four days a week. When we think of the life ahead of us, we see a constructive future. We hope that we can afford for our children to go to college.* (Chinese)

The egalitarian life-style is best illustrated by two questionnaire items, both involving responses to the sharing of family decision-making power or influence by the spouses. Multivariate analysis of the data revealed that children with higher GPAs came from homes where (1) there was strong agreement that both spouses should participate equally in decisions involving employment and (2) strong disagreement with the statement that a wife should be subservient to the husband's wishes. Children of respondents who said that the wife should be consulted regarding whether or not a husband should quit a job had an average GPA of 3.19, compared with 2.81 for the children in families in which the respondent said that the wife need not be consulted. Respondents were also asked if the wife should always do "as the husband wishes." The children in the homes in which the respondent disagreed with this item averaged 3.16, compared to 2.64 for children in homes in which the respondents agreed. Thus, two of the stronger GPA predictors from the questionnaire pertain specifically to the relative equality in influence of the spouses. The differences are sizable and statistically reliable; thus, it appears that when attitudes in the home are nonegalitarian, the scholastic performance of the children suffers.

Two additional items contributing to the explained variance in GPA pertained to whether the husband helped with some of the household chores. If the husband participated in doing the dishes and the laundry, particularly if he did it in the United States but not in Indochina, the consequence for GPA was positive. These items explained 0.16 of the variance.

These egalitarian attitudes extend to the sex roles and expectations for children in the family, as well as to the adults. Here egalitarian parental attitudes toward housework and education in which both boys and girls participate equally, rather than a more traditional sex-based allocation of housework for girls and college for boys, predicts higher GPAs. One way to show this egalitarian approach to sex-role socialization and expectations is to look at bivariates involving these two items on children's participation in housework and education. Children of respondents who rejected the idea that a college education is more important for boys than for girls had GPAs that averaged 3.14 as opposed to an average GPA of 2.83 for children of parents who advocated a promale bias in college education. Similarly, in those families in which housework was not strictly limited to the females, the GPAs averaged 3.15 versus an average GPA of 2.85 for children in families in which males did not participate in any housework. Although we lack the data to know exactly what sex-role attitudes these parents had in Indochina before being exposed to the travails of migration and the influence of American culture, it appears that they are currently working under very egalitarian views and expectations, which make best use of the human capital within the family unit and promote the growth and development of all members, regardless of sex.

Finally, the fact that we found no sex differences in academic achievement in overall GPA or CAT scores, nor in math GPA or CAT scores (traditionally a subject in which men predominate as a result of preference, socialization, or special cognitive skills), might be attributable to the lack of differences in gender-based role expectations and behaviors in these refugee homes.

Parental Involvement

Reading to children. We asked the parents if they read to their children, meaning the younger children. Response to this single item proved to be one of the statistically purest and most reliable predictors of GPA. Forty-five percent of the parents said that they read to their children, and the average GPA for all children in those households (not only those being read to) was 3.14 versus 2.95 for those in homes where the parents did not read to their children. The effect, therefore, appears to be spread across all children in the home and is not particular to those who are younger.

In the absence of additional data, any interpretation of the reason for this impact on achievement would be speculative and indirect. The problem of interpretation is even more confounded by finding that the consequence for education is unrelated to the language used by the reader. Of those parents who read to their children, twice as many read in their native language (68 percent) as in English (32 percent). Interestingly, those children who are read to in their native language have a higher mean GPA (3.16) than those who are read to in English (3.09). Though this difference is not statistically reliable, the direction of difference is intriguing. At a minimum, this finding suggests that English literacy skills of parents may not play a vital role in determining school performance, that the affective or emotional components associated with reading to children and, very likely, the cultural wisdom shared in stories read in the native language have a positive carryover to the school.

We also would venture the hypothesis that reading to children early in life makes the boundary between home and school less obvious and less forbidding. More specifically, the valuing of education as expressed by the presence of books in the home and the family interactions centered around reading and homework activities make learning and education a normal and familiar part of children's lives. Possibly, this learning and the learning to learn that takes place early at home through reading make it more likely that these children will feel at home in school and, in turn, more comfortable with the formal learning experience there.

This finding on the differences in GPA among children who are and are not read to at home, as with those on spelling ability and on family size and GPA, are intriguing. They cannot be elucidated more fruitfully on the basis of our data but certainly deserve serious consideration for future research.

Discipline and control. Modes of discipline to influence children's behavior in desired ways also contribute to the amount of variance explained. Children from homes where parents take an active role in influencing their children have significantly higher grades than those from homes where there is no parental effort at control. Seventy percent of the respondents reported that they disciplined their children at levels ranging from "very often" to "hardly ever," and the average GPA for children in these homes was 3.18, regardless of the level of discipline. Thirty percent of the parents responded that they never disciplined their children, and the mean GPA of their children was 2.80. The difference is sizable and statistically reliable. Parental discipline, however infrequent, therefore is apparently important to school performance.

In the main, parental control is firm but not harsh, as can be seen by the responses to an item asking parents to describe how they discipline their children. The methods cited most often are the following (in percentage):

1. Urge children to do well in school for the   87
   honor and pride of the family.
2. Build self-confidence by telling them they have   71
   the ability to do well.

3. Reward good performance (i.e., money, presents, special privileges).   57
4. Stress shame if grade falls below expectation.   55
5. Grant special privileges.   47
6. Take away privileges for less than acceptable   37
   grades.
7. Spank.   7

Because families often used more than one method of discipline, it was not possible to partial out the differential effects of one kind versus another on achievement. But, as stated previously, parental involvement in at least some type of disciplining effort appears important to school achievement. The efforts at control that predominate are neither punitive nor physical. The most frequently cited means of influencing school performance is the appeal to family honor, cited by almost nine out of ten respondents. This item is in keeping with the cultural value system and the family-based achievement factor. But it should also be noted that this emphasis on family identity and pride is not stressed to the exclusion of positive appeal and support at the individual level; seven out of ten respondents reported attempting to influence their children by building up their self-confidence. The remaining items are more typically negative sanctions; slightly more than half stressed shame, one in three took away privileges, and, finally, 7 percent reported that they spanked their children.

Homework. We questioned parents about their role in encouraging and assisting with homework, and, not surprisingly, those children with better grades came from households where parents were most involved. The main role of the parent appears to be that of facilitator; that is, they assume responsibility for the practical conditions that permit homework to take place and operate smoothly rather than directing the preparation of assignments or providing pedagogical help. Their lack of an American education or facility with English precludes active involvement in the content of homework. This lack, however, seems not as crucial to success as is the parents' interest in their children's education and concern that their children do their homework.

Commitment to education is evident in the number of hours of homework reported by parents and students. Parents reported that an average of two hours, fifty-four minutes is spent at homework by all children in the family during weeknights. Data gathered independently from the children are basically the same: students in high school reported an average of three hours, ten minutes; junior high students reported an average of two and a half hours; grade school children reported an average of two hours, five minutes.

These figures are comparable to homework time reported by Nakanishi (1982) of two and three and a half hours outside of school on weekdays for students in Japan at the junior and senior high school level. On the other hand, Timmer, Eccles, and O'Brien (1985) reported that American students in their sample studied about one and a half hours a day at comparable levels of school grade and age. It is important to bear in mind that our data on homework include all students in the household, even those in kindergarten and elementary school, who are assigned little, if any, homework. On the other hand, because homework is a total family commitment, the kind that results in high GPAs regardless of sibship size, then it is understandable that all the children stay involved equally, regardless of their grade level. It suggests that a great amount of learning goes on in these homes in terms of course content and study habits, and it becomes understandable that children socialized in these settings would feel at home in school.

Because homework dominates the home milieu during the evening hours and simultaneously involves all children in the family, we could not tell how much time was spent on what subjects or relate the expenditure of time to the educational performance of individual pupils. These are important issues, but it also should be recognized that the type of experience children have in connection with homework is also an important consideration. Although we are unable to penetrate the more subtle interactions between older and younger children and are not in a position to make sensible comparisons with other groups, we believe it would be a mistake to assume that homework is viewed as bothersome or drudgery. Even though their roles differ, all family members become full participants in the educational process and appear to find satisfaction in doing so.

Efficacy and Family Identity

Efficacy has long been thought to be an important ingredient in achievement motivation. If people believe that they have fate control, control over the forces that influence their lives, it will affect their view of the future and produce expectations for success, which, in turn, will motivate them to make an effort to achieve goals. The belief in the value of hard work, being planful, even optimistic about one's future, all pivot on one's perceived ability to be efficacious. Respondents thus were asked a series of questions about the site or locus of control in their lives, that is, internal or external, and the degree to which they believe they have mastery over their own lives.

Efficacy. The refugees score high on efficacy when measured directly, and there is evidence that such items have consequence for economic and academic performance: those highest on these measures are more likely to succeed. The direction of the relationship is a positive one: the higher the scores on the efficacy items, the higher or better the outcome. The following illustrates the strength of association with both poverty-level standing and GPA. Respondents were asked, "Do you get to carry out things the way you thought, or do things usually come up that change your plans?" For those who said that plans went according to the way they thought, the mean household poverty-level standing was 120 percent and the mean GPA for the children was 3.12. For those whose plans were changed, the corresponding means were lower: 69 percent for poverty standing and 2.97 for GPA.

For all efficacy items the relationship to educational outcomes was stronger than that for the economic variables. This difference in impact probably realistically measures the actual situation of the refugees. They do not have much say over the kinds of jobs they can hold; they are more vulnerable to the ebb and flow of the economy and to other structural factors outside their control. In education, however, perceived as dependent on their own efforts or the efforts of their children, there is scope for personal control to effect desired outcomes. Thus, we see, for example, for children from homes where parents reported that good luck affected their lives in a major way (i.e., an attribution for success with an external locus of control), the mean GPA was 2.96. On the other hand, the mean GPA was 3.17 for children in households where luck was viewed as less important. The poverty standing for these households, however, was virtually identical. Finally, children of parents who believed that they had a great deal of influence on them did better in school than those of parents who believed they had little influence.

Causal attributions. Another way to look at efficacy is to measure the attributions that people make to explain events in their lives. Such explanations are interpreted as efficacy constructs because they attempt to assess responsibility for causation or locus of control. The data below show that the refugee parents and children alike credit scholastic achievement more to variables under the control of the individual ("Love of learning," "Hard work," and "Perseverance") than to variables beyond the control of the individual ("Luck" or "Fate").

	Percentage Who Agree	
	Parents	*Schoolchildren*
Love of learning	99	91
Hard work	97	93
Perseverance	94	89
Excellent teachers	89	92
Intelligence	86	67
Excellent schools	86	88
Luck	56	37
Fate	46	41

Additionally, we asked about factors that hindered academic performance. Only a few attributions were cited as impediments to educational performance:

	Percentage Who Agree	
	Parents	*Schoolchildren*
Lack of English	65	98
Disruptive behavior of nonrefugee students	24	20
Lack of transportation	21	25
Family responsibilities	16	21
Poor schools	8	5
Illness	7	18
Fate	7	4
Bad luck	3	7

The most important hindrance to their children's school progress in the view of two-thirds of the parents was a lack of proficiency in English language skills. The data from the children were even more emphatic, with 98 percent citing lack of English as the prime roadblock to improved educational performance. Unlike English acquisition, the remaining items are less likely to be under immediate personal control. But these tend to be comparatively less important than lack of English and, in most instances, realistic and straightforward commentary on the real situation in which parents and students find themselves. From the standpoint of efficacy, it is important to note that fate and luck, the least controllable attributions, are seen as least important as causal determinants of success or failure.

Family identity. As products of Western education, particularly Western psychology, in initial reaction to these data we thought of such items as love of learning, hard work, and efficacy as person-centered qualities. No doubt, to an important degree, this view holds some credence. Intrinsic gratification is certainly felt when a problem is worked through and the correct answer found. And, no doubt, hard work is a sign of strong commitment at the individual level. But as greater experience and contact with the refugees were gained, there came a fuller appreciation of responses to these items and an interpretation that took family-based identity into account. That is to say, joy of learning has come to mean not only the joy one gets from learning but the joy of a collective learning experience—joy not only for the learning one acquires but also by seeing it take place in others, in part perhaps as a result of one's teaching effort, and from pride in the family because others in one's family are doing well in school. Similarly, the meaning of hard work applies beyond the individual level. It also refers to the family unit, in which all members are expected to (and generally do) pull together, in which both spouses work, all members share in the housework, and older children teach the younger. Thus, we interpret these results on efficacy to be derivative from family involvement and refer to a family-level identity as well.

In the classic study by Coleman et al. (1966) on the effects of desegregation, several efficacy measures were used: "Good luck is more important than hard work for success"; "Every time I try to get ahead, something or someone stops me"; and "People like me don't have much of a chance to be successful in life" (p. 320). They found that children who responded with a strong sense of environmental control (i.e., efficacy) also had a higher level of achievement in school than those who believed that they were less able to influence their lives. The authors reported these measures "extremely highly related to achievement" (p. 325), so high, in fact, as to override variations in school and a host of geographic and demographic factors. Our results lend support to the perception of control over external events as playing a determining role in achievement. Our data, however, do not give it such singular importance. In addition, we interpret its origins differently. It may appear to be a person-centered variable, but, as with cultural values, children are not born with such beliefs about their relationship to the outside world. These beliefs are acquired, and, in our view, this sense of environmental control can be traced back to the family setting, that is, relational efficacy in contrast to personal efficacy, as treated in Western social science literature.

Culture as Life-style

In this section, we present excerpts from three life-history interviews. These descriptions have been translated from the native languages of the respondents by our interviewers. The material pertains largely to parenting practices and, therefore, relates more often to educational performance of the children than to economic outcomes. Had we included complete life histories, such as refugee efforts to enter the labor market, adjustment of personal lives, interactions with sponsors, service agencies, the Indochinese community, and so on, the length of the manuscript would have been prohibitive. But the brief segments of family life presented here nonetheless provide a good sense of what goes on in the family when interaction among all members is at its fullest, during the late afternoon and early evening hours.

The excerpts come from three respondents, a Lao, a Chinese, and a Vietnamese. The Vietnamese family had been in the United States the longest, three years at the time of the interview, with both parents employed, and, in addition, the father and his young sons engaged in yardwork on weekends for additional income. The Lao family had been in the United States for two and a half years with only one parent, the mother, employed. The Chinese family is the most recent arrival, having been in the country for one year, with neither parent employed. There are seventeen children among the three families, and, with one exception, those attending school are doing well, getting A's and B's.

The Lao Family

The first description of family life is by the Lao mother. There are five children in the family, three boys and two girls, who range from four to eighteen years in age. The two girls are the youngest.

Every weekday afternoon, all my children go home right from their schools. They change their clothes, then go watch TV. I come home right after them, and some of them help me clean house and prepare dinner. We have dinner together, and then, while I do the dishes, the boys help clear the table, then play together about one or two hours. Then, when it is dark, they get back to their schoolwork. Only my oldest son has much schoolwork to do; the rest are too young and don't have as much as their brother.

When I get home, I always ask my children about their homework and ask them to finish doing it. I also direct them to do the house chores and not let them do as they wish. That is our culture: the young ones have to listen to their parents. Of course, I ask them to help with cooking and doing the house chores with me. Our culture doesn't let the male in the family do house chores, but now, here in this new society, the female has to take a job, too, and everybody has to help at home.

My husband is the one who decides what chores the children are to do, especially the important things or the hard, heavy things. My oldest child is a boy; he has responsibility for the other kids. When my husband is not home, I direct them; but I always respect the males in the family, and we still do it here. My husband always tries to show our kids a good example, and he is the model for the kids to follow.

Only my oldest son has much homework and lots of books to read. He spends about two or more hours on his homework. The young ones spend only about half an hour. They do their work by themselves, or the oldest one helps his brother and sister if they have any problems. We don't know how to help them because we don't have enough education, but we always ask them to do their homework. Well, sometimes they forget to do it; perhaps the homework is too hard, or they may be too lazy and don't want to do it. That is what I guess; I don't know for sure. But I know that the Laotian instructional assistant sometimes calls my kids, talks to them, and re-minds them to do their homework and explains to them about the importance of doing it. I only can remind them to do it in front of my eyes.

I know my children never get any awards from school, but their report cards show me they get mostly B's and some A's, with written praise from their teachers. My husband and I think that they are doing OK in school. We take them out to McDonald's every two weeks, and these eat-outs are our rewards for them.

When they are not doing well in school, my husband and I talk to them seriously. We don't spank our kids. We think that spanking is old-fashioned and has no effect. We express more love than any other expression, to show our kids that we do care for them and so want them to be good. For me, I cry when I see them not doing well, and they are very sad to see me crying and promise to be better. I think that is the good way to keep the kids doing well.

All my children get along with each other very well. They listen to their eldest brother, who always helps his brothers and sisters in almost everything, housework or schoolwork. He is responsible for others in the family regarding schooling. According to our culture, the eldest son is always responsible for others in the family.

We don't read to our children, because we don't read English. The kids can read for themselves [in English]. But we tell cultural stories to them, in our native lan-guage [Lao]. We tell stories about half an hour on week-days or about one hour on the weekends.

My kids like TV very much, and they spend most of their leisure time watching TV, cartoons, special pro-grams for kids. Of course, we limit their TV time. They can only watch TV after school before doing homework and another hour after dinner. We don't use TV as a reward for good work.

I know that here in America, without good education, you cannot get a good job with better salary. We tell our kids about this and ask them to study hard to get a good job. We need to learn more English, but we have to work first to feed our kids. How can I go to school while working all day long and after work I also have my family to take care of? The only thing I can do is work and get money to support my family.

We talk to them very often, about once a week. We want to remind them about the importance of education. I don't know for sure whether they understand or not, because they are still too young. But my husband and I always remind them to study first, study hard, not play, not go out without permission from us. We tell them that we want to go to school, too, but we have to work to feed them. We sacrifice for them, and the only thing they can pay back is to study well.

My husband and I wish our kids to have good jobs, but we don't know what kinds of jobs are good for them, or what jobs they are good for! Right now, I don't know yet, and even my eldest son told me that he wants to be an engineer but doesn't know what kind of engineering he can learn! When we talk about this, my husband says that he wants his eldest son to become a mechanic; that is it. I really don't know what careers my kids can do. I think they can study a skill and get a good job; that is enough for me. Becoming a mechanic is good, but, of course, an engineer is better. I wish my eldest son would be an engineer, my second son a mechanic, my third son an accountant, my daughter a nurse, and the youngest [a girl] a teacher. But who can tell for sure what they will be?

If my children had remained in Laos, I could never have hoped for the same careers for them, because in Laos we didn't have to compete with any others, and we preferred to live a quiet and peaceful life in the countryside, to farm or have a small business only. We did not have the ambition to be in high society. Here, if you don't get enough education to get a good job, you cannot go to the countryside and do farming. There is one way you must follow: get a good education to survive.

The Chinese Family

The next picture of family life was reported by a Chinese woman from Vietnam. There are seven children in the family, ranging in age from ten to twenty-four. Those children still in school are doing outstanding work. All were getting A's in math and B's in other subjects, English excepted. Neither parent is employed.

> *When the children come back from school, usually they watch TV or video. If they have schoolwork close to the due day, they do it. I am a housewife, and I take care of the family and decide most of the chores the children are to do. My husband is unemployed, and he helps me around the house. Most of the time we don't have to be involved with the children. We let them do as they wish.*
>
> *They can watch TV or video while helping me clean the house or prepare dinner. I ask the girls to do cooking, dishes, washing clothes, cleaning house; and the boys do yardwork, mowing the lawn, taking care of the garbage. The eldest son and the eldest daughter have special tasks, driving us around when we need it, taking me shopping because my husband and I don't drive.*
>
> *But I only decide on small things [food, clothes]. My husband decides bigger things such as buying a TV, a VCR, a car, or whatever. We just got this low-income housing unit about one month ago.*
>
> *Generally, my children do their schoolwork after dinner, right on the dining table because we don't have a place set aside for them to study. The young ones spend only about one hour or so for their schoolwork. If one of them wants a private place to study, she or he can go into one of their bedrooms.*
>
> *The big ones spend more time on their schoolwork, from one-half to three hours every day and night. My eldest son, who is in college, helps them sometimes, but generally they can do their schoolwork by themselves. My husband and I cannot help them, and we really don't*

do anything to get them to study; they know their responsibilities.

My husband and I don't give any rewards to our children for doing well in school or tasks around the house. We only tell them to try to imitate other good students. We treat them as adult persons and always show them love. My husband and I rarely spank our children, even when they were young in Vietnam. For me, I think that spanking is a good way to keep children in good behavior, but I don't need to do it because my husband and I always show them our good example.

Besides, there is another important thing you should know. After years of living with the Communists, the children realize that they are lucky to live in a country of freedom. They can become whatever they want to be, and their futures are in their own hands. We don't need to remind them, and you should know that almost all of the refugees from Vietnam have known that, too.

My children get along with one another well. They are responsible for others in the family regarding both schooling and housekeeping.

We are Chinese from Vietnam. All members of the family can speak both Chinese and Vietnamese. I was born in Vietnam. My husband was born in China. We met each other in Vietnam and have our family there. I can read and write Vietnamese better than Chinese. My husband tells old Chinese stories to them but does not read to them. They like to watch Chinese videotapes, read fiction or nonfiction such as Kung Fu and stories about Buddha. The children don't want to read either Chinese or Vietnamese books. They are free to do so most weekends, but on the weekdays they have to finish their schoolwork first; then they can watch TV about one or two hours. They go to bed about 10:00 P.M.

According to our culture, a well-educated person always gets respect, even when not rich. But this country is different; education goes along with the wealth. I would like my children to be well educated, both to be respected *in our community and also to get a high position in this society.*

Our generation is different. We didn't get much education, but we could do business and get rich. Here education goes along with higher position, higher careers.

I wish my children to get enough knowledge, to have a skill to survive, to get a good job. The boys can get a higher education and higher position, but the girl belongs to her own family and doesn't need to go too far. My husband and I let them choose their own careers. We only want them to be happy and to have an easy life.

If my family had remained in Vietnam, my children would not have been able to complete their education, because the Communists would not have let them study. Instead, they would have just learned to praise socialism and go to the labor camp.

My children are happy here. They can do whatever they want to and learn whatever they want to. They are doing pretty well at school. The teachers like them because they are so eager to learn. The schooling system here is more open, easier, the discipline not too serious. The students are being treated equally, no discrimination about sex, age, or race.

The Vietnamese Family

The final report on family life comes from a Vietnamese father who was employed and also did yardwork on weekends. The mother is also employed. There are five children in the family, ranging in age from four to thirteen. The oldest, a boy, is a straight-A student. The others are doing well, except for a nine-year-old male whom the father views as lazy.

After school, my children always look for something to eat first, usually a light snack such as ice cream, popcorn or something left over from last night. My wife and I are not at home at that time, but my children have things to do at home. My oldest son does his duty, cleans the living room and his bedroom and cooks the rice in the electric rice cooker. My third child, also a boy, has to help his brother. My second child, the oldest daughter, has to clean her room, too, with the help of her younger sister. They also have to do the laundry for the whole family and clean the kitchen. My wife gets home around 4:30 or 5:00 after work, with our youngest boy, a four-year-old, from the child-care center. She has stopped to get the groceries on the way home.

My two daughters fix dinner for the whole family. Then they have dinner without me, because I always get home late, about 7:30. After dinner, my oldest does dishes while my wife takes care of the little boy and watches TV.

When I get home, my children are studying at the dining table. I find a corner right next to them and have my dinner. Usually, they do their schoolwork by themselves. For the schoolwork, my oldest son is in charge of his little sister [the fourth child], but she is doing well enough to be responsible about doing her schoolwork without being told. My oldest daughter [second child] has to take care of her little brother [third child]. This boy is the laziest one I have ever seen. He always forgets to take his homework home and tries to avoid doing anything, including chores.

Every evening, my children study about one or two hours, depending on their work, then go take a bath and get ready for bed around 9:00 or 9:30. I don't let them watch TV at night, but I know they turn it on in the afternoon right when they get home and watch it while doing their schoolwork and house chores. My wife likes to watch TV and video, too, and the kids sneak out to join her if they finish their work.

About decisions in the family, I have to assign tasks to them, including my wife. Of course, those tasks are given on the basis of age: the older has more responsibilities; the boys have to do heavy tasks [cleaning the yard and doing the garbage]; the girls do cooking and dishes and the laundry.

The kids always listen to me or their mother and don't need help to make decisions. They have to listen to their parents; that is the rule in my family.

About rewards for doing well in school or tasks around the house, I use different ways for each child. My oldest son is doing well in school; he gets straight A's, and I let him have the right to play the video keyboard game at home when he finishes his work. His brother is too lazy and doesn't do well in school. He always gets C's or D's and some E's, always forgets his home chores. He is not allowed to play the keyboard games or to watch TV (but he always tries to sneak out and do it!).

I also use money to reward them: a dollar for an A, for a B nothing. They have to save money, because when they get a C their savings must be debited a dollar, and if there is a D, a dollar plus a spank. The other way to reward them is to take them out to McDonald's or Burger King. I always arrange a time to come to the PTA meetings and keep in touch with my children's teachers, especially the Vietnamese instructional assistant at school, to make sure that my kids are doing well at school. They listen to this teacher and respect her well. They don't want to be reported on badly.

I spank them when they really do very bad things— impoliteness, fighting, being too stubborn, and so on. Kids are afraid of spanking, but spanking alone is not a good way. While I spank my kid, I always talk to him or her, explain the reason for my feelings. I think that I am hurting myself, too, and I explain it to my kids, to try to help them understand the reason for this punishment.

I also keep in close touch with the Vietnamese instructional assistant at school. The kids have to listen to her. I know that she also gives them special praises, some gifts for their birthdays, and talks to them when they are not doing well.

I know that my kids are growing in a new society that has plenty of freedom but less responsibility. They are too young to understand the good and the bad, the rights and the wrongs. Besides, imitating bad friends is another

*way they are affected. I have to keep them in good be-
havior even though I have to use serious punishments
like spanking. But besides spanking, I also treat them
well and respect their personalities. My oldest daughter
is a teen now, and I don't spank her but talk to her more
sincerely, seriously, and closely.*

*I have another job doing yardwork on the weekends,
and my three big children help me very well. But I know
that at home without me, the two boys always have problems—yelling, fighting. At school they are better; they
always support each other side by side when they have
problems on the playground. The older ones are made to
be responsible.*

*I tried to teach them to read Vietnamese last year, but I
have been too busy to do it, and the Vietnamese class at
church [Vietnamese Church] is too short to cover the
reading program. They have some Vietnamese books
written in English, too. Those are stories and nonfiction.
When I have the time, especially when I take them out to
eat or do yardwork, I tell them stories from our country,
of course in Vietnamese.*

*At school they have their reading program every day
and have to read books every week, doing book reports,
too. They check out books from school and take them
home to read. They read about one hour each day; the
two big ones have to do book reports and have to spend
more time on reading at home. They do it either in the
afternoon after school or after dinner. Most of the books
they take home are stories or nonfiction.*

*The children are not allowed to watch TV at night, but
my wife does it, and the kids sometimes sneak out to join
her. TV is limited, but they do it in the afternoon after
school anyway, and there is nobody there to control it.
On the weekends they can watch TV as a reward for good
work or play the video keyboard game at home; we have
one.*

*I think that education is very important to everyone. It
is the most important thing for us, the refugees. I myself*

want very much to go back to school, but I must work hard first to provide everything for my pretty big family with five children. I don't have a good education, and my English is too poor to get a good job. I talk to my children about the hard life without a good career and a high education. If I could finish school here, I would get a better job, better career, better position with better money. I always remind them not to spend time playing and fooling around but to study, because only a good education can help us to get out and get up higher and higher.

I tell them that there are millions of other Vietnamese kids around the world who cannot go to school because of this or that or whatever: no opportunity, no schooling, and, therefore, nothing to eat. Besides, lots of young students came here without parents. They don't have the good care of any relative; they have to work hard to go to school. That means that we have to help ourselves first; if we don't, nobody wants to help us. I also tell my kids that people value those with an education, with degrees and certificates. Asian people with black hair, black eyes, and tan skin cannot survive in a strange country if they don't try hard to get a good education. This society still has plenty of discrimination; education is the best way to get respected.

I have to tell you that our generation has to sacrifice for the next generation. We have our dreams, but we cannot make ours come true. We pass our dreams to the next generation and ask them, push them, help them to make it; is it right?

Three Families in the Cultural Present

These are three cohesive families with members working hard, meeting reciprocal obligations to deal with the burdens of daily life and to reach mutually shared achievement goals in their new homeland. The three families represent diverse ethnic and language backgrounds, different religious customs, different levels of work-force participation, and varying lengths of residence in the United States. Yet the life-style and content of family life are strikingly similar and reveal a blending of Confucian and Buddhist tenets.

Probably nowhere else is the role of these parents more important than in taking the upper hand to transmit the message embodied in the cultural values. Parents clearly believe that the past is as important as the present, and, as carriers of their heritage, they work hard to bring its lessons into the present to instill continuity and direction to family life. They have faith that the cultural foundation on which their lives rest will support them through the vicissitudes of resettlement. Although these short excerpts cannot show how every value item influences the family in all domains of family life and achievement, they demonstrate that the basic tenets and norms are acquired by the children and relate directly to achievement in school and the management of the day-to-day routines of family life.

Cultural literacy is spread in the home by a variety of techniques, ranging from storytelling to high-tech VCRs, where Confucian analects compete for time with Kung Fu. The Lao mother talks of frequent family evenings spent in storytelling. The Chinese mother reports a variety of activities from the telling of traditional stories to the showing of Kung Fu videotapes. The Vietnamese father tells his children stories from "our" country and uses weekend yardwork with them as occasions to infuse them with their cultural heritage. The core values, emphasizing education, achievement, hard work, and cohesiveness, virtually epitomize home-life activities among these three families.

In the Vietnamese family, both parents are employed, with the father also doing yardwork on weekends and the boys helping. The mother in the Lao family is employed but not the father. Even though the stereotypic vision of the father as breadwinner is no longer maintained, his position of parental authority and status is not weakened. The Chinese family has been in the United States for less than one year, and both parents are unemployed. All the children in these rather large families are doing well in school. The one exception, the second son in the Vietnamese family, is a major source of concern to the father, who repeatedly describes the boy as lazy. He attributes the poor school performance to lack of effort. This causal attribution is basic to Confucian thought and represents a theme that is commonly shared among all our respondents, regardless of ethnic or religious background. It is also of interest to note that the parents do not boast of their children's grades. The Lao children are getting A's and B's, which the mother views as "OK." On the other hand, when a child is not doing well, such as the one boy in the Vietnamese family, it is a major source of distress and preoccupation.

The parents in these interviews repeatedly refer to the importance of getting ahead with respect to their own lives as well as those of their children. They see their own efforts and sacrifices to gain an economic footing as a trade-off for their children's chances to advance through education. The Lao mother talks of working all day long and sacrificing for her family, asking only that her children study hard in return. The Vietnamese father also poignantly states his strong desire to go back to school, while recognizing his responsibility to work hard to provide everything for his family. They also make the connection between education and social and economic advancement explicit to their children. The Lao mother talked to her children often on this point, reminding them about the importance of education and the need "to study first, study hard." The Chinese mother reports that years under a Communist regime have etched the point indelibly in the minds of her children. And, finally, the Vietnamese father proclaims that education is the most important thing for refugees. He tries to get this lesson across to his children often. He talks to his children about the importance of a good education as the family's means of getting out of poverty, hoping and working to pass his dreams on to the next generation. Achievement, hard work, willingness to sacrifice the present for the future, a place for the family in the community, and a secure and comfortable life are made particularly evident. From the perspective of the factor analysis, the factors involving cultural foundations, family-based achievement, hard work, and self-reliance and pride are evident.

These same attitudes are common to the entire sample and to the schoolchildren as well, as shown by the household survey data discussed earlier. But values are the subjective side of culture; they are content, not process. Like expectancies, they must be translated from intentions into effective actions, and it is the family life-style of the refugees, particularly its emphasis on hard work, cooperation, willingness to take responsibility for carrying out obligations, and respect for the authority of family members, that mediates this relationship between the desire to get ahead and making the most of available opportunity.

The repeated reference to hard work cited above by the parents is clearly extended to the children in the form of household chores and the amount of time spent on homework. The routinization of family activities around the burdens of household chores and other obligations is strikingly similar across the three families. When the children return from school, they have a brief respite during which they may have a snack and watch TV. After that, everyone takes part in carrying out day-to-day chores, such as cooking, shopping, transportation, cleaning, laundry, mowing the lawn, clearing the table after dinner, and doing the dishes, before turning to their schoolwork and helping their young siblings with their homework assignments.

The burdens of household chores and other obligations are assigned with striking similarity across the three families. Everyone takes part in the day-to-day chores, with roles defined by age and gender. These activities, like school, provide opportunity for the children to engage in efficacious behavior. As the mother in the Chinese family puts it, "We treat the children as adults." Chores also serve as an occasion for the parents to share stories and advice aimed to impart cultural heritage, as in the case of the Vietnamese father and sons doing yardwork together.

The fathers play a dominant role in family life. Although most of the responsibility for seeing that household chores and schoolwork get done by the children falls upon the shoulders of the eldest son, fathers do engage in housework. Resiliency in role sharing is explained by the Lao mother: "Our culture doesn't let the male in the family do house chores, but now, here in this new society, the female has to take a job, too, and everybody has to help at home." All three parents comment on the importance of love in relation to their children, and two speak of taking the children to McDonald's as rewards, but otherwise the methods for controlling and influencing the children's lives vary. The Vietnamese father will spank when necessary. The Chinese family does not spank and appears to be the most democratic in child-rearing practices, the mother explaining that the need for discipline is minimal because their children know the advantages of living in a land of freedom and opportunity: "We don't have to remind them." The Lao mother also expresses little need for discipline, views spanking as old-fashioned, but is not above using tears to influence the behavior of her children. The Vietnamese father is the most explicit in describing his various approaches to discipline. Although he spanks the younger children, he shows understanding when dealing with his older children, whom he talks to "sincerely, seriously, closely." The tie between school performance and earning a living later in life, so important in all three families, is made explicit in his reward contingencies for grades: a dollar for A's; nothing for B's; C's will cost the child a dollar; for a D the child is debited a dollar and receives a spanking.

Nowhere is this commitment to the children's education more evident than in the pooling of family resources for the purposes of homework. Between dinner and bedtime, it is the main household activity. TV watching is curtailed. Particularly telling is the scene in the Vietnamese household where space is left for the dinner plate of the father, who routinely arrives home from work at 7:30, after the children have begun doing their homework at the dinner table. Upon sitting down to eat, he also proceeds to oversee the children in their schoolwork.

All parents express gratitude for the educational opportunities for their children and speak favorably of the school system and teachers. Two parents mention the contribution of Indochinese educational assistants. After stating that her children are doing well in school, the Chinese mother reports that "The teachers like them because they are so eager to learn." Transcripts and report cards collected for our research, particularly those of children at the primary level, are replete with anecdotal teacher comments that attest to this view, raising the possibility that a halo effect may operate in favor of these children; while in the same school as other children, they may in fact be treated to a learning environment different from that of children who exude less enthusiasm to learn.

Although these families seem much alike, the children are not carbon copies of one another and are reported as being happy. The Chinese mother says her children are happy here because of the freedom they have to do and learn whatever they want to. But each of the three parents expresses a recognition that his or her own chances to advance socially and economically are bleak and that the family's future rests in the hands of the children. The Vietnamese father states this most explicitly and wonders aloud about the fairness of it all: "We have our dreams, but we cannot make ours come true. We pass our dreams to the next generation and ask them, push them, help them to make it; is it right?"

The level of commitment to homework, along with the multiple job holding, illustrates the family-based achievement factor of values at work. There could not be a high level of success in these activities, however, were it not for a strong sense of family loyalty, respect for elders, reciprocity, and a willingness to delay immediate personal goals and gratification in the interest of long-term family goals and objectives. Somehow, factors 2, 3, 4, and 5, pertaining to individual- and family-level imperatives, seem to fall harmoniously into place. It goes on without comment by the respondents, as if everyone knows by nature what has to be done. But this behavior, too, is an achievement derived from a deliberate and planful effort of cultural learning and expression.

Opportunity

The fish's strength lies in the water. (Vietnamese proverb)

My thanks go to the generous American people who allowed us refugees to come to this land of opportunity. Once we start working, we will be happy to contribute back to this country and take our turn in helping other unfortunate peoples. (Vietnamese)

I always remind my children that good education always helps one to get a good career, high position, better life. This country has many opportunities to get a good education. The only requirement is your goodwill. You have to put in your own energy, your own time, and your own effort to get what you want to have. (Chinese)

I expect more of my children as a result of living in America. Most of the Vietnamese refugees here came to expect more of their children to get good opportunities for a good education. People paid to come here to study, and now that we are here, why not take that good opportunity and push our kids to take it? (Vietnamese)

I realized that America is a big and civilized country. Their culture, living, and way of communicating are very different from ours. In my opinion, I feel that Americans have an attitude to be self-sufficient and to be oneself, to survive. I therefore, in my point of view, in terms of being in the United States, should work hard and be able to support my family. (Lao)

We have accounted for the achievements of the refugees by emphasizing cultural values and the family setting in which these values are transmitted and carried forward to their fullest development. From the standpoint of what the refugees brought with them, these items best explain resettlement successes. The fruits of their labor, however, would never have materialized in the absence of an opportunity structure and an environment responsive to such goals and efforts. To credit the Indochinese completely and solely for their achievements in the United States is to lose sight of important structural, system-level factors that have telling impact on their lives.

The schools attended by the children were not the best, but neither were they the worst. They were in urban areas attended largely by the children from disadvantaged homes. And even though the refugee children did better than many would expect possible in such schools, the fact is that the educational health of the school systems was a lot better than the economic health of the country when the refugees arrived. So, although the economic progress of the refugees may appear less dramatic than their success in school, it is no less an achievement given the state of the economy when they arrived. Nevertheless, as grim as the economy may have appeared at the time, it still afforded some opportunity for economic advancement—not optimal conditions for producing economic self-sufficiency, but better than what the refugees had known in their native countries—and the refugees appear to have made the most of it. As one Chinese male in Seattle commented:

> When I read Chinese newspapers [printed in the United States] reporting that there were twelve million persons unemployed, I felt consoled and proud of my effort. Because having been just less than three years in this country, at this recession time I am employed.

Taking Advantage of Opportunity

The Boat People arrived in the late 1970s and early 1980s during the very depths of a recession. Unemployment was the highest since the Great Depression. Despite the recession, certain types of job opportunities were available, although many were jobs that others were unwilling to take. Even though the work was hard and the pay low, the refugees took them, and their rate of unemployment steadily declined. In some instances, the refugees were preferentially hired because they could be depended on. For example, in January, 1984, the *Washington Post* carried a feature story on the hiring of Indochinese Boat People by companies that contracted to clean government office buildings, mostly in the evenings or at night. Absenteeism had been a constant source of frustration to the management of these companies, because it meant an increased work load for others and overtime pay rates. The owners of the cleaning companies, however, noted that there were never absences among Indochinese refugee workers. Even if one of them fell ill, another refugee, a friend or relative, would show up and fill in. Thus, in addition to being conscientious hard workers, the refugees had developed, on their own, a strategy to ensure employment by innovatively accommodating themselves to the available opportunities.

An event of a similar nature was witnessed by one of the authors, who was invited to sit in on an informal celebration held at a refugee employment agency located in one of our sites. A personnel administrator representing a coalition of fast-food firms in the area took great pleasure in explaining to the researcher the decision to rely on the agency as the sole-source supplier of future employees. He brought a bottle of champagne along to toast ceremoniously the pledge of employment and spoke at length on the business benefits that accrued from hiring the Indochinese, whom he described as diligent, hardworking, courteous, reliable labor. He emphasized that he was not doing this for humanitarian reasons or because of prejudicial attitudes against those who had traditionally made up their labor pool; his actions, he emphasized, were motivated purely on the basis of what he called sound business practice.

Thus, within the limits of a very narrow range of existing opportunities, the refugees have forged ahead. They operate within an opportunity system that has allowed them the scope to make the most of their attributes, however narrow the existing range of job opportunities. Can they continue to advance themselves economically? Probably, but lacking language and job skills, self-sufficiency can be gained only nominally, and then mainly by more persons in the households finding employment and not by individuals advancing up the job ladder. Therefore, because the adults, in the main, hold entry-level jobs at the periphery of the economy and without much opportunity for occupational mobility, there may be added incentive to work with and motivate their children to excel in school. The refugees have an appreciation of what is educationally possible, and this awareness, coupled with the knowledge that their chances to improve their own lot further are restricted, has probably deepened their commitment to their children's education. Explicitly or implicitly, each of the three parents whose reports on family life were presented earlier in this chapter attests to this view.

Opportunity for educational advancement is more egalitarian in America than it was in Indochina, and, as with jobs, the refugees are taking advantage of the opportunity for academic advancement. For them, the U.S. educational system is an equalizer for the inequities of privilege that existed in Indochina during the colonial period and those of political allegiance under recent conditions. In consequence, the opportunity for schooling may have assumed a new significance for these refugees. The practical significance for achievement of the basic cultural values, motivations, and family-life factors shared by all of the refugees remained latent in their native countries. In the absence of opportunity, there was no way to establish functional interconnections between their attributes for success and the means for getting ahead. But, given an opportunity in the United States, the refugees become active agents in their own progress by manifesting their attributes and linking them to the existing system. Their accomplishments are impressive, and yet even more interesting is the normative nature of their progress. Bedrock socioeconomic class standing and other related family background variables were *not* found to be major predictors for the educational achievement of these children: the children perform very much alike in school, regardless of the family's past economic or social standing in their native country. Judging from the progress achieved during the early stages of resettlement, the results are outstanding.

Refugee and Mainstream American Values

One reason the refugees are able to take advantage of this opportunity is that the values they bring with them are consonant with those mainstream middle-class American values considered to be chiefly responsible for the prosperity and high level of life quality in the United States. The emphasis on education and achievement through hard work and the willingness to delay immediate satisfaction for future gains are at the heart of the belief system one associates with the American dream. In one sense, it is heartening to see that these beliefs still work to reconcile differences in cultural heritage and to restore tolerance to people's lives under such difficult economic and personal circumstances as those faced by the Indochinese. These beliefs stand for more than myth and cliché; they are the standards that guide behavior in a variety of ways, and they work to the benefit of those who strive to improve their lot.

The newly arrived refugees live in low-income areas, and, presuming that their nonrefugee neighbors do not represent success stories, it is of interest to note that the refugees impute as important to these neighbors the very values that they themselves consider least important, namely "Material Possessions" and "Fun and Excitement." We did not interview the nonrefugee neighbors, and conflicting value systems, if they exist, may not be their only impediment to success. On the other hand, this cross-cultural assessment by the refugees may indeed have some truth in it. Seeing Americans at the same or a not much better station in life as themselves and possessing values that they eschew may serve as a standard of measurement, a motivating force to protect, to reinforce faith in the pragmatic utility of their own cultural values, traditions, and practices.

It has often been assumed that successful adaptation by refugees was, in large measure, the result of their willingness to adopt the ways of their American neighbors. But the successes of these refugees, at least to some degree, may have occurred for very opposite reasons. A parallel may be made to a factor perceived by the Indochinese as responsible for holding their children back in school. As noted earlier, they cited disruption by nonrefugee children second only to lack of English proficiency as an impediment to educational performance. Thus, again, the implication is to reject rather than to emulate the ways of their nonrefugee neighbors. Perhaps the refugees see not only the necessity to rely on their own cultural value system for guidance but also the need to insulate themselves from the behavioral and value standards of their nonrefugee neighbors.

Although there are certain basic similarities between Indochinese and American middle-class values, such as the motivation to achieve through hard work, optimism, and the forward-looking can-do attitude, there are also important differences. These refugee values differ from mainstream American values particularly with respect to the strong emphasis of the latter on individualism and competitiveness. Leading theorists on achievement motivation, such as Joseph Schumpeter, Max Weber, and David McClelland, have traditionally interpreted the "need to achieve" along lines of the Protestant ethic, or "new spirit." This underlying motivation was characterized as a preoccupation with the need to better oneself through hard work, risk taking, reliance on individualism, and a strong commitment to standards of excellence. Although the negative rating by the refugees of "Fun and Excitement" and "Material Possessions" is not unlike the Protestant ethic prohibition against hedonism and the taking of pleasure in material comforts and possessions, we did not find evidence among the refugees of a competitive drive to rival or surpass others in order to get ahead.

By contrast, the refugee value system places emphasis on collective rather than individualistic achievement. For them, collaboration and cooperation are emphasized over unbridled ambition and competitiveness. This collective cooperation is apparent in the value items dealing with the family (cooperation, collectiveness, harmony, and respect). It also may be seen in the economic strategies employed by the refugees, as noted earlier.

The Indochinese Ethnic Community as an Emotional and Pragmatic Boundary Spanner

The Indochinese refugees underwent a radical transition during resettlement. Faced with language and cultural barriers and often with meager financial resources, refugee families were particularly in need of others for both social and material support. Also needed from supportive others was information on which to premise coping strategies that would allow them to negotiate safely through the cultural and bureaucratic mazes of their new homeland. The Indochinese community constituted a vital and trusted resource with which to span the boundaries between the family and the external opportunity structure. And the family that accepted the importance of anchoring itself in the larger social unit was able to enhance its ability to cope successfully as a consequence. Just as one's individual identity is inextricably bound to the immediate family, there is a similar tie that relates that individual and family to the larger Indochinese community. The role of the Indochinese community in facilitating resettlement was most evident in two areas: easing the culture shock and providing local knowledge.

Supportive Buffer

The literature on refugees (and immigrants more generally) has placed emphasis on the destructive aspects of culture shock. What has been stressed are the trauma and disruption of displacement and sadness over the prospect of never seeing one's native country and loved ones again. Chaos and confusion, paranoid tendencies, inability to concentrate, suspicion, distrust, malaise, and depression are the more typical dysfunctional mental states attributed to the shock of finding oneself a refugee faced with adapting to a setting vastly different from one's native homeland. Kunz (1973) stresses the refugee fear for safety, the trauma and disruption of displacement, and depression over the prospects of never seeing homeland and family again. Zwingman (1973) describes a variety of dysfunctional behaviors, such as guilt, loss of vitality, paranoid tendencies, inability to concentrate, low tolerance for frustration, and decreased working efficiency. Chu (1972) describes their mental state as one of confusion and chaos. This position on the mental health of the Southeast Asian refugees runs through the literature on the wave of refugees that arrived after the fall of Saigon. Mortimer and Simmons (1978) emphasize the destructive aspects of "reality shock" and the refugees' "fellowship of suffering." Ishisaka (1977) stresses malaise and depression. Mental health professionals have also commented on the challenge posed by the demands of the more recent second wave of arrivals (Williams and Westermeyer 1984). Lin, Tazuma, and Masuda (1979) find evidence of dysfunctional thinking among the refugees and attribute it to deeply rooted beliefs in Buddhism and Confucianism—the very beliefs we find important to success in resettlement. But in general, the types of disorders that have been reported seem less serious than those associated with refugees coming out earlier as a part of the first wave. The most prevalent complaints have been somatic, headaches and insomnia, with almost no reports of addictive disorders such as alcoholism, drug abuse, or obesity (Nguyen 1982; Kinzie and Mason 1983.) Nicassio (1985) found evidence of alienation among ethnic groups within this more recent wave of Indochinese refugees and goes on to comment that their experience provides "a natural laboratory for the study of phenomena, grief, depression, stress, anxiety, etc." (p. 170).

We do not believe that serious mental health problems are a distinguishing feature of the refugee community—at least not for the post-1978 arrivals we studied. Our interviews contained sets of items concerning perceived happiness and life quality, causal attributions of success and failure, and estimations for future well-being. There was some evidence of adjustment problems, but we do not believe these problems to be characteristic mental health features. We do not imply that maladaptive behavior is absent, but in the aggregate, the refugees appear to be adjusting quickly and with success. They do not ruminate or rail against the events of their past; they recognize the sharp differences between their culture and that in the United States, but they are not thrown into a state of shock as a result of it. On the positive side, as indicated earlier by the data regarding efficacy and locus of control, they see themselves as masters of their fate. One reason for this chin-up, can-do orientation is that the refugees are able to see that the larger Indochinese community has achieved a cultural anchoring and that they themselves are embedded in this larger social unity. As a consequence, they are encouraged to think affirmatively about its benefits in terms of their future prospects for resettlement.

Information Resource

Kinship and social groups, newsletters, refugee-owned businesses, and religious institutions all help to make life in the United States appear less foreign. Additionally, the Indochinese refugee groups in our sites set up neighborhood centers to help deal with a wide variety of needs and services, such as legal clinics and guidance in obtaining health and welfare assistance, and social support groups. These centers helped greatly to define the situations in which the refugees found themselves and to decide what could be done. Thus, families who saw threats to their well-being could find among their own people likely ways to mobilize resources in defense. Such help in forming an accurate appraisal of threatening events is a crucial step in determining what is required to handle the situation. In this way the refugee community itself becomes a built-in resource by blunting the edge of culture shock, reducing dysfunctional behaviors, and promoting a degree of flexibility and adaptability to allow for the beneficial selection of behaviors, goals, and beliefs, to guide the newly arrived refugee family in its efforts to adjust.

A boundary-spanning function with a more tangible consequence results from the sharing of job-related tips and information. Refugees reported that they were twice as likely to find employment through friends or relatives than by way of formal employment services (see the App., p. 217). We doubt that the reason for this is entirely a matter of failure on the part of the public agencies. Information of all types may flow more efficiently when networked among individuals of similar linguistic and ethnic backgrounds. There is also the matter of self-help and the feeling of pride in having ownership and control over one's own fate. Most often, what anthropologists refer to as local knowledge allows a community or group to gain that sense of mastery over external forces, and for recently arrived refugees, nothing could be more vital than the pooling and sharing of information about getting ahead. Thus, local knowledge in the refugee community is likely to go beyond where one can get a job. Also included are strategies for pooling resources communitywide, such as holding employment by controlling absenteeism, as illustrated by the press report described earlier in this section. We would also expect that strategies such as multiple job holding and the availability of singles to provide a period of combined income in the transition from cash dependency to earned income among nuclear families are but two among a number of techniques in the local information repository shared by the refugees for linking to the opportunity structure.

Asian-American Achievement

The successes of the Indochinese refugees are, in a broad framework, also part of the overall achievement of Asian-Americans. Jayjia Hsia's (1987) work notes that a considerable portion of this latter minority group "is more likely to have good jobs, earn above-average incomes, and live in affordable housing in communities with academically strong schools for their children" (p. 6). As she states, "Asian Americans have become the best educated Americans."

All of these accomplishments have not been without obstacles and discrimination, which worked against their efforts to become economically and educationally successful. For example, immigrants who were other than Asian were eligible for American citizenship after five years. Asian immigrants, however, were not eligible for citizenship regardless of how long they remained in the United States, a condition that remained basically unchanged until 1952 (Kim and Kim 1977). Moreover, evidence of discrimination continues to emerge, as in the case of the issue of quotas for Asians at major universities (Bell 1985, among others). Asian-Americans make up 10 (Harvard) to more than 20 (Berkeley and UCLA) percent of the student body and even 30 percent at Juilliard School of Music. Yet they constitute only about 2 percent of the U.S. population (Hsia 1987).

Asian-American success stories are fairly common even in the news media. Generally, they attribute Asian success to hard work. Indicators of success are usually comparisons by income, occupation, and education with majority Americans, that is, all whites not of Hispanic origin. On all such measures, Asians are found to be disproportionately at the higher end of the scale. The relationship, however, is not linear: Asians earn less than whites with comparable education, thus possibly attesting to evidence of residual discrimination. An exhaustive review of these results, particularly from social science and professional publications, may be found in the September, 1980, publication of the U.S. Commission on Civil Rights entitled *Success of Asian Americans: Fact or Fiction?* An updated report, *The Economic Status of Americans of Asian Descent*, has also been published by the commission (1988).

In their 1980 publication, the commission reported that even at the Ph.D. level, a 1977 National Academy of Sciences study found salary discrimination. In a study of thirty-three thousand persons who received Ph.D's in 1970 or later, Asians with the same qualifications for comparable work were found to have the lowest median salary in 1975. Thus, a socially secure environment for the refugees and their children is still a long way off in the future as they push ahead. Their success story notwithstanding, Asians appear not to be treated equally by the majority of Americans.

In view of these exceptional achievements, it would only be natural to raise the question of personal cost—achievement at what price? Could the successes of the Indochinese in particular and the Asian-Americans in general have occurred and continue without an obsession to get ahead at greater expense and sacrifice than should be demanded of one's self? Are the trade-offs so overwhelming as to cut out important areas of enjoyment in life? Are we dealing with neurotic achievers? The answer, at least with regard to the Indochinese refugees, appears to be no.

In fact, the opposite may be true, and the Indochinese may point the way to understanding the success of Asian-Americans, particularly those from East Asia (China, Japan, Korea, Vietnam). When asked why their children do well in school, the most salient and most frequent response given by the refugee parents was, "They love to learn." These parents thereby imply that there is something intrinsically gratifying in learning, carrying with it the motivational reinforcement to continue learning independently of outside demands to achieve. It is a learning style characterized by outside help and encouragement but not domination or unbridled ambition from within.

These remarks can also apply to economic achievement. The drive to achieve self-sufficiency does not carry with it a concomitant set of social pathologies and breakdown in mental health at the personal and family levels. Again, the opposite may be true in that these people take satisfaction in having made their values work and in being efficacious. In such a way do the Indochinese and other Asian-Americans overcome any racial barriers and work to gain access to the opportunity available here.

Refugees and Society: What Approach?

Given the successes the Indochinese refugees have had in the United States, how should we plan to handle newly arriving ones? The two prevailing theories on refugee resettlement implicitly or explicitly carry with them notions about the opportunity structure and what is needed to gain access to it.

One position may be labeled the immersion theory of refugee resettlement; the other may be called the staging theory.

The immersion or, more appropriately, submersion theory is the sink-or-swim view. It posits that the best way to facilitate economic and social adaptation is to plunge the refugees into the new setting immediately and let them fend for themselves with minimal or no outside assistance. The logic relies heavily on the assumption of incidental learning, assumes a high degree of elasticity and flexibility in the ability of refugees to adjust, and requires access to other resources and opportunities appropriate to the theory. Two suppositions underlie this position. The first is that learning takes place best by doing and that outside assistance cannot substitute for or, worse, will retard the advantage of real-world experience. As painful and difficult as it may be for the refugees, it is presumed that such experiences will foster independence and that those who make it will be far better off in the long run if they find their own way. The second supposition, in keeping with Western individualism and the Protestant ethic, derives from a conviction that once on welfare, that is, cash assistance and ameliorative programs, refugees will grow to enjoy the luxury of being cared for and will eventually sink into the cesspool of dependency.

The staging approach argues for a graduated introduction into the setting, a planful sequencing of programs and services in keeping with the development of the requisite competencies for gradual integration into the work force and new social environment. This approach requires needs assessment, cash assistance, work training and counseling programs, language training, and an array of social service programs. Although costly in the short run, it is argued that the long-term payoff will more than offset the initial expenditures necessary to ease the refugees into the new setting. By contrast, submersion is quick, not costly, and without need for a complex of backup agency services and the like.

The two positions are stated here as if they represent irreconcilable differences. And, in fact, legislators, policy implementers, or the general public do tend to fall rather neatly in one or the other camp and conveniently justify it on political, economic, social theory, or cost-benefit grounds. More often, what is done for refugees is that which is possible. In the absence of a definitive victory by those holding one or the other position, refugee policy is almost always in a state of flux, moving toward one or the other extreme, depending on changes in the political, social, and economic climate rather than the outcome data.

Immersion might work for those refugees with a strongly individualistic orientation to achievement and acculturation. Such persons would resist outside assistance and choose self-sufficiency on their own means. As detailed in the Appendix (pp. 214–16), we searched our sample of respondents for such bootstrappers and found no evidence of persons who are making it totally on their own, at least in numbers sufficiently large to be detectable. Yet these are refugees who are industrious, frugal, and hardworking and whose accomplishments are exemplary. The vast majority got off welfare as soon as possible. We see enough evidence in these data on multiple-wage-earner strategies and the various trajectories of self-sufficiency measures to infer independence, self-direction, and perseverance. Yet even where jobs were available, they were entry-level jobs requiring at least two persons to be employed per household in order to achieve an income level above the poverty level. "Making it" requires both spouses in a nuclear family setting to be employed, with either no children under school age or some arrangement for very young children to be cared for. Thus, other than for singles with English language skills, it would seem unrealistic to expect immersion to work.

A variation of the immersion approach would be to provide low levels of assistance for a short period of time (for example, three months) and then to cut off the refugees from assistance, leaving the former recipients to sink or swim. This alternative presumably would allow refugees time to settle in before being required to enter the work force, while preventing them from initially entering the welfare system. Here the underlying assumption is still that once refugees enter the welfare system they will hold on to its benefits as long as possible. Were we to apply this approach to the refugees under study, they would have gained nothing by being forced off assistance and into the work force. When jobs were available, the Indochinese took them as soon as possible, regardless of the quality of employment; they could be trusted to be self-reliant. Worse, immersion would have placed them in grinding poverty for a protracted period. Equally serious, the inferences upon which these ideas are based constitute a grave injustice to these people. They can be trusted to know what is best for themselves, to show respect for the work ethic, and to persevere in the pursuit of self-sufficiency in the face of overwhelming obstacles.

In fact, the assistance program under the staging theory of refugee resettlement is meant precisely for such people. The Indochinese come from cultures that stress resourcefulness and achievement, employing an orientation that takes advantage of the family and community to best exploit the opportunity structures in which they find themselves. Using whatever resources are within their reach, they have attempted to attain and maintain their footholds in society. However, no matter how resourceful they (or any group of refugees or immigrants) are, they cannot control the structural variables that impinge so tellingly on their economic progress: the availability of jobs and the ways and means by which to learn of them and to secure and keep them. Because of these factors, they need some time in which to learn about their new homeland, to assess their skills and fit with the environment, and to learn how they can find and maintain jobs. A policy of gradual integration would permit the Indochinese the time and support in which to settle during a period of great stress and overwhelming strangeness, mindful all the while of their full intention to gain economic self-sufficiency as soon as possible and respectful of the integrity of their culture and their worth. Their cultural values, their collective achievement orientation, and their patience and perseverance notwithstanding, the Indochinese could not have made it without some level of outside help.

Programmatic Assistance in Other Countries

As pointed out earlier, in many important respects the resettlement of the refugees is like a natural experiment in that they arrived in the United States with no material resources and were distributed into five sites, each varying in economic and educational opportunities, physical geography, social climate, and demographic milieu. Therefore, getting ahead was dependent on what they brought with them by way of cultural and personal traits in conjunction with external opportunities. By comparing the resettlement progress of refugees from the same Boat People pool sent to other countries, it is possible to gain insight into the consequences of different political and economic systems with regard to achievements in resettlement. The closest we can come to making such a comparison between the United States and other countries comes from the data on Boat People refugees who resettled in Great Britain (Jones 1982) and Australia (Viviani 1984).

The study in Great Britain examined sixty-six hundred Indochinese refugees who arrived at the same time as those we studied (from 1978 on) and who resettled mostly in large cities such as London, Birmingham, Newcastle, and Manchester. These refugees have almost identical characteristics to those in our sample with respect to past occupation, education, and English proficiency. Therefore, from a practical standpoint, they may be considered equivalents. Implied here is the belief that differences in resettlement in the different countries may be attributed to macro- or system-level differences between the two countries rather than to inherent differences in the two refugee groups.

Jones concentrated on economic and social progress. The most telling difference is in the unemployment rate. The overall refugee unemployment rate in Britain was 84 percent, twice as high as the 42 percent for refugees in the United States. For those in Great Britain the longest (the 1978 arrivals), the rate was 29 percent, compared to around 30 percent for those in our survey with an equal length of residence.

Thus, the refugees in England had a higher initial level of unemployment, but by the end of three and a half to four years the rates are identical.

On balance, however, Jones provides a very negative portrayal of resettlement progress in England, which he attributes primarily to poorly organized assistance programs. The main burden for assisting the refugees fell on local volunteers, who had either little or no communication or coordination with any centrally located administration at the national level. In consequence, there was great emphasis of "front loading," efforts to get the refugees job-ready almost immediately, with little help with respect to housing, medical, ESL, and other forms of assistance efforts or ameliorative programs to help with the difficulties of resettlement.

Comparison of the data for the refugees in these two countries would suggest that the assistance programs in the United States were far better organized and were more appropriate to the needs of the refugees. The consequence was that economic progress was made earlier here than in Great Britain, even though employment levels were eventually the same for both countries. We have no way of knowing if employment opportunities were also identical, but clearly the data from Great Britain would suggest that the refugees eventually succeeded in advancing themselves, largely because they were able to fall back almost entirely on their own resources. These data also show that immersion or front loading, efforts to throw refugees immediately into the work force with little consideration to other needs, does not produce immediate results.

For her report on Indochinese refugees in Australia during the 1978–81 period, Viviani reviewed several employment studies conducted in that country. These studies varied with respect to sampling procedures, site location, and time span. Unemployment rates ranged from 27 to 40 percent, depending on time of arrival. About three out of four were employed as unskilled workers ("factory fodder"); the remainder were largely in skilled work, with less than 5 percent in clerical and professional jobs. In general, the findings examined by Viviani do not differ appreciably from our aggregate data for the United States and broadly confirm the picture of the refugees as an industrious group making remarkable headway into the work force under rather difficult circumstances. These circumstances included lack of skill in English, lack of coordination of support services, and personal problems associated with the hardships and trauma of escape, family separation, and a lengthy stay in crowded and unsanitary refugee camps.

The data on employment in England from Jones and those reviewed on Australia by Viviani would be easier to compare with our data if theirs were longitudinal and reported in greater detail. But the aggregate pictures do appear similar to our own insofar as employment is concerned. In terms of personal and social adjustment, things seem to have been worse in the United Kingdom and Australia, primarily because of the lack of coordination, equity of access, and resources among the agencies that provide welfare assistance, ESL, and employment-related programs. Viviani mentions that even the mastering of Vietnamese names was a major step forward for the Australian agencies. Yet it appeared that, on balance, they did a better job than those in the United Kingdom described by Jones.

The strength of the U.S. refugee program lies in its unique combination of private and public efforts over a period of time. The American requirement of sponsorship for all incoming refugees lessened the isolation of and increased the contact for these refugees. The pattern of federal, state, and local assistance programs here may not directly predict refugee economic and educational success, yet their lack would certainly have led to greater problems for the refugees, as seen in Australia and the United Kingdom. The American assistance programs have provided a supportive and encouraging context for the refugees to take advantage of the opportunity available here and to move ahead quickly in this country.

Summary

From chapter 1 we have followed the course of the Boat People leaving Indochina through their early stages of resettlement in America. Despite personal hardship and trauma, they have endured without being irreparably scarred. We do not find overriding demoralization, lamenting of fate, and indulgence in self-pity. Instead, we find an aspiring, upbeat people who have made some rather remarkable economic and educational achievements.

If asked how we could have identified their predisposition to success, our reply, if limited to one factor, would be cultural compatibility. These refugees brought with them a mixture of Buddhist and Confucian values and traditions that have provided a source of motivation and guidance with which to successfully steer the course of their lives in America. Their values emphasize hard work, education, achievement, self-reliance, steadfast purpose, and pride—values that closely resemble those viewed as traditional middle-class American prerequisites for success. The major differences between the Indochinese and American values pertain to identity and orientation to achievement. The American value system stresses independence and individualism, encouraging all to seek out competition, to compete, and to win. In contrast, the Indochinese value system places emphasis on interdependence, stresses a functional interconnectiveness among individuals, with a strong, family-based orientation to achievement. This orientation is evident in their cooperative pooling of resources in employment and in education. With respect to income-related achievements, pooling is evident in multiple job strategies, guarantees against absenteeism, and the willingness of unrelated singles with earned income to combine their income with that of families on cash assistance, to help achieve economic self-sufficiency for all household members. In the area of education, cooperative strategies and pooling of efforts are most evident in a homework strategy whereby the older sibling teaches the younger. Judging from the finding that school performance is independent of sibship constellation, birth order, gender, and size, these children appear to learn as much from tutoring one another as from being taught. Not all of the 1,384 households studied were families as defined by consanguinity. Yet in terms of the types and levels of cooperation, and regardless of the nature of the household composition, most were not very different from the subsample of nuclear households used in order to concentrate on school performance.

The family is multifaceted in the roles it serves. Among them, it is a source of identity, support, authority, and order. And in all of these, the importance of the family as a carrier of the culture is evident. To know who you are is to know your cultural background, who your family is, and your relation to both. To show veneration for your ancestors' memory is to learn respect for their prudence as well as to acquire a sense of continuity and order that carries into the present. Such knowledge does not occur in a vacuum; it is learned in the context of family life. But the family does more than maintain the cultural core; it also connects the cultural values to the living present through the development of strategies to survive, to get ahead, guided by the ethical and practical doctrines embedded in the culture. We can only infer obliquely how these strategies evolve, but we have learned something of the characteristics of the families that function best in using the cultural heritage to make the most of available opportunity.

These are cohesive families with the burden of household chores and other obligations shared by all members. They stress and expect a high level of achievement, especially evident with regard to school performance. Typically, three hours are devoted to homework each evening, with the older children being responsible for working with the younger. Schoolwork is the chief activity in these homes from the completion of after-school chores to bedtime. TV watching is tightly controlled. Parents are actively involved in the lives of their children, with encouragement and support appearing to play a more central role than corporal punishment in discipline. Telling stories and reading to the children appear to be of special importance to cultural and educational development. Children who are read to by their parents do better in school than those who are not read to; this effect holds up regardless of whether the children are read to in English or in their native language.

The males in these families, specifically the father and oldest son, appear to assume the major responsibilities for the conduct of family activities. Yet the families with the highest levels of achievement are the more democratic in decision making and also in role sharing. They are also marked by a stronger sense of gender equality. In short, equality, flexibility, and resiliency are positively associated with achievement.

We cannot overstress the situational determinants: getting ahead requires not only motivation and knowledge but opportunity. The effectiveness of programs designed to facilitate the linking of refugees to employment appears not to be as helpful as informal sources such as friends and sponsors. But once the connection is made, with respect to either employment or education, the most is made of it, despite economic recession and low-income-area schools. One final point deserves attention in order to illustrate the significance of opportunity as the great equalizer. Past occupation and past socioeconomic status played a role in determining who got jobs first and who got into employment and ESL programs; those from less advantaged backgrounds failed to gain equity of access (see the App., p. 219). Past SES measures, however, did not account for variation in outcomes when the school performance data were submitted to multivariate analysis. Thus, because of equality in educational opportunity for children, we can expect the advantage of past economic and social circumstances to be wiped out in one generation.

In short, rather than think of high versus low classroom achievers, it is more fruitful to think in terms of a family's educational competence. An educationally competent family depends for its effectiveness on a life-style within the home, premised upon a set of cultural values, the implementation of which allows for a good fit or interface with the available educational opportunity. The same applies for the achievement of economic status. It is the family's ability to translate cultural values into a life-style, not its surface or demographic features, that helps its members to confront adversity and prepares them for future success.

Chapter 5

Achievement in America

We have looked long and hard at the data we collected on the Indochinese Boat People in order to document as accurately as possible what the refugees have accomplished in the brief period of time that they have been in America. Their success in resettlement has not been insignificant. As a group, they have accomplished a level of economic and scholastic achievement that few would have predicted, given the unpromising economic circumstances facing this country and the material deprivation of the refugees at the time of their arrival. Possessing only what they had within themselves, their cultural heritages and experiences, their desire for and determination to create a place for themselves in this country, they have prevailed to write another successful chapter on immigrants in America.

The research findings on these recently arrived Indochinese refugees have many ramifications. Depending on one's interest and perspective, this concluding chapter might have focused on a number of different topics. It could have been a commentary on immigration policy and programs, on large-scale research methodology in the open community, on the socialization of cultural literacy, on the etiology of Asian achievement, or, most obviously, on the story of the Boat People in America. But as we examined the data on the determinants of economic and educational achievement, it became increasingly evident that these findings tell us as much about America as they tell us about the Boat People. The refugees have shown the strength of the system by their ascendancy at a time of severe economic recession, when few would have expected them to succeed and some questioned this country's capacity to support them.

The Refugees and Their Road to Achievement

Much of this chapter is devoted to explicating the findings in this light and exploring their implications. And in the end, it will argue for reconsideration of the importance of cultural pluralism and the role of the family in economic and educational achievement. But first we present a review of the more prominent factors influencing the attainment of resettlement goals. Figure 15 is a conceptual framework that recapitulates the findings and the chain of relationships among them, beginning with premigration factors, through arrival in the United States, and finally the desired outcomes of economic self-sufficiency and scholastic achievement.

Premigration

Here we have what the refugees brought with them from their past. Unlike the more privileged wave of Indochinese refugees who came into the United States with the fall of Saigon in 1975, this post-1978 wave came with no material resources, minimal prior contact with Western ways or language, and little education or transferable occupational skills. In terms of material belongings, what they brought with them consisted almost entirely of the clothes on their backs. Of greater significance, however, was what they carried in their heads, namely a sense of their cultural heritages and, in particular, time-honored cultural values, as indicated by the first category under "Premigration" in figure 15. Like the "invariants under the diversity of its aspects," which philosophers have searched for since ancient times, these values work independently of time and place of their application. For the present circumstance, their importance is that this blending of Buddhist and Confucian values is not an esoteric memento of

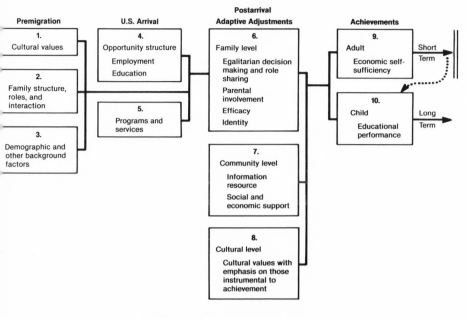

Fig. 15. Factors influencing refugee achievement

their past, alien from the perspective of what are considered American middle-class values. Rather, they are vitally important to and in synchrony with the requirements for accommodating to the present. In fact, it is their similarity and compatibility that appear to be the basis on which the success of the refugees rests.

The second category under "Premigration" variables involves the family. The importance of the family as a central institution of Asian life is critical to understanding the refugees' mobilization and organization of human capital in order to make the most of opportunities in the United States. Traditionally, family members are bound together into a social unit that provides meaning, direction, and order to the lives of its members. It is in this setting that the cultural values are instilled, transmitted, and implemented. Also, we cannot overstress the resiliency of the family unit to adapt and press on, regardless of the stark reality in which it finds itself as newcomers to a strange land. Despite the fact that we have shown that life inside the households is very similar, there are distinctive characteristics of family life among the Vietnamese, Chinese, and Lao in their native lands. The similarities in family life-styles as presented here attest to their resiliency in the face of the common and overriding problems they share in the challenge of resettlement. It is this similarity at the core regarding the importance of the family and their cultural heritage that has allowed them to restore a balance to their inner and outer worlds and attain a wider use of resources.

The demographic category is the last set of premigration variables we looked to in order to understand refugee achievement. Because of the acute and radical changes brought upon these refugees in the course of flight and resettlement, variables such as educational background, sex, urbanicity, and age did not prove to hold much explanatory value. Although some differences in outcome measures were found in association with variations on these items, they were not robust in their influence. Where associations were found, such as between past occupation and current employment and between past socioeconomic standing and classroom performance, the effects are either insignificant or the result of collinearity with other variables whose contributions to resettlement outcomes are unique and independent. We found two such past demographic variables to be important here: "Arrival English" and "Number of children in family." A third demographic variable, but not one from the distant past, was "Length of residency in the United States." Those here the longest did better than those who had arrived more recently. Other than for these three measures, the benefits of demographic items are small and may be expected to fade out with the present generation.

Left out between the points of premigration and U.S. arrival are the events associated with the perilous escape of these people from Indochina and the painful months in overcrowded and unsanitary refugee camps. These people suffered but appear not to have been permanently scarred by the trauma. Conceivably, the experience may have enabled them

to deal more effectively with later stress and thus not be over-
whelmed by the challenges of early resettlement. We chose
not to gather data on personal experiences in this regard and
can only speculate on its significance for survival and adaptation.

U.S. Arrival

Here we look at situational and programmatic factors in the
United States that may have influenced progress in resettlement. Box 4 in figure 15 depicts the opportunity structure. No
matter how motivated the refugees may have been, the fruits
of their labor would not have paid off in the absence of opportunity and access to it. Economic recession and low-income-
area schools notwithstanding, opportunities for achievement
in the United States were better than anything known to the
refugees previously; thus, the potential existed for upward
mobility for these former farmers and fishermen. What must
be credited specifically to the refugees, however, is the inge-
nuity and hard work they exhibited in assessing and making
the most of these opportunities.

Box 5 refers to federal, state, and local programmatic
efforts to facilitate refugee resettlement in the United States.
Although English language and employment programs were
provided to move the process along, we were not able to detect
their effects. Admittedly, our measures were ex post facto, and
in the absence of a carefully orchestrated before-and-after
research design with control and experimental groups, program effects are very difficult to uncover unless they are substantial. Cash assistance programs, however, were critically
important to the refugees, who used such welfare as a temporary support until they could earn income in the labor market.
We found no evidence of protracted reliance on such support.
Finally, although we did not include measures to assess sponsorship, our own observations and the statements from the
life-history reports indicate that the patronage and help of
sponsors were important. They provided refugees with material help and emotional support and served as a connection to

informational and other resources beyond the capacity of the formal service organizations.

Postarrival Adaptive Adjustments

This column of items in figure 15 represents an emergent product of the previous two. It is here that the means-ends connections and strategies converge and enable the refugees to become the artisans of their own fate in their new homeland. It is the instrumental side of their cultural heritage expressed in accord with existing conditions and opportunities. Listed as family-level adjustments are two factors that would normally be considered person-centered or individual-level, namely efficacy and identity. To view these items from a Western perspective when looking at the refugees, however, may not only be wrong but would also obscure their importance in achievement. The effectiveness of any group is strongly influenced by the degree of interdependence and versatility of its members in mobilizing their energies, and these refugees have moved ahead largely because of a group-based sense of identity and efficacy that promotes achievement strategies premised on interdependence and reciprocity. There is pooling of human resources and teamwork as they avoid conflict and find ways to cater to their needs and priorities, as they maintain their cherished cultural values and begin to apply them purposefully and creatively in building their future. At the family level we see this in the multiple-job strategy and in homework practices. At the community level we see it in the temporary help provided by single individuals who move in with families to combine earned income with cash assistance for the mutual benefit of all parties, in the stand-ins who guarantee full manpower to employers and job security and income to the refugees, and in the provision of procedural and employment-relevant information.

This group-based sense of identity and efficacy dictates that one think in terms of an educationally competent family or an employment-competent family, and not a set of individual high achievers. Similarly, one has to think of an efficacious family rather than a collection of individuals, each scoring high on measures of personal efficacy. A similar set of parallels applies to the refugee community. Efficacy is relational rather than personal, in the sense that for the refugees, both children and adults, group-based efficacy reflects the difference between what they can achieve as individuals and what they can achieve by pooling their human capital. Basic to this efficacy experience is an optimistic view of future prospects and confidence that their values and cultural beliefs and practices will facilitate adaptation. It is this interpretation that is critical to understanding our findings on achievement.

Items pertaining to gender equality, role sharing, a tendency toward democratic decision making in the family, and parental involvement are typical of the higher-achieving refugee households. Although common here in the United States, these appear to have been less characteristic of the same families back in their native countries. Thus, again, they attest to the level of resilience mentioned earlier and figure prominently as determinants of economic self-sufficiency and school learning. It argues for an understanding of culture-as-lifestyle, because family life among the refugees is strongly guided by their heritage, including their ability to bend and adapt. As bearers of the culture, the parents serve as a constant reminder to the children of their origins and heritage. The children internalize the culturally based code of precepts and prohibitions that, accordingly, shape their view of the world.

In box 7 of figure 15, we refer to the refugee community, which is a repository of procedural information about how things work in this new country, where employment can be found, and tactics for getting ahead. It is also an important source of social support, where similar cultural perspectives and expectations are understood and problems encountered in the transition of resettlement are shared. There is a close parallel between what was said about the family and what can be said of the community in which it is embedded. It, too, is part of the collective identity.

We have come out of this study with the conviction that cultural values are as important to successful adaptation as gravity is to physics. It is to them that we refer in box 8. On some value items—those that pertain to achievement, hard work, and family life—the respondents were identical in rankings on perceived importance, with virtually all in agreement that these are of utmost importance. We view these as cultural givens and, from the standpoint of resettlement, necessary but not sufficient. In addition, we were able to identify a set of value items in which variations in perceived importance were associated with variations in economic or educational performance or both. We label these instrumental values. These items appear to be most important in extending the core values into the present. These instrumental values connote a willingness to face new challenges, the delay of immediate gratification for later gain, the importance of family respect in the community, and a negative affinity for two values that the refugees described as being of paramount importance to their nonrefugee neighbors: material possessions and hedonistic indulgence.

What we see here is not so much the deeper wisdom of the refugees' heritage but clear evidence that they are not held back by the stifling bonds of moribund tradition. Their values have an important pragmatic side which can serve them well as newcomers adjusting to a land with customs and language unlike their own, a land very different in time and space. It is the compatibility of these values with the basic American beliefs about what is needed to get ahead that makes them relevant to issues of resettlement. These values, as discrete items, have only limited significance. More important is their combined effect as a system of values whose breadth and hierarchical ordering provide us with a sense of the goals and priorities of the refugees. With respect to culture, its importance in resettlement and adaptation is on the milieu that it shapes, which affects the way families solve problems, on the study habits of children, and on the etiology of achievement. Values are content and preoperational intentions, but not the process; for the latter, we must look to culture.

Achievements

We have looked at two particular resettlement efforts in our study: economic self-sufficiency on the part of the adults and educational achievement on the part of their children. These are indicated under the "Achievements" column of figure 15. Although the adults climbed out of poverty and economic dependency with dispatch, they find themselves in low-paying jobs. While alleviating themselves of their most immediate economic problems, they have moved in the process from being dependently poor to working poor. So long as they have limited facility with the new language, their main hope for improving their immediate economic position is by having more adults per household enter the work force. Such a strategy may help in terms of short-term economic advancement, but the chances for extending their advance to full participation in American life and opportunities are bleak in the long run. They are sufficiently wise to know that their goals cannot be reached in one generation; the sole avenue to extended further advancement is through their children. The dashed line in the figure, from parental to filial achievement, represents a mark of acuity and ambition in that regard. It indicates that the achievement of the children in school is undergirded by strong parental commitment and sustained support for the mutual benefit and a better life for all family members in the long run. Although the state of the economy is beyond their control, these parents hold a strong belief in the economic importance of an education and trust in their ability to affect the outcome of their children's learning. They are willing, therefore, to expend the effort needed to ensure their children's success in school. We are not able to penetrate into all the subtle influences of the home on the children's accomplishments in school, but surely its importance for the long-term economic well-being of the family is one reason for the strong commitment to education, a commitment these Indochinese most certainly share with waves of other immigrants who preceded them to this country.

From the standpoint of the children, there must be a

great deal of "oughtness" associated with the expectations placed on them. To many outsiders, it would seem that nobody could enjoy the household responsibilities placed on them or the amount of time spent on schoolwork, especially with the difficult and demanding nature associated with achievement in math or the acquisition of English. Yet in the data gathered independently from the schoolchildren and from the parents, as well as in the life-history data, we find no evidence of an unacceptable or damaging manipulation of their lives. They are not carbon copies of one another, nor are they merely cheerful robots. The fact that "Love of learning" is cited as the chief reason for doing well in school would argue for an opposite interpretation. Whether such a feeling state is the result of intrinsic gratification associated with learning, an understanding of the out-of-school relevance of learning to the long-term well-being of the family, pride in sharing in the teamwork responsible for making the family educationally competent, conviction that things will work in their favor if guided by the wisdom and constructive influence of their cultural background, or some combination of such variables is beyond the limits of our data to explain. But, for whatever the reason, this causal attribution for their success in school is in accord with our observations of their life: they enjoy learning and feel at home in school.

A Contemporary Concern: Underachievement in America

Increasing numbers of reports and books have appeared in recent years on what is viewed as the dangerously declining level of achievement in the United States. Assessments of present and future states are gloomy. The focus is mainly on economic decay, usually political economic treatments such as Paul Kennedy's *The Rise and Fall of Great Powers,* David P. Calleo's *Beyond American Hegemony,* Mancur Olson's *The Rise and Decline of Nations,* and Walter Russell Mead's *Moral Splendor.* These are scholarly works, not just faddish talk pieces about American decline. Basic to each is the conviction that we are falling behind not only economically but in a qualitative sense; other nations seem more industrious and are building better reputations for high standards, diligence, and discipline. It is alleged that we have become indifferent to these virtues and are declining in a calamitous way toward lower levels of economic and educational status nationally and a loss of economic and military power worldwide. Our political and economic dominance has slipped since World War II. The Vietnam conflict greatly aggravated this slide, raising much concern and instigating much soul-searching.

Most critics believe that the economic problems are acute and chronic, caused by the loss of American standards of excellence in industry and education. There is concern with respect to the workplace over the erosion of the work ethic, falling productivity, absenteeism, the use of alcohol and drugs at work, and unwillingness on the part of blue-collar and white-collar workers to accept jobs and working conditions that their parents and grandparents would have been happy to take.

These views on the faltering state of the economic structure of the country and its educational system are not ones to excite enthusiasm; according to them, the collective prospect is dismal. The refugees, however, may hold quite a different view. Although the United States falls short of being the promised land, they would be more certain to see the most prominent trends as upward and positive. Those conflicting viewpoints bring to mind Toynbee's (1972) observations on the flow of cultures within a society:

> ... *fresh challenges are perpetually evoking fresh creative responses from newly recruited minorities, which proclaim their own creative power by rising, each time, to the occasion. The drama of challenge-and-response continues to be performed, but in new circumstances and with new actors.* (p. 228)

We will leave such broad and encompassing sweeps of the goings and comings of cultures to the historians and extend this concern with America in decline to our schools.

In education, the lines of argument and recommenda-
tions for reform are easier to follow. But the results of the
diagnosis and their projected outcomes are no better and
perhaps even gloomier. For three decades, since the Soviet
Union's Sputnik soared into outer space in 1957, we have
been bombarded by an unending series of reports and warn-
ings from political or educational leaders and blue-ribbon
commissions to the effect that American education is in serious trouble, particularly urban secondary education. Reports of meltdown of our educational systems grab headlines
and high visibility in the news media. Like the economic assessments, these assert that we are lagging behind, particularly with respect to mathematics and the sciences, by international comparison. More often than not, such commission
reports, speeches by officials, and editorials are then followed
by a miscellany of unpromising suggestions and reforms to
revive public education.

Indeed, the problems are chronic and urgent, and perhaps the best grasp of the overall situation was set forth in the
National Commission on Excellence in Education report published by the Department of Education in 1983. It is one of the
few documents of this type that recognizes explicitly the tie
between educational and economic standing.

> *Our Nation is at risk. Our once unchallenged preemi-
> nence in commerce, industry, science, and technological
> innovation is being taken over by competitors through-
> out the world. This report is concerned with only one of
> the many causes and dimensions of the problem, but it is
> the one that undergirds American prosperity, security,
> and civility. We report to the American people that while
> we can take justifiable pride in what our schools and
> colleges have historically accomplished and contributed
> to the United States and the well-being of its people, the
> educational foundations of our society are presently be-
> ing eroded by a rising tide of mediocrity that threatens
> our very future as a Nation and a people. What was
> unimaginable a generation ago has begun to occur—*

others are matching and surpassing our educational attainments.

If an unfriendly foreign power had attempted to impose on America the mediocre educational performance that exists today, we might well have viewed it as an act of war. As it stands, we have allowed this to happen to ourselves. We have even squandered the gains in student achievements made in the wake of the Sputnik challenge. Moreover, we have dismantled essential support systems which helped make those gains possible. We have, in effect, been committing an act of unthinking, unilateral educational disarmament. (National Commission on Excellence in Education 1983, p. 5)

As the above quote asserts and as we believe, the state of the nation's school system and that of the economy go hand in hand. The following discussion rests on the assumption that success in the economy lies ahead for those who do well in school and that progress in alleviating the nation's economic decline is intimately linked to progress in solving the problem of our schools. This connection appears to be obvious, but a review of the achievement literature reveals that economists and educationists do not talk to each other, at least not on professional matters that ought to be of mutual concern. The literature on achievement in economics and education would indicate that the two professions clearly are in separate intellectual worlds, with different languages, different ways of thinking about causality, different lines of approach, and different audiences. The long-term economic health of any nation depends on the ability of its schools to fulfill upcoming occupational demands, and therefore, at the public policy level, the two are tightly connected and rooted in the same fertile ground. Thus, we take a holistic approach to achievement and to getting ahead. Similarly, because the student needs first to be educated and developed in order to become a fully productive worker, and because the future of any nation depends on what it makes of the productive potential of its citizenry, we focus most strongly hereafter on educational achievement and the implications of our study for achievement in America.

Implications of the Study for Achievement in America

The main implications of the findings of this study regarding achievement in America are (1) the need to be more accurate in defining the problem of nonachievement in our schools, (2) the need to rethink the critical importance of the role of the family and cultural pluralism in American education, and (3) the need to recognize the potential of the family and its culture to promote and produce achievement in its children.

Schools Do Teach

Contrary to the common view, we do not believe that the nation's schools are educationally bankrupt. The schools across the country, even in low-resource urban areas such as those attended by the refugee children, respond remarkably well to children who come prepared and willing to learn. If the first-order objective of education is the teaching of literacy, numerical skills, and the like, our data suggest that the schools can meet those goals with a higher level of effectiveness than is commonly appreciated.

Moreover, our schools do well in teaching children from backgrounds that are disadvantaged in many ways. The refugee children in our study generally did not come from single-parent, broken, or divorced home settings. Yet apart from the traumas and loss of loved ones associated with their escape, they also were limited with respect to past educational experience and English language proficiency. Except for mathematics, what education the children had in Indochina involved non-Western languages and content. Indeed, although the Vietnamese do use a roman writing system, the Chinese and Lao employ completely different scripts. Additionally, many children had little or no schooling during their months and years in the camps. The children arrived in the United States completely unaware of such basic knowledge as George Washington, baseball, and pizza. Nor did they fare well economically once in the United States. More than 60 percent of the refugees in our study lived below the poverty line. Many came from large families and lived in crowded home conditions. Nevertheless, the level of school learning among the children was outstanding. If measured by performance on nationally standardized achievement tests, used by many education officials as the major criterion for evaluating school systems across the country, these refugee students achieved levels of learning equal to the national norms or better, particularly with regard to math and spelling. These successes indicate that their schools are succeeding in educating this group of children from diverse and disadvantaged backgrounds.

If our schools can teach, if they can carry out their pedagogical objectives, how then have we come to believe that there is a full-alarm crisis in American education? The public perception of the inability of our schools to educate may stem from an overreliance on the educational institution to deal with urgent and pressing social service needs, such as keeping children off drugs, dealing with teenage pregnancy, preventing violence in the schools, promoting safe sex, teaching how to get and hold a job, and a myriad of other tasks and responsibilities that have been placed within the jurisdiction of schools. As the human needs have moved into the classroom, the school's educational function and purpose have become background, leading us to doubt the capacity of our schools to teach. Thus, we have on the cover of national news magazines the spectacle of principal with baseball bat as a symbol of the determination to achieve social management in our schools.

At issue here is the merging of the two quite different purposes by our schools and our failure to separate (1) pedagogy from (2) social service issues when assessing the crisis in American education. In our zeal to condemn and revamp the entire system, we have failed to identify the essential problem in our nation's schools: the presence of social service needs in the schools and their inability to deal effectively with them. Whereas the problem is not one of pedagogy per se, yet issues that figure prominently in reform efforts are overwhelmingly in that direction. Curriculum changes in combination with single- and multitrack programs, teacher accountability, and competence certification plans are major elements in efforts at educational change these days.

More to the point for us are the scientific pilgrimages made by researchers in a variety of fields to the Orient to learn how the Asians do a better job. Educationists have gone abroad, too, to seek solutions to the problems of American schools. In *Japanese Education Today,* the U.S. Department of Education (1987) described the structure of learning in that country. Like others, this study concentrates on the results of the system and the structural and behavioral elements related to them. They mention but do not attempt to emphasize the social and cultural foundations that underlie the described structural patterns. Even though Secretary of Education William J. Bennett took the opportunity to stress the significance of Japanese parental involvement and student character and motivation in the success of the Japanese system, we are left to try to emulate the Asian educational systems and their behaviors with little sense of their sociocultural basis or their relationship to the social service problems in our schools.

Our study has dealt not with educational systems and their pedagogy but with the sociocultural patterns that encourage learning and study. The Indochinese refugees did not come from highly developed school systems as did the Japanese. They arrived here with no material resources and little English. Nevertheless, their children's scholastic achievements seem to rival those of their more settled Asian neighbors. Why? Because, as we have argued, their values and familial efforts strongly encourage the type of learning and study that has led to the Japanese school system. Here we find, if you will, the philosophical and behavioral core of the East

Asian systems being employed within our own schools, and not only within our own schools but, some would say, among the worst of our schools. The results are similar to those in Japan. Thus, we need not necessarily go abroad to seek answers for scholastic excellence. Our own traditions of cultural diversity and educational opportunity currently provide food for thought here at home.

From the standpoint of the three R's, the impact of pedagogical reforms we attempt may be marginally positive or even negative, but from the opposite perspective, that of human needs, these reforms are completely irrelevant and therefore unable to remediate the problems stemming from this source. A more accurate definition of the crisis in American education begins with the separation of pedagogy and its academic purpose from social management and the provision of social services. From there, we can assess the true ability of our schools to accomplish these two sometimes contradictory functions. Should we decide that our schools ought to undertake both functions, we shall then need to decide what requirements and support these two functions will need from society in order to accomplish their aims. Clear about their two separate roles in our schools and fully supported by the system, each function can be carried out, then, without impediment from the other and with full recognition of its place in the education of our students.

Our study does not deal with the social problems that have come to overwhelm many of our schools and cannot be ignored if we are to make progress in improving the education of our children. We have to leave these issues to other studies and other specialists. Our concern, as our study has taken us, is with the learning process and how, with better cooperation between school and family, it may be improved.

Debasing Family and Culture

Throughout this book we have discussed the role of the family in the success achieved by the Indochinese refugees in the

United States. The message that comes through clearly and unambiguously is the fundamental and overriding effect of family life and basic values on achievement. By comparison, the impact of remedial programs and related efforts to help in both economic and educational spheres seems insignificant. The impact is so profound and direct that based on the findings presented in this book, we would venture that concerted family effort and commitment to school achievement could lead to success even in the face of formidable obstacles outside the home. Conversely, no reform effort, particularly those intended to produce widespread improvement in school learning, is likely to succeed without the cooperation of the home. Yet when one looks through the social science literature on motivation and economic success or on educational performance and ways to improve it, the role of values and family life appears to have receded in importance.

To use a medical analogy, most intervention efforts appear based on inoculation models designed to protect students from the influence of their families and cultural backgrounds. Effort is made to build elements into school life to overcome the home environment and family background, to disengage the educational system totally from any direct influence of the social and cultural system from which its students originate, to obliterate the role of the family and its cultural imperatives on achievement. Parents acquiesce to this view by abdicating their political and intellectual responsibility for public education or, alternatively, by joining those who in increasing numbers seek out costly alternative forms of private education for their children. Our data would argue strongly that the effectiveness of schooling and the educational system cannot be detached from the social and cultural systems of its students. More specifically, the data presented here strongly support the position that the effectiveness of schools can be increased positively and substantially by the integration of its functions and goals with the social and cultural system of its schoolchildren. Why, then, is an effort made in most reform programs to diminish, even obliterate, the role of the family and cultural heritage in education? Here are some reasons.

The Melting Pot

> *For a festival sponsored by Henry Ford during the early
> 1920s a giant pot was built outside the gates of his factory.
> Into this pot danced groups of gaily dressed immigrants
> dancing and singing their native songs. From the other
> side of the pot emerged a single stream of Americans
> dressed alike in the contemporary standard dress and
> singing the national anthem. As the tarantellas and the
> polkas at last faded away only the rising strains of the
> national anthem could be heard as all the immigrants
> finally emerged. The enormous pressures which created
> this vast transformation amounted to a forced conver-
> sion.* (Bellah 1971, p. 181)

Typical of societies at the height of their social, economic, and
political powers, Americans have long believed that other
backgrounds and traditions are culturally backward and in-
ferior to our ways, that getting ahead in our success-oriented
society requires one to behave like Americans, to give in to the
pressures toward conformity, and to assimilate. Adoption of
the new culture, however, carries with it the rejection of and
alienation from the old. There is no room for bicultural reso-
lutions or compromise, at least not with respect to what is
presumed necessary to achieve the American dream. Indeed,
the Americanization of immigrants through their schoolchildren was an explicit mission of public education earlier in this
century. Wittingly or unwittingly, explicitly or implicitly, that
objective is promoted still.

By contrast, the Indochinese refugees may have succeeded for the very opposite reason: by holding to the world-
views and values of their own cultural heritage, and perhaps
even by insulating themselves from the ways of their nonrefugee neighbors. This is not to say that these refugees represent ways that are antithetical to basic American beliefs
about success; to the contrary, what is remarkable is that their
values and the coping strategies that evolve therefrom are
entirely compatible with basic American notions about the

work ethic, the motivation to succeed, optimism about the future, and the challenge of new experiences.

Educational Elitism

There is an intellectual and professional elitism associated with reform. Professionalism and political impression management make it desirable that ideas on educational change be new, innovative, exciting, and even high-tech. By contrast, concepts such as culture, values, and family life seem mundane and old-fashioned, pre-Gutenburg notions at a time when computers and an accumulation of technological gadgetry proliferate in the classrooms as if technological abundance, rather than human qualities or moral substance, were the index of cultural progress. In addition, educationists seem obliged to prove their authority over the home with scientifically based teaching methods, such as those based on operant conditioning, in the effort to show that in-school learning can be achieved independently of outside help.

It does not seem too adventuresome to hypothesize the overriding influence of the family and its value priorities over in-school instructional innovations. The rationale for this view is quite straightforward: the children we surveyed attended schools in five metropolitan sites across the nation and were exposed to many variations in pedagogical qualities, procedures, and settings. Yet they performed alike and performed well, these differences in educational experiences notwithstanding. These "normative" results stem from such noncognitive factors as the home and cultural background.

A parallel argument may also be made with respect to economic achievements. Similarities in the ways the refugees in our study found employment and achieved self-sufficiency across the nation are notable, given the diversity in physical geography, climate, economic conditions, and local demographics. They show the power of the family and its cultural background not only to press for success but to find ways to achieve it. Perhaps our failure to find any significant impact attributable to the intervention programs designed to facilitate employment and English language acquisition may have resulted from the effectiveness of home and community life and not programmatic failures.

How could we have known the predispositions of the refugees toward success in the absence of their response to economic and educational opportunities? The parents had nothing to recommend themselves for economic accomplishment in conditions of high unemployment and an unknown labor market. Similarly, on the basis of prior schooling or the lack thereof (whether in the refugee camps or their homelands) and English language deficiency, one would hardly have predicted success in school for the children. As with the parents, the obvious prediction would have been one of great difficulty and failure, regardless of the level of effort.

Many different factors go together to produce the success described here. Faced with the task of predicting the response of the refugees, those concerned with these issues would have bypassed culture and the family in favor of culture-free tests emphasizing cognitive abilities. Yet in terms of the type of characteristics routinely assessed in predicting achievement behavior, such as intelligence testing, aptitude measures, and even motivation, no such set of scores would have been as useful as an assessment of their values, possibly in conjunction with some simple measures of efficacy. A set of items such as these could be administered quickly and easily to persons with limited language facility and could be expected to yield information about their potential for success and consequences for the success orientation of their children. We would argue for more assessments of this type, in which culture and family interactions play a central role, and a lessening of the emphasis on IQ-type testing and other culture-free tests of primary mental abilities which, despite decades of research showing low correlations of such measures with actual performance, still dominate psychometrics in education.

Victim Blaming

Any explanation of behavior has at its foundation some theory about human nature. Additionally, that which explains the most with the least complexity and effort is generally the favored folk explanation, especially if it seems intuitively correct. These axioms on theory building are true whether we are searching for a disciplinary base to account for falling in love or for underachievement.

Concerning the latter, the "just world" interpretation, with its victim-blaming orientation, fits the criteria of folk theory: by a process of causal inversion, the victims are treated as if they are the cause of the situation in which they find themselves, because in a just world people get what they deserve, good and bad. When applied to situations where it seems particularly apropos, not only does this perspective of the world come to be believed by those it favors—that is, the relatively advantaged segments in society whose myths and clichés it reinforces—but, to a surprising degree, it is also believed by those subject to the definition of their predicament. This acceptance of blame by the victim lends further credibility and legitimation to what is done or not done by way of remediation.

Narrowing our attention and scope to person-blame explanations frees us from having to explore a multiplicity of structural and difficult to perceive alternative explanations. We need only to trust our eyes to what appears self-evident. Those who hold this position believe the poor are poor because they deserve it, for their breach of the dominant norms: they lack the work ethic and ambition; they are immoral and are unable to limit the number of children they produce, children who share the same incapacities as their parents. When such a theory for underachievement is held, it comes as no surprise that the role and responsibility of the family in education is not promoted. On the contrary, it would seem wiser to disengage all efforts at remediation from such families and their backgrounds.

Granted, it is difficult to know where structural determinants end and where culture begins, where culture ends and where the family begins, or even where the family ends and where the individual begins. But sufficient research exists to show us that it is incorrect to hold people entirely responsible for the problems that beset them while ignoring causal determinants external to the individuals, their family, or even their culture. Similarly, while it may seem just to ignore the family and culture when undertaking corrective reforms, this perspective rests on an erroneous and self-serving causal attribution that determines what one does or does not do by way of remediation. What definitely is not done as a result of this viewpoint is to consider the strengths and positive aspects of the family and cultural background which, as our data show, have a positive and substantial impact on school learning.

Social Science Support

There has also been support from the social sciences to place blame for economic and school failure on cultural factors. For example, the theories of cultural deficit, culture of poverty and similar derivations hold the position that children in low-income areas fail to develop the cognitive, language, and social skills, aspirations, impulse control, or the proper frame of mind necessary to adapt to and succeed in school and life. Thus, it is argued that they fall prey to a cycle of poverty whereby successive generations fail in school and take up low-level jobs, only to wind up unemployed and, finally, dependent on welfare. The poor perpetuate their condition through cultural learning: children, as cameras of their culture, are socialized by their parents to adopt the very attitudes, values, and behaviors that maintain the cycle of poverty into yet another generation. These views espouse the presence of an alternative belief system, not necessarily antiachievement in orientation but a subculture that survives and sustains itself with its own rewards and incentives, quite independently of the dominant achievement-oriented host culture. It is this culture that is held primarily responsible for people either not caring or being motivationally unable to participate wholeheartedly in activities directed at getting ahead (Lewis 1968a, 1968b; Reisman 1962; Banfield 1970; Wilson 1987). While not entirely ignoring structural determinants, these views come close to the position of victim blaming on a more sophisticated intellectual level.

A More Positive View: Culturally
Responsive Education

There is something superficial about one-sided views that stress negative relationships of culture and family life to achievement. More often than not, they refer only to limited facets of a complex set of phenomena. To characterize and label these as culture, and even then to focus only on their negative aspects, is seriously misleading and damaging to those groups subject to the interpretation. It fails to take note of the strengths of the culture of even an underclass and how its positive aspects may be used to raise achievement. We would venture that no set of people, regardless of race, ethnicity, religion, or social position, is disinterested in its own social and economic betterment and the future well-being of its children. Despite vast differences in external appearance, there is an astounding amount of agreement among the great diversity of world cultures regarding family organization and what is valued. There may be great differences in how they go about attempting to get what they want, whether successful or not, determined, in the main, by physical setting and opportunity factors, but not in their goals. Even at deeper levels, there is similarity, as Jung and others have noted, in dreams and myths. People may find themselves engulfed by impossible beliefs leading to all sorts of outrageous behaviors against one another by day, but at night they dream like dreams. Our purpose here is not to attempt to illuminate the wide-ranging nature of human behavior at the deepest recesses of the soul. The point here is that the kinds of values that have emerged as important to the refugees probably transcend cultural differences and are most prevalent and obvious in the nuclear family, where the basic similarities pertain to economic well-being and good education.

If one were to query any economic subclass segment of the U.S. population, regarding hopes and aspirations for their children, there would not be great differences between their responses and those from the Indochinese parents. Yet we would expect major differences between the Indochinese refugees and these other parents on the perceived likelihood of ever achieving those goals and objectives and, in turn, the behavioral intentions to act on those objectives with strategies that are likely to have them materialize. These depend on the presence of opportunity, perceived accessibility of that opportunity, and expectation for success by following a set of prescribed guidelines and strategies. For the Boat People, these factors fell into place because their core, normative, and instrumental values were compatible with the requisites for employment and education. For many Americans, native-born and otherwise, the power and connections may have eroded away because of long-term discrimination and denial of the right for full-scale participation in American life. The Indochinese refugees, on the other hand, arrived suddenly, with much history and tradition behind them but little history here. They brought their cultural patterns to America and defined their new reality in their own terms, according to these cultural beliefs. They then proceeded to act on this reality: they see opportunity here and construct their own fate, within the limits of their new circumstance.

By contrast, other groups with longer histories of interacting with American society and culture have seen their definitions of reality distorted by the clash between the dominant culture and their own. When the definition of one's culture is imposed from the outside, its integrity is weakened, in contrast to the strengths that it may derive from an internally derived, self-determined definition. An outward frame of reference seems to weaken the group's pride and confidence in itself; the concomitant restrictions on avenues for success imposed by the dominant culture and the resultant lowering of expectations for success by the dominated sap its energy and drive necessary to succeed. Under these circumstances, minorities are appreciated for their expressive distinctiveness that are entertaining and even fashionable but are not similarly encouraged to give expression to their values pertaining to intellectual and economic pursuits. Instead of participating fully in society and coexisting with mutual respect and equality with the dominant culture, the position of minorities in society takes on the character of a sociological bazaar at the group level and as hyphenated Americans at the individual level. Aesthetic pluralism may afford certain benefits, but it does not carry with it an appreciation that intellectual and economic capabilities, and the basic values that inspire them, are embedded in these cultures as well.

We would not deny that alternative goals and behaviors can have a strong and detrimental effect on school learning. We do not doubt that the learning of cognitive styles and linguistic patterns takes place in the environments of children in disadvantaged areas which can relate negatively to school learning and ultimate socioeconomic advancement. But these are probably guided by adults and siblings who are effectively disengaged from the means and avenues for conventional achievement. Their cultural-based sense of efficacy or confidence has been diminished or, if intact, is allowed rein by the larger society only in noncognitive, expressive domains.

These expressive behaviors, however important as reifications of a culture, are again only limited aspects of the complex. To understand why we accept the validity of this expression of a group's cultural heritage but not the validity of their values for conventional achievements would require deeper treatment than can be attempted here. It would require an exegesis on the nature and determination of dominant/subordinate group positions in society relative to their political and economic power. What is of importance here is that cultural pluralism in our schools, apart from sidestepping the denigration or destruction of cultures incumbent with narrow assimilationist attitudes, would permit teachers to harness the press for achievement that exists in all cultures, however differentially defined or expressed. The result would be a constructive partnership between the family and school which would further their mutual goal of educating students and promoting their long-term economic advancement.

From the standpoint of the school, there has to be an understanding that education is a reciprocal process and that the home should be involved in ways that go well beyond an annual parents' night or parent-teacher conference. It also requires an understanding that cultural differences are not necessarily a barrier to education and that, in fact, American education has much to gain from multicultural education. Most critical is an approach to education that is culturally responsive, whereby attempts must be made to identify and incorporate into its philosophy and pedagogy those aspects of the students' cultures that are central and conducive to learning. In so doing, care has to be taken to ensure that minorities do not equate the school and school learning with a loss of cultural and ethnic identity, that such an approach does not carry with it the specter of assimilation. Finally, we should emphasize that just as schools cannot work without the support and cooperation of students and their families, these same schools cannot work without the support and cooperation of the larger society in which they are embedded. At the very least, this relationship must involve the financial support with which to deal with problems in our schools, be they academic or social, and a "kinder and more gentle" attitude toward all members of society. Given such support, all citizens may come to believe in the equality of access to the economic and social structures of the country and value of an education, by which their potential might be realized.

From the standpoint of the home, the school is to be seen as a resource in an additive sense: that it does not threaten to absorb or to replace its culture and ethnic identity, that the school's recognition of cultural diversity goes beyond the level of festivals, entertainment, and fashion, to extend to basic intellectual skills and the motivation to achieve. With society's support for the well-being of all members, parents will believe in the out-of-school relevance of an education and trust that they will gain something by way of postschool opportunities for themselves and for their children. To the degree that is possible, parents will need to appreciate the importance of education and that they themselves will gain from the investment of time and energy devoted to preparing for and following through on the school learning of their children. Finally, and most importantly, children have to feel at home with learning. For this important prerequisite of education, only the parents or their proxies can bring it about; they must become more involved in the education of their children.

We use the word *family* with full awareness that the typical home today may mean a single parent, divorced parent, adoptive parent, grandparents, extended family, or any combination of these. While a family headed by the biological mother and father may have important advantages, what is of importance for successful learning is the control over the milieu and the determination of whose values prevail, those of the adults committed to education or others. Just as schools must grasp the irrefutable importance of the child's home on in-school learning and the ways in which cultural ideologies are embodied in human lives, it follows that adults in the family must come to understand and believe in the power of the home environment for promoting competence and belief in the governability of their lives and aspirations, particularly with respect to the learning of values that have consequence for achievement.

The schools cannot teach values by rote memory and expect them to produce the kinds of impact on learning reported in this study. They could be no more successful in that regard than they could be in force feeding formulas and facts to develop a taste for learning. What is essential to the transmission of the values that give priority to education is their early and deliberate promulgation by the adults in the family. We have probably gone too far, however, in the direction of believing that low-SES, single-parent homes with large numbers of children cannot succeed in school. The critical issue is not the number and relationship of the adults in the household to the children but rather what dominates and who determines the nature and character of the milieu, its beliefs and behaviors. It means that the values and aspirations linked to student learning have to be instilled early and that an environment promotive of learning must be supported by families in a society concerned with the well-being of all of its members.

Conclusions

Churchill once said, "Men occasionally stumble over the truth, but most pick themselves up and hurry off as if nothing had happened." So it is with the empirical support we provide on cultural values and family life and the determining role they play in achievement. The ideas are hardly novel or surprising; they are long-standing. Genuinely independent minds would move on, assigning such notions to the tyranny of common sense or considering them too close to the stifling bonds of tradition to have a place in the contemporary world. But in the end, there is a price paid for ignoring the obvious. It may seem strange that at a time of deemphasis on cultural background and a diminution of the family's role and responsibility, we should find reason to emphasize their importance and argue the case for culturally responsive education. It may seem equally strange that at a time of increased concern with our economy and schools, we find reason to affirm that opportunity and the practical conditions for getting ahead still work. This is why we choose to reiterate our findings once more here—not out of partisan favor to the Boat People, nor to argue that America is still a land of opportunity, but simply because it is the most straightforward and pertinent interpretation that we can make of the data.

These Boat People have endured a calamitous course of events. Their native countries have been torn apart by war and political upheaval. Their escape was perilous, and those who survived spent months, even years, in crowded and unsanitary refugee camps. They arrived in the United States with virtually no material possessions, little education, little or no English language proficiency. Yet in a few short years, they, as a group, have achieved some extraordinary successes, wrought in the main through hard work and determination. Although not everything they may have wished for and not entirely under circumstances they would have chosen, to a surprising degree they have achieved a high level of control over their own history.

We have endeavored to use a variety of quantitative and

qualitative data to gain a cumulative insight into the factors responsible for their achievements. We place great confidence in our explanation of the role of cultural values as implemented through family life-style. The values essential to promoting achievement are simple and direct. Those that work for the Boat People are not exclusive to them or absolutes, do not require a burst of transcendental wisdom or metaphysical understanding or a grounding in non-Western thought for understanding and application. What we find working for them in terms of achievement outcomes are the practical side of values they share in common, however heterogeneous they are and remain with respect to spiritual, aesthetic, and other values. Moreover, these values of practical significance to achievement are, if not identical, congruent with what have been viewed as mainstream middle-class American beliefs about getting ahead.

But the values would not have been kept alive if they were not sensible and appropriate. Perhaps a heightened consciousness of and reliance on cultural values for guidance is an outgrowth of the crises they have experienced. The history of their experience and survival may well be a testament to the functional utility of their common beliefs. Certainly, the relationship of values and the family life-style that transmits and implements them to successful outcomes during the difficult years of resettlement in the United States is compelling enough for us to appreciate their importance.

A constant give and take occurs as people and the world in which they live interact. This interaction is enhanced if pluralistic attitudes pertain, allowing people to retain their ability to define the reality they face, to make sense of their world. The Indochinese brought their cultural patterns to America and used them to define their new world in their own terms. They then proceeded to act on this reality, seeing opportunity and access to such opportunity. The family is the major vehicle by which the Indochinese define and come to grips with the world they face.

Cultural pluralism in America means not forcing on each

of its groups a single view of how the world is to be seen and lived. In such a society, minority groups do not lose their distinctiveness in order to participate fully and to coexist with mutual respect as members of the larger union. Under this condition, ethnic groups can advance simultaneously and on equal footing with the dominant culture, creating in the process a heterogeneous society.

The dismal assessments and predictions about the states of the economy and of public education notwithstanding, these refugees from Indochina prevailed. Their own attributes have played a major role in determining their achievements, but their effort would nót have paid off had there not been doors to opportunity in the work force and in the schools. In particular, the educational performance of the children clearly demonstrates that schools can be used more effectively than is commonly believed, at least in regard to meeting pedagogical objectives. From a definitional standpoint, the problem appears not to be a need to refashion and reform institutional arrangements and their primary objectives, particularly with respect to the schools; they perform well in teaching those who come prepared and willing to learn. We should not abandon what we have; public education still has direction and effectiveness. The problem is how to improve the response to it, how to clarify and to rein in the pieces that work, and how to deal effectively with the social and human problems that impede the in-school learning.

The central issue can be put simply and directly: how do we make children feel at home in school, at home with learning? The problem is not that our schools cannot teach, but to teach effectively they cannot go it alone, independent of the diverse social and cultural systems with which they interact and the input and cooperation of families from whom the students originate.

Schools can start by becoming more aware of the cultural backgrounds of their students and employing those values and other cultural aspects that promote learning. They can also help themselves and their students by enlisting the cooperation and involvement of parents in the education of the children. Similarly, parents and adults in the families of children should recognize and carry out the vital role they play in establishing the family milieu, values and behaviors that bring learning into the home and prepare their children for learning at school. Nationally we must value and work toward a society that assures the productive potential of all of its members. Building an active, working partnership among all parties involved in the education process will be a first and important step in dealing with the crisis in American education.

It is in the public interest to give priority to the two ingredients that, for a variety of reasons, have been disregarded in studies in achievement and achievement motivation, namely the family and culture. We argue for a reappraisal of the strengths in these components of social life and for the development of programs aimed at (1) forming a constructive partnership with the family as a basis for promoting achievement and (2) allowing more rein for opportunity to groups with diverse cultural backgrounds in ways that engage values basic to those cultures for advancement in intellectual and economic pursuits and culturally responsive pedagogy.

It is ironic and paradoxical that these refugees from Indochina have achieved economic and educational success at a time when our level of performance in these areas is an issue of concern high on the national agenda, a time when scholarly books, political debates, and blue-ribbon committees address themselves to the foreboding prospect of what many have come to refer to as America in decline. The irony is especially deep because the major reasons for the refugees' success can be attributed to beliefs and family practices that, although non-Western in origin, coincide closely with traditional, mainstream, middle-class American presumptions about the values and means-ends relationships necessary for achievement.

Appendix

The Study

Data Sources

The procedures used to develop and field the study are those generally followed by the Survey Research Center at the University of Michigan, with respect to questionnaire development, pretesting, interviewer training, sampling, verification and quality control, and coding. But, because of the special nature of the sample and languages involved, special steps had to be taken. In addition to the survey, extensive background and demographic data were collected for each site from various administrative sources, and, finally, several life histories were collected using a social anthropological approach. These life histories pertain primarily to leaving Indochina and initial experiences in the United States and family life during resettlement.

Three ethnic groups were studied, representing the major elements of the second wave of refugees at the time of the study: Vietnamese, Sino-Vietnamese, and Lao. Few of the refugees were proficient in English. Therefore, it was necessary to interview them in their native language—Vietnamese, Chinese, or Lao. Questionnaire items were translated into each language, pretested with refugees, then back-translated into English to be checked by other translators, interviewers, and respondents for fidelity and meaning. That task was arduous, often requiring many versions of the same item before consensus was achieved. In addition, many special problems

181

arose, one such being to locate a Lao typewriter. The inter-viewing took place in five sites across the country, and we had at least one Ph.D. or a near-equivalent research coordinator working full-time in each to supervise sampling and data collection. Native-speaking interviewers were carefully se-lected and trained at each site. The training paralleled that used to train professional interviewers at the Institute for Social Research of the University of Michigan and involved classroom instruction and many supervised practice inter-views.

Sampling was particularly difficult and costly. Initially, we had been led to expect that administrative lists were accurate and complete, or at least nearly so, and could serve as a sam-pling base. This information, however, proved to be grossly inexact. In the end, it was necessary to select most respon-dents on the basis of an area probability sample. That meant knocking on doors to conduct enumerations of residents in our sample areas, developing a pool of eligibles on the basis of the enumeration, selecting respondents from that pool, using randomized probability procedures, and, finally, returning to the address to interview the designated respondents. Respon-dents were cooperative, and the refusal rate was quite low, about 4 percent, which is comparable to that usually experi-enced in national studies. A detailed treatment of survey and other data-collection procedures, site selection, and sampling procedures follows.

Site Selection

The five sites in which we sampled for respondents were Boston, Chicago, Houston, Orange County (California), and Seattle. These sites contained major ethnic concentrations of Vietnamese, Sino-Vietnamese, and Lao, as well as Hmong, Mien, Khmer, or other groups we did not study. They were selected because we wanted sites in different parts of the country, with different patterns of service delivery and assis-tance programs, and with different demographic and eco-nomic climates as well. Finally, we attempted to ensure that there would be different balances in the ratio between the first and second waves of refugees across the five sites, that is, between the 1975 refugee population that arrived shortly after the fall of Saigon and those who have arrived since 1978. Accordingly, candidates for research sites were identified and evaluated on the basis of the following profile items:

- Wave I refugee population (arrived in the United States April, 1975)
- Wave II refugee population (arrived in the United States starting October, 1978)
- Secondary migration
- Wave II ethnicity
- Unemployment rate
- Job climate
- Cost of living (Consumer Price Index, CPI)
- Cash assistance (CA) levels
- CA eligibility criteria
- Nonrefugee demographics
- Physical geography

As the refugees scattered across the United States, either by initial sponsorship or by secondary migration, the respondents came to be located in the five sites selected for this study. Here we give capsule descriptions of each of these sites and of the Indochinese communities within the sites.

Orange County. This California site had approximately sixty thousand Indochinese refugees at the time of the study, which made it by far the largest of the five sites. Many of the refugees who left Vietnam at the fall of Saigon in 1975 were temporarily housed at Camp Pendleton, which is just south of the county. Many found sponsors among the local (Los Angeles–Orange County–San Diego) residents who had helped them in the camp, and they quickly established a sizable community in Orange County. Family reunification, good weather, a reasonably good employment situation, and the availability of Asian cultural centers have drawn many others, both in their initial resettlements and via secondary migration.

Though Orange County is almost entirely suburban, refugees live primarily in the more urban areas—Westminster, Garden Grove, and Santa Ana. There are hundreds of refugee small businesses, a Vietnamese Chamber of Commerce with more than one hundred members, and a variety of trade and professional associations. The Lao, Cambodian, and Hmong communities are reported to be fairly well organized and politically homogeneous, though they possess little political or economic power. Conversely, the Sino-Vietnamese are said to have considerably more economic power but seem to be organizationally fragmented, with no association speaking for all and considerable internal competition. Ethnic Vietnamese are reported to be roughly between these extremes, in both economic power and political unity. It was also reported that several Saigon black-market rings have reconstructed themselves in Orange County, adding both color and conflict within the refugee community.

Virtually all officials reported excellent cooperation among the individuals and agencies responsible for aiding refugees and a high level of service coordination as a result. There appears to be little duplication of effort and few gaps left unfilled. The Orange County Refugee Forum is the primary vehicle for coordination among the agencies. The major service providers are the six Volags operating in the area (Church World Service, U.S. Catholic Conference, International Rescue Committee, Lutheran Immigration and Resettlement Service, World Relief Services, and the Presiding Bishops Fund), a funded Mutual Assistance Association or MAA (the Lao Family Community), the County of Orange, and several school districts (Pancho Santiago Community College District, Coast Community College District, Garden Grove Adult School, and the Huntington Beach Union High School District). Various other MAAs, church organizations, and civic and charitable organizations provide services on a smaller scale.

In 1982, the Cost of Living Index (CPI) in Orange County was three to five points above the national average. The unemployment rate was 5.4 percent. Although considerably better than the national average, it shows the area to have been affected by the recession.

In December, 1981, the ethnic composition of the refugee community was estimated as follows: Vietnamese, 31,800; Chinese-Vietnamese, 5,200; Lao, 6,000; Hmong, 6,000; Khmer, 2,500.

Houston. Since 1975, Texas is second only to California in the total number of Indochinese refugees who settled there, and Houston (Harris County) has one of the largest refugee populations in the country. By January, 1978, the state total had grown to almost 12,800, which made up 9 percent of all refugees in the United States. From June, 1978, to July, 1981, the second wave of refugees brought another 26,000 to Texas directly from Southeast Asia, as well as a net gain of about 7,000 from other parts of the country. Houston's total Indochinese refugee community of 30,000 to 35,000 thus included a large number of secondary migrants. The refugee community appears to be more homogeneous—that is to say, ethnic Vietnamese—than elsewhere in the five sites. State sources estimated that two-thirds (20,000) of the refugees living in Houston came from Vietnam, 7,000 from Cambodia, and 3,000 from Laos.

Given Houston's geography, the Indochinese refugee community lies scattered about the outskirts of the city and is not concentrated in any one section. The refugees live in both single-family residences and small-unit, low-income housing. The major problem here is a lack of public transportation, for which Houston is notorious. For refugees without the ability to buy a car and drive, getting around is difficult. Houston was understandably highest among the sites in which respondents had driver's licenses (79 percent) and in households owning a car (81 percent).

The region around Houston has been the site of some of the more brutish refugee-community conflicts in the country, such as the well-known shrimp boat conflicts between Vietnamese and Texas fishermen. Perhaps as a result, the city's officials have gone out of their way to welcome the refugees. In March, 1982, the city of Houston hosted the National Association for Vietnamese American Education (NAVAE) conference, and the mayor praised the refugees as "law-abiding productive citizens who contribute to the total well-being of our city." In addition, the superintendent of schools gave a keynote address at the NAVAE conference and praised the academic success of the refugee students.

Until the middle of 1982, Houston's economy was booming. It was the energy capital of the world and the end of the pipeline for petrochemicals. But by the time of the study, the world oil glut had begun to have its impact on the Texas economy. The unexpectedly sharp downturn of the local economy in the summer and fall of 1982 strongly affected the work force. Houston's unemployment rate doubled from 4 percent in October, 1981, to 8 percent in October, 1982. The Houston economy was still in better shape than those of the three northern sites, but the boom was over. Its fall 1982 CPI figure (317.6) was highest among the five sites and well above the national average.

The refugees have been a major force in convenience stores. Wrangler, Totem, and Seven-Eleven stores were dominated by them. Also, a Houston shopping arcade called the Glass Palace contained twenty to thirty shops owned by Vietnamese. The influx of the refugees also contributed to the revitalization of the urban Chinatown area. Many Indochinese immigrants found work as assemblers in high-technology manufacturing industries. Their progress, however, was dubious as Houston's economy entered a decline.

Seattle. The Seattle–King County area had a relatively small influx of refugees after the fall of Saigon in 1975. The refugee community here remained small until the 1979 arrival of the Boat People, who were resettled here in considerably larger numbers. At the time of the study, approximately twelve thousand refugees lived in the area, primarily ethnic Vietnamese and Lao, with many Hmong.

The Seattle–King County area had approximately 1.2 million people in 1980, making it roughly twice as populous as the Boston–Suffolk County area and half the Orange County area. Blacks, the largest minority group, comprised about 10 percent of the city and 5 percent of King County. A large Asian, primarily Japanese-American, community in the Seattle area (nearly 10 percent) gives refugees some access to

Asian cultural and culinary resources. The refugees tend to live in the poorer urban areas.

Most officials report excellent cooperation among service providers who have developed an extensive network of voluntary resettlement services to complement funded programs. The central service providers are the Washington Association of Churches (a joint effort of Church World Services, the U.S. Catholic Conference, the YMCA, and the Hebrew Immigrant Aid Society), other Volags (mainly Lutheran Immigration and Refugee Services), the state-run Economic Opportunity Center, the Asian Counseling and Referral Service, and various community and private colleges. The Refugee Forum has served as the primary vehicle in the development of a well-integrated system of programs.

The CPI in 1982 showed Seattle to be about four to five points higher than the national average. As of December, 1981, unemployment was 9 percent, placing Seattle near Chicago as the two sites with the highest unemployment rates. The recession hit the Seattle area relatively late, but it hit hard. Boeing, which employed about 10 percent of the labor force, got a boost when it received the AWACS contract but did not receive the hoped-for MX missile contract. Timber and construction, the other major industries, were not doing well at the time and were not expected to recover until interest rates turned around. There was relatively little refugee-owned business activity: about a dozen Vietnamese-owned stores, three or four Vietnamese restaurants, and a Vietnamese newspaper. Thus, though not grim, the employment picture for refugees was not bright.

Chicago. Even though the city economic problems and its weather can be fearsome—especially for those accustomed to gentler climes—Chicago's refugee community is still growing. Whether this growth is because of its liberal public assistance levels, excellent public transportation, or its heritage as a city made up of people of diverse ethnic backgrounds, Chicago appears to be a congenial place for refugees to begin their life in the United States.

Our 1981 estimates for Illinois indicated that approximately 20,000 Indochinese refugees lived in the state. Beginning in 1975, there were 3,696; by 1978, a modest increase to 7,385 was seen. However, in the space of just one year, 1980, the refugee population almost doubled to 14,085. The 1981 estimates suggested the statewide refugee population to be 18,619. Of that number, it was approximated that in 1982 Chicago was home to some 12,000 Indochinese refugees, mostly Vietnamese and mostly living in the Uptown area. The Lao have tended to congregate in the Elgin and Hanover Park areas of the Chicago region.

When, in 1975, Chicago had suddenly been faced with resettling two thousand Southeast Asian refugees, the Refugee Social Services Consortium was formed to handle that crisis. It consists of Catholic Charities, Jewish Family and Community Services, Jewish Vocational Service, Lutheran Child and Family Services, and Travelers Aid/Immigrants' Service League. This consortium and the programs provided by the city colleges of Chicago (especially Truman College) form the core of services offered to refugees in Chicago. Refugee programs in Chicago appear to be very well coordinated, with excellent cooperation among service providers as well as citizen groups.

Several refugee groups had managed to organize support groups for themselves by 1981, when we first went into Chicago. The Vietnamese Community Service Center opened in 1980; the Cambodian Mutual Assistance Association, the Hmong Center, the Lao Center, and the Association for Chinese from Indochina were also active by 1981. These centers performed a number of services, including orientation for newcomers, classes for the elderly and the young, cultural activities, English classes, and employment orientation and information.

The CPI in 1981 for Chicago was three points below the national average. The unemployment rate was 9.3 percent, which was slightly above the national average and the highest of all five sites. As a result, entry-level jobs in manufacturing industries were scarce and virtually nonexistent for those without English ability. But entry-level positions in the service sector were available, albeit at minimum wages. By 1981, a good number of refugee-owned businesses had sprung up in Chicago's Uptown area, which is the center of the refugee community. Most prominent are Vietnamese and Chinese-Vietnamese restaurants, retail stores, and import/export businesses.

Boston. Suffolk County was ranked seventeenth nationally in arrivals (4,866) from mid-1978 to mid-1981, but it was very high in the ratio of second-wave refugees to first-wave refugees. Additionally, among the five sites, Boston had the greatest number of recently arrived refugees. This fact has implications for the general level of economic self-sufficiency for the refugee community as a whole.

Another characteristic unique to Boston was the presence of a large number of refugees, primarily men, who had come to the United States alone. Nearly half the refugee households in Boston (47 percent) included at least one such single, and fully 16 percent of the households there were comprised of just a single or of unrelated singles living together.

The refugee resettlement program started slowly in Massachusetts, given the small number of refugees from 1975 who settled there. Most of the effort was left in the hands of the voluntary agencies. In 1982, the International Institute of Boston was serving as the main program center for refugee services. It ran the major ESL program and provided employment services and vocational training. The United Community Planning Corporation also worked with a local Vietnamese group to provide ESL, job counseling, and vocational training. Two other programs, working in conjunction with local Asian-American organizations, provided counseling and social adjustment services. They were the Research for Social Change and the Chinatown Consortium.

The CPI for Boston in December, 1981, was the lowest for all five selected sites. In breaking down the CPI figure, food, housing, medical, and other expenses were low compared to the other sites; utilities and transportation were high. Clothes and entertainment were about average. The unemployment rate for Boston in 1982 was 7 percent, below the national average.

The ethnicity of the refugee population in Boston is largely Vietnamese. The initial period (1978–80) saw 75 percent of refugees coming from Vietnam to be of Chinese descent. Some Hmong came in 1977, and Lao began to come during these years as well. Additionally, there was a spurt in the number of Khmer in 1981. In the main, however, ethnic Vietnamese dominated the late arrivals. In December, 1981, the estimated total of the 6,500 refugees living in Boston was broken down as follows: Vietnamese, 3,500; Sino-Vietnamese, 1,000; Lao, 800; Khmer, 750; Hmong, 450.

The refugees in Boston remained a small minority, scattered in different sections of the city. Community reaction ranged from support to harassment, depending on specific situations. Some racial incidents took place in 1981 and 1982, but in general attitudes in the wider community were good.

Overview. Site-specific effects are identified and discussed where relevant. In most instances, however, we have combined the data across sites because (1) the analyses indicate greater similarity among refugees and their resettlement experiences than initially expected, irrespective of site location, and (2) percentage factors specific to the sites can be easily isolated by applying deductive logic to simple bivariate comparisons.

The data are presented unweighted statistically. Many analyses were run using weighted data (weighted by probability of selection by sampling frame for each respondent and each household), and, with only minor exceptions, the weighted and unweighted analyses show the same pattern and magnitude of relationships. Not only is this important because unweighted data are far easier to present and understand than weighted data, but it means that the combination of area probability and other sampling procedures used have resulted in a data set relatively free of bias sampling error. Thus, with few exceptions, the data are presented unweighted with respect to sampling procedures and variations across sites.

One additional comment on the relative importance of site characteristics needs to be made: the site that is most distinct from the others on important economic variables such as employment and cash assistance is Houston. It is also the site where we had the greatest difficulty locating respondents in our sample. This difference sometimes makes it difficult to distinguish variation in policy (e.g., cash assistance) at the site level from individual differences among refugees. Compared to refugees in other sites, those in Houston fared well. But we caution against rushing to conclusions regarding Houston, since we know too little about those refugees who either left the site or, for whatever reasons, could not be traced by our interviewers. We also know that Houston was settled earlier than the other sites; therefore, the refugees there had greater time to adjust. Those who were resettled in Houston also had better English proficiency upon arrival in the United States than refugees at the other sites. English proficiency, as we have seen, is an important predictor of economic self-sufficiency. Thus, this combination of greater length of residency in the United States and greater English skills would have improved the chances for success during resettlement regardless of site location.

Sampling

A dual sampling frame approach was used for this study: (1) lists comprised of data from government agencies, public resettlement agencies, refugee mutual assistance (MAA) organizations, and support service organizations; and (2) area probability frames.

List frames. Lists of refugees maintained for administrative purposes offered certain advantages. They could provide respondent addresses and additional information, such as date of arrival and ethnicity, which could be used to stratify the sample. In each of the five sites, an effort was made to determine what administrative lists existed, their completeness, their currency, and their availability. After obtaining the lists, we estimated the proportion of the site universe covered by the names on all the lists, the proportion of the site universe covered by the names on each individual list, and the extent of overlap among lists. Such information provided the basis for developing procedures for selecting respondents from each list.

Often there were statistical and practical problems associated with using the lists. Each list provided only partial coverage of the study population. Furthermore, the addresses and other information provided on the lists were not always current, and concerns about confidentiality prevented the staff from gaining access to some lists of eligible respondents. Having encountered such difficulties, it became necessary to resort to area probability sampling. The major portion of the sample came from the area frame.

Area probability sampling. The area frame is a consistent, well-structured tool for developing probability samples of general household populations. If conducted properly, the area frame approach provides the best coverage of the survey population and permits more generalizable findings and safer inferences. However, it is very costly and time-consuming because it requires the use of household enumeration and screening methods. In studies like this one, where lists, for a variety of reasons, have their limits, the area probability approach is the best supplemental sampling procedure to maintain scientific integrity. Thus, at each site, when the limits of available lists were reached or if conditions precluded the practical use of the lists, we shifted to area probability sampling.

The actual enumerations and screenings were conducted by the interviewers under the supervision of field coordinators and the University of Michigan staff. The problem of determining how many and which persons should be interviewed by area probability procedures was based on the success of the list sampling frame at each site. Where necessary, by relying heavily on the area probability sampling and by reducing dependency on available lists for single selection, there can be no doubt that sampling error was reduced.

The dual sampling frame described above was the basis

for identifying the households and individuals for the first round of interviews. A subsample of nuclear families was drawn from this primary sample for the second round of interviews. Specifics of that selection procedure will be described later.

How representative is our sample for the refugee communities of the Vietnamese, Lao, and Chinese from Vietnam in the United States? Our site selection procedure focused on counties having high concentrations of Southeast Asian refugees, and the five sites chosen are all areas of urban and suburban nature. Based on data from the Office of Refugee Resettlement (HHS), our sample is representative of the Vietnamese, Lao, and Chinese from Vietnam who live in large American cities and the suburban areas surrounding them. But the results of this survey may not carry over to refugees living in medium and small towns or in rural areas. Nevertheless, the findings reveal a great amount of commonality for the refugees across all five sites and therefore indicate a broader relationship and greater generalizability than initially foreseen.

At places in the tables, the numbers used will vary, because all 1,384 questionnaires do not contain uniform data for all their questions. Indeed, the respondents were told they did not have to answer any questions they did not want to. Thus, any one topic is likely to have missing data from certain questionnaires. The N will represent the number of those households or individuals for whom data exist in the questionnaires on the topic under discussion.

First Survey

During the first round of interviews in 1981, one person was identified to be interviewed in each household on the basis of the sampling procedures. That person was interviewed at length with regard to his or her personal views and circumstances. This respondent was then asked to provide more limited information on all other members of the household. In all, we gained data on 6,775 individuals in these 1,384 households. The data on the person interviewed (the respondent) is, of course, more extensive than that for other household members. We have used households and, when appropriate, individuals as the unit of analysis. In some instances we have data only on the main respondent, and in those cases the 1,384 main respondents constitute the unit of analysis.

All interviews were conducted and recorded in the respondent's native language—Vietnamese, Chinese, or Lao— by a native-speaking refugee interviewer of the same ethnicity as the respondent. These interviews were then back-translated into English by the native-speaking interviewers. The interviews averaged around two hours, fifteen minutes and covered the following topics:

- Household information: background information on each household member.
- Employment: jobs and employment facts and history on each person in the labor force.
- Nonemployment: data on all household members not in the labor force.
- Income: data on income from all sources other than employment.
- Expenses: data on household needs and strategies to become self-sufficient.
- English ability: fluency level and participation in English classes.
- Use of program services: types and degree of involvement in assistance services.
- Health: health problems and care.
- Attitudes and social behavior: perceptions of problems faced in resettlement, quality of life, interactions with refugee community.

Second Survey

The second round of interviews was conducted in 1984 with a subsample of nuclear family households. The project began with the data base encompassing the 1,384 households across the five sites. Of these households, 781 had school-age children (six to seventeen years old) for the 1983–84 school year. We drew an initial subsample of 358 households. Once the field survey was under way, we replaced unlocated households from the remaining households sampled in the earlier study. Respondents were interviewed in a subsample of 200 of these households, which contained 536 school-age children. The number of school-age children per household ranged from one (forty-five households) to eight (one household). Fifty-five percent of the children were male, 45 percent female. The distribution of children by grade is fairly even. Forty-two percent were in the six grades of secondary school and 58 percent in the seven grades of elementary school, with each grade from first to eleventh having between 6 percent and 11 percent of the total. Only kindergarten (5 percent) and twelfth grade (4 percent) had smaller numbers.

As with the first-round interviews, these second interviews were conducted with the main respondent and in the native language by trained interviewers. The interviews averaged one hour, thirty minutes and focused on the following topics:

- Cultural values: assessment of the relative importance of a set of value and goal items.
- Perception of neighbors: perceived characteristics of nonrefugee neighbors and other Americans.
- Locus of control: degree of perceived control over events that affect one's future, particularly with regard to educational achievements.
- Family roles and parenting: role sharing, decision making, and division of labor among family members.
- Background demographics: more explicit data on SES-related items than obtained in the first interview.
- Economic update: changes in economic status and work-force participation since the initial interview.

In addition to the interview questions, the respondent, in all cases a parent or guardian, was asked for written permission to allow the school(s) attended by the children in the family to release transcripts to the researchers. As with the interview material, respondents again were guaranteed confidentiality and anonymity. Statements of permission for each child were presented to the respondents in English and in their native language for their signature. These were presented to the schools and the relevant data provided without significant exception across the sites.

In addition to interviewing parents, we also obtained self-administered interview forms from ninety children in grades seven through twelve. These interview forms were printed in English. The questionnaire included items that referred to the students' values, attributions, and ethnic heritage and, in abbreviated form, was patterned after the second round of face-to-face interviews conducted with their parents. Unlike the other interview data reported in this study, these data on the students are not treated extensively but are used mainly for the purpose of underscoring a particular point in the discussion. Even though we do not make a claim for sampling precision, these ninety cases do not differ in age and educational performance from their grade cohorts for whom we do not have questionnaire data. What distinguished those on whom we have these data is that the questionnaires were retrieved before a cutoff date dictated by coding schedules.

Data Base

What follows is a brief description of the major predictor variables studied in relation to the two main outcome variables: economic self-sufficiency and scholastic achievement. They are presented under headings that follow the stream of events ranging from background factors before migration to recent data on economic and educational achievements in the United States. The most significant stages of their migration and events affecting their lives in the United States are used to designate these categories, namely premigration, migration, entry (U.S.), resettlement, family life, social interaction, coping mechanisms, and outcome measures. The following gives some idea of the items studied under these headings.

Background Variables

Premigration. An important aspect of this study was to examine the effect of background demographics, cultural background, and family life on adaptability and success in the United States. Background data collected include the family's past socioeconomic status, going back to the colonial period in Indochina, and degree of contact with modern Western culture and values. We looked at a variety of cultural traditions existing among the three ethnic groups: Vietnamese, Chinese-Vietnamese, and Lao. The three groups have different languages, including writing systems, and they vary in their social and cultural patterns. Vietnamese civilization received major influences from China, and, as a result, the cultural patterns of the Vietnamese and the Chinese are relatively more similar to each other than they are to those of the Lao.

The question of family socioeconomic status is also important because the higher-status families were more likely to take part in the ideal cultural pattern of the society. From our knowledge of the family's socioeconomic status in Indochina, we wanted to estimate the importance of different patterns of achievement for the family relative to the society's traditions. Presumably, members from the lower levels of society would be less likely to have participated in that society's ideals of advancement than those at the upper levels, though the former may still hold close to the ideal itself. Of interest here were the middle classes of society, particularly those in commerce, and the adoption of their former society's ideal.

From these background variables comes a sense of the cultural contribution to achievement and adaptation. Does the emphasis on a particular pattern of achievement in an ancestral culture affect a refugee's performance in our society? What are the differences in performance, if any, among those of Vietnamese, Chinese, and Lao descent? Do these differences vary within each culture according to socioeconomic status therein, variations in cultural value systems, or patterns in family life that they brought with them?

Migration. The refugees have gone through a traumatic set of experiences to reach this country. They chose to leave their homeland, did so in more or less grave circumstances, survived the flight (whether as Boat People across the sea or as escapees across the Mekong River), and settled in different refugee camps for varying lengths of time before coming to the United States. For a variety of reasons, we did not probe the respondents' reasons for leaving or the difficulties undergone during the flight as part of the survey questionnaire. Admittedly, only passing attention is given to the events on the open sea and the attendant horrors. Nothing could be so sobering and touch the depths of the human spirit so much as the knowledge that the refugees had, at best, about an even chance of being raped, murdered, abducted, tortured, and robbed at sea. But we felt the respondents were rightfully entitled to their privacy concerning such experiences, and even had they been questioned and willing to discuss them, it would be obscene to subject their trauma to calculation and analysis.

The incidents of atrocities among those who fled by sea vary greatly. A major problem in assessing the extent of hardship endured is that there is no count of the number of boats sunk by pirates or storms with no survivors or witnesses. Some estimates of the number of boats lost at sea go as high as 50 percent. It was estimated also that of those boats not lost on the open seas, about 80 percent were attacked by Thai pirates at least once. The Thai pirates were particularly vicious in their treatment of the Boat People. Many individual stories were told of unimaginable brutality—such as young girls being abducted and repeatedly raped and bartered for fish from one pirate boat to another. Rape, murder, and robbery were common outcomes of pirate attacks.

Although we did not question the refugees about their reasons for migrating and the events associated with the escape, we did gain such information through the gathering of life histories from a number of our respondents. In addition, we also collected data on the length of time spent in the camps and the programmatic assistance (e.g., English, vocational training) used while in the camps. Some of these experiences were presented earlier.

Entry. Date of arrival is one potentially significant variable, to determine both how long the refugees have been in the country and the economic conditions, service programs, and other forms of assistance existing at the time of their arrival. We have also looked at the health of the families on arrival and particularly at the level of English held by the refugees when they first set foot in the country. Another significant element at their point of entry is the general refugee community existing at the resettlement site, and more particularly the friends and relatives there.

Resettlement. In order to describe the present conditions of the refugees, we compiled community profiles, including demographic data and local attitudes, of the five sites. We gathered data on secondary migration by recording which of our respondents stayed in their initial resettlement sites and which left their initial sites to come to one of our five sites. About 15 percent of our sample had taken part in the secondary migration of the refugees within the country by mid-1982. We also asked about continuing health problems in the household since arrival in the United States and whether any new problems had arisen.

More important, however, is the record of employment and income for the households. The first survey concentrated on the labor-force status of all adults aged sixteen and older in the household, as well as on the total income (both earned and cash assistance) coming into the household. Thus, we had a great deal of data on these matters, which we later updated at the time of the second survey in order to accurately measure the economic situation in which the refugees were living. At the time of the second survey, we also collected data on the academic achievements of the children, including grades and standardized test scores. Details of the economic and scholastic achievement measures are described later under "Outcome Measures."

We also examined the social services used by the refugees. Most particularly, we looked at programs offering English language training, employment services, and vocational training, as well as information on what refugees were using which service. We were interested as well in English acquisition outside of formal programs and the different means refugees employed to learn English.

Family life. Very important for the study is the household composition. The households studied were made up of nuclear families, extended families, and single, unrelated individuals. Within these households, we examined the patterns of interaction among the adults. How did they relate to each other? What part did sex roles have in these relationships? We examined how the households reacted to the children's schoolwork and searched for a sense of parent-child interactions, the nature of parental efforts to influence the children, and the family life-style.

We examined the patterns of cultural achievement motivation among the refugee families. Here we looked at the clusters of beliefs and values held by the refugees and how they compared with the cultural patterns brought from Indochina. We hypothesized that the family is the repository of such patterns, which they employ innovatively to adapt and achieve in the United States.

Social interaction. Going beyond the family and the household, we gained information on the types of organizations to which the refugees belonged and the ties of the respondents to the refugee community, temples or other religious organizations, and to established communities (Lao, Vietnamese, or Chinese) in the cities where they live. We sought to trace the contacts made by the refugees to these ethnic sources of social, economic, and informational support.

Extending this point, we explored the more general area of social contacts. We examined the refugee patterns of socializing (with other refugees, others of Asian background, and Americans, minority or otherwise). Perceptions, too, enter into the question of social relations. In the second set of interviews, we asked the refugees about their perceptions of American schools, American teachers, and the nonrefugee families and children in the immediate neighborhood and for the nation as a whole. Here we looked more generally at adult refugee perceptions of American society, as well as feelings about assimilation.

Coping means and mechanisms. Major mediators of the coping process, which have such telling impact on adjustment, are the social support resources available to the individual and the family. To a large extent, they determine the capacity to withstand stress and include those personal and family characteristics that promote good adjustment, such as a flexibility to flow in the face of adversity, as well as a cohesiveness and integration to buffer the family in chaotic times. Reference back to the refugee communities as support sources are also intended here.

In this connection we used attribution and efficacy measures to detect refugee effort at finding meaning in crises through causal interpretations of their situation and at restoring a sense of mastery and control over their own lives. We also sought information about the continued maintenance of cultural customs within the home and the extent to which the families value their cultural traditions and work at preserving and transmitting them. We asked about goals and expectations for their children.

Outcome Measures

Economic self-sufficiency. We defined the degree of economic self-sufficiency achieved by the refugee households in three ways: (1) by income source (i.e., earned, cash assistance, and various combinations thereof), (2) by official poverty-level standing, and (3) by various measures of work-force participation. These data are presented with emphasis on changes over time for these measures and the trajectory (i.e., slope and direction) of those changes.

Scholastic achievement. The degree of scholastic success achieved by the Indochinese refugee children was determined from actual school transcripts from kindergarten through twelfth grade. We established the success (or lack thereof) for each refugee student by relative ranking in comparison with school grades at the local level (GPA) and standardized achievement test scores, especially the California Achievement Tests (CAT), at the national level.

Statistical Analyses

A number of multivariate analytical techniques were employed to assess the size and character of the relationship between a set of predictors taken together and our measures of economic self-sufficiency and scholastic achievement.

Multiple regression was a basic tool used in our analyses. In general, it computes the fraction of variance of an outcome measure which is accounted for by a group of predictors taken together and apportions the shared variance to the predictors in proportion to the magnitude of their individual relations to the outcome measures. Thus, if each of two predictors accounts for 10 percent of the variance in a self-sufficiency measure, and together they account for 15 percent, then 5 percent is shared. To the extent that predictors account for shared variance, they can be viewed as alternative measures of the same thing; and the extent to which such shared explanatory power should be attributed to one, to the other, or divided between them becomes a matter of theoretical interpretation. Although we are interested in the total shared explanatory power for the set of variables under study, the primary focus of the discussion will be the amount of variance contributed independently by each variable to the total. Multiple regression analyses, which assume linearity and additivity, investigate the degree of shared variance or "multicollinearity" and the relative importance of predictors when taken together.

In our analyses, we have also attempted to determine whether there are interaction effects among the predictors in their relations to economic self-sufficiency or academic achievement. An interaction effect exists when the relationship observed between one predictor and the outcome depends on the values of a second predictor. For example, large households might fare better than small ones among the Vietnamese, but household size makes no difference among the Lao. We have employed three strategies to detect interaction effects: (1) direct comparison of bivariate relationships within various groups, (2) multivariate analyses of the outcome measures with a technique called SEARCH (see below) which successively partitions the sample into groups by maximizing the variance for which each such partition can account (asymmetrical partitions thus indicating the presence of interactions), and (3) comparison of the proportion of variance which can be explained by SEARCH (which is sensitive to interaction) with that accounted for by multiple regression analyses (which are not sensitive to interaction) using the same predictors. All of these strategies suggest the presence of relatively minor interactions: the strength, but not the existence or direction, of many relationships vary within different parts of the sample. However, there appear to be no major interaction effects that must be taken into account in order to describe the basic relationships of interest in this study. Furthermore, we have not detected any sizable curvilinear relationships that need to be taken into account. It appears that the relationships can be adequately described by models that assume linearity (that the relations can be approximated by a straight line) and additivity (that there are no pronounced interaction effects).

Because the SEARCH technique is not as well known as multiple regression analysis, it requires some additional comment. Derived from a multivariate analysis of variance procedure developed by Morgan and Sonquist (Sonquist and Morgan 1964; Sonquist, Baker, and Morgan 1973), it parallels that strategy of an exploratory researcher engaged in a series of primary and secondary search processes to find the best way for isolating homogeneous subgroupings in a body of data. The procedure permits a number of systematic data combinations and permutations to be examined for their power to increase variance between high and low groups on a dependent variable.

In brief, the statistical analysis operates sequentially. First, the computer simultaneously scans all predictor variables until it determines the one predictor variable split leaving the greatest reduction of the unexplained variance on the dependent variable—namely the split producing the largest sum of squared deviations by a single division of the total sample. Next, the computer again scans all predictor variables to locate best splits for each of the two subgroups resulting from the initial split. This iteration procedure continues to operate until all dependent variable divisions accounting for a variance reduction of one or more percent of the unknown variance are detected. Technically, it is a binary segmentation technique that explores for structure in data.

The approach we used to obtain a factor-analytic understanding of the values was to submit rating scores for the twenty-six value items to a series of principal-components factor analyses, employing Kaiser's criterion to determine the number of factors, iterating the communalities from unities and rotating the factors orthogonally, based on the varimax criterion. Six factors or groups of values resulted from the procedure. Items selected for inclusion in a factor were those with loadings of .40 or better (Gorsuch 1974).

Further Economic and Scholastic Data

Labor-Force Status

Employment History

Once they arrived in the United States, it took the refugees an average of eleven months to land their first jobs. Of the respondents employed at the time of the interview, two-thirds (64 percent) had held only one job in the United States—their current job; 26 percent had held one previous job in addition to their present job; 9 percent had held two or more previous jobs. As expected, those who held only one job had been in the United States less time (twenty-seven months versus thirty-three months for those with more than two previous jobs) and had a shorter history of employment in the United States (fifteen months versus twenty months for those who held more than two previous jobs).

The jobs of our employed respondents were classified by occupational category as follows:

Professional	2.5%
Semiprofessional	5.1
Managerial	2.0
Clerical	9.3
Sales	2.0
Crafts	10.2
Operatives	40.0
Service	23.9
Labor	5.0

In the United States, the refugees held a broad variety of occupations, which for ease of preparation and discussion we have collapsed into the broadest census job families. Most were employed as operatives, in service industries, or in crafts. More specifically, 21 percent of the working refugees held jobs in factories, 12 percent in restaurants, 17 percent as janitors or maids, and 4 percent as machine operators or mechanics. Only 14 percent were operatives, service workers, or crafts people in their native countries, but these categories accounted for 74 percent of those working in the United States. Put simply, for all former occupational groups, the jobs most often held in the United States were as operatives or in the service sector. Tables A-1 and A-2 show the occupational status, economic sector, and wage data for the jobs held by the refugees.

Income Source

Table A-3 illustrates the point that the households that received public assistance, cash or food stamps or both, often depended on more than one kind (i.e., 57 percent of the sample). In contrast, only 18 percent of the sample received only one type of assistance; 25 percent received no assistance at the time of the study. The combination of assistance received by the refugees included both food stamps and RCA (25 percent). And when only one type of assistance was received by a household, it was most frequently food stamps (10 percent).

By identifying the groups that had cash assistance, earnings, or some combination of the two, we are better able to focus on the household features that set these income groups apart from one another.

Poverty-Level Standing

Household income is defined as money income from Refugee Cash Assistance, Aid to Families with Dependent Children,

TABLE A-1. Employment by Socio-Economic Index and Hourly Wage

SEI Status	Percentage	Mean Hourly Wage
Low	71	$4.62
Medium	19	5.24
High	10	6.74

TABLE A-2. Employment by Economic Sector and Hourly Wage

Sector	Percentage	Mean Hourly Wage
Core	45	$4.68
Periphery	55	5.53

TABLE A-3. Percentage of Households Reporting Different Combinations of Assistance (1,384 households)

	N	Percentage of Households
No assistance	342	25
Food stamps only	138	10
RCA only	45	3
AFDC only	52	4
SSI only	20	1
Food stamps and GA	20	1
Food stamps and RCA	342	25
Food stamps and AFDC	260	19
Food stamps and RCA and AFDC	40	3
Other combined	125	9

General Assistance, and Supplemental Security Income (SSI), as well as earnings, that is, the sum of labor, capital, and cash assistance of all household members. In-kind income (e.g., food stamps or Medicaid) is not included.

Poverty level, poverty line, and *poverty need standard* are used interchangeably. The basic explanation for this measure is set forth by Orshansky (1969) and is calculated on the basis of Department of Agriculture data on food needs by age, sex, and family size, corrected for inflation and published each month by the Department of Labor in the *Monthly Labor Review.* The official federal poverty level for each refugee household was calculated by first assigning a monthly need amount to each household member by gradation of age and sex. These individual need amounts were then summed to a household total and adjusted for household size to reflect economies of scale. The poverty-level standing then was calculated by dividing each household's total monthly earnings by its need standard. A household with a value of 1.0, or 100 percent, on this measure is therefore precisely at the poverty level; a value of 0.5, or 50 percent, would place it at one-half its poverty-level need standard; and a value of 2.0, or 200 percent, would mean it earned twice its poverty-level need standard. It should be pointed out that this standard is a very conservative estimate of self-sufficiency (the monthly need standard for a "typical" family of four was approximately $800 in 1982).

Scholastic Achievment: Standardized Tests

The California Achievement Test (McGraw-Hill, 1986) is the most widely used test to measure scholastic achievement in the United States. It has undergone more than fifty years of psychometric and standardization development. The CAT tests are grade-equivalent for kindergarten through grade twelve and reflect mainstream objectives: reading, math, and language skills. (See Willson 1985, Rodgers 1984, and Bunch 1985 for reviews of recent studies on the CAT and the basis for standardizing normative distributions nationally).

Initial Efforts at Explanation

We searched for the bases of the extraordinary progress of the Indochinese Boat People in this country. This section focuses on the standard demographic items, those that social scientists look to first for explanation, applying them to both economic and academic outcomes. We end with an analysis of the impact of intervention programs targeted specifically to aid the refugees; we examine to see who used them and with what results.

Demographics

Ethnicity

The difference in level of employment across the three ethnic groups is small. The Lao were somewhat more often employed than were the two other ethnic groups: Lao, 60 percent; Vietnamese, 57 percent; Chinese, 55 percent. But the jobs held by the Lao were lower-paying and more likely to be in the periphery rather than in the core of the economy when compared with Vietnamese and Chinese. By contrast, the Vietnamese tended to have higher wages and better jobs than their Lao and Chinese-Vietnamese counterparts. On the average, the Vietnamese earned $5.26 per hour, the Chinese-Vietnamese earned $4.89, and the Lao earned $4.76. Also, the Vietnamese were more likely to hold professional, semi-professional, and managerial jobs (15 percent versus 9 percent for the Chinese and 2 percent for the Lao). The three ethnic groups did not show major differences, however, when compared on poverty standing or length of time on public assistance. On the other hand, analyses of variance show a clear distinction in the mean GPA among the ethnic groups.

On GPA we found statistically reliable deviations among the three ethnic groups. On the overall GPA, the mean GPAs for the Vietnamese, Chinese, and Lao were 3.17, 2.99, and 2.63, respectively; the mean for the total group of refugee children is 3.05. The science GPAs by ethnic groups are as follows: Vietnamese, 3.08; Chinese, 2.87; Lao, 2.17; the science GPA mean for the total group is 2.97. The difference by ethnicity on math GPA was as follows: Vietnamese, 3.35; Chinese, 3.23; Lao, 2.82; group mean was 3.18. All differences on ethnicity and GPAs shown are statistically reliable (p = < .01), the Vietnamese getting the higher grade scores, followed by the Chinese and Lao in order.

The order of the three ethnic groups—Vietnamese, Chinese, and Lao—remains the same for all the different types of grades we have. A look at differences in circumstance in Vietnam among Vietnamese and Chinese helps to explain their differences in academic achievment in the United States. As indicated in chapter 2, only the Vietnamese had a major interest in and the possibility of advancement through higher education. Government and academia were open to them. On the other hand, commerce was the road of advancement for the Chinese, and a secondary education filled the needs for such advancement. Among the Lao, only the privileged had access to education above the primary level. Those in our sample were from the lower-SES segments of that society. In addition, the Lao were in camps the longest, up to three years. Thus, their children arrived in the United States late and with a greater deficit in formal education compared with the two other ethnic groups. Yet the results at the national level for those who took the CAT show no such differences among the three groups. When judged against the common standard of national norms, the differences in performance and ethnicity were not maintained.

Religion

Refugees indicated their religious beliefs sufficiently to be identified as Buddhist, Christian, or Confucian. Among the Buddhists, we distinguished the Mahayana from the Theravada sect from Laos. Those from Confucian backgrounds had the highest GPA (3.37), followed by Christian and Buddhist groups (see table A-4). These differences between religion and GPA, however, are small but statistically reliable. There is, of course, some overlap and blending of religion and value items, but what the analysis tells us is that some differences in these religious beliefs remain intact and that they are somewhat associated with academic achievement. No relationships were found between religion and measures of economic outcomes.

Sex

Females in the work force were more likely to have jobs than males, by 61 percent to 56 percent. This may be so because women tend to classify themselves as housewives rather than unemployed when work is not available to them. Interestingly, women and men were about equally likely to have high-status jobs (13 percent of women versus 11 percent of men). But at all points on the time scale, women who have been employed the same number of months as men earned 20 percent less per hour than men for jobs at each skill level. The mean hourly wage for men in our sample was $5.36 versus $4.47 for the women.

We found no statistically reliable difference between the sexes in educational data, either on overall GPA or CAT data, even when compared by subject area such as mathematics, a field that is traditionally dominated by males. This finding is discussed further in chapter 4, where we look at the family characteristics of high-achieving students who tend to hold an egalitarian approach to sex roles and expectations deriving therefrom.

TABLE A-4.   Mean GPA by Religion
(349 schoolchildren)

	N	Mean GPA
Confucian	58	3.37
Mahayana Buddhist	127	3.13
None	31	3.05
Catholic	62	3.03
Protestant	35	2.94
Theravada Buddhist	36	2.47

Socioeconomic Status: Past Education and Occupation

Past education. Variables pertaining to past socioeconomic status were of little practical significance in determining economic standing during the early years of resettlement. Although households of singles with the highest level of past education have the highest percentage above poverty, 81 percent, there are comparatively few (4 percent) in our sample, and their current economic standing may be more a function of their employability and lack of dependents. The level of Indochinese education has a correlation of .24 with poverty-level standing and .13 with receipt of cash assistance. These are positive but not strong relationships. Past education did not emerge as a variable with explanatory power for economic achievement when the data were submitted to multivariate analysis. These results showed that past education correlated with our measures of self-sufficiency because of its intercorrelation with proficiency in English; that is, it was a means by which some refugees had acquired English proficiency before arriving in the United States. Those with less education but as good proficiency in English did just as well economically as those with high past education.

Past and present occupation. Former managers, semiprofessionals, professionals, and clerical workers had more success finding work in the United States than those in other occupations, with an unemployment rate of 39.5 percent. In contrast, farmers, laborers, and fishermen had the highest unemployment rates, at 55.8 percent. During the early stages of resettlement, current unemployment and underemployment among the different occupational groups may be a rather poor guide to their eventual self-sufficiency. They had not yet been able to bring their background skills fully to bear on their circumstances, and, therefore, the transferability of skills was low. An ironic illustration is the employment and occupational status of former operatives. Despite the strong tendency for employed refugees to find jobs as operatives in the United States, those who worked as operatives in their homelands were comparatively unsuccessful at finding jobs here—only 25 percent were employed.

Past SES and GPA. The vast majority of the parents of refugee students came from low-SES backgrounds, the poorer and less educated segments of their society. But sufficient variation in SES was represented in our sample of households with schoolchildren to permit us to look for relationships of past socioeconomic standing to educational outcome measures. Additionally, because of the disruption of the war years in Vietnam, we decided to trace SES back to the French colonial period and obtained data on the grandparents as well as the parents of the students. But again, as with income, no independent or unique contributions to GPA variation could be identified using past SES for either parents or grandparents.

Arrival English

English proficiency and outcome measures. The influence of English proficiency among parents on the GPA of their children is less clear. Nuclear families were lowest on "Arrival English" among the categories of household composition, with 80 percent reporting that no household member knew any English upon arrival. As already indicated, this deficiency posed a serious handicap to prospects for economic advancement. The children in these households, however, do not appear to be so handicapped in their academic pursuits; we found no correlation between GPA or CAT and English literacy levels among the parents.

Importance of literacy in the home. Nonetheless, the importance of English is an overriding concern in the refugee households. When asked what played the major role in holding children back in school, virtually all parents and children cited "Lack of English" as highest in importance. Also, as mentioned earlier, children performed less well in subjects that involved English language components. Thus, a relationship may be inferred, but it is not one that is simple or easily understood. The relationship between bilingualism in the home and school performance further illustrates the complication. We found that the children of parents who read to their children did better in school than did children who were not read to. But it made no difference whether the children were read to in English or in the native language of their parents. They did better as long as they were read to, regardless of the language employed. This finding is discussed further in chapter 4, but it, along with the CAT data on spelling, raises many interesting questions regarding the relation of language skills and school performance.

Other Factors

Health. About a quarter of the refugees reported health problems, but the only variable associated with health was age: older people have more health problems. We found no association between health and economic self-sufficiency for the refugees considered in the aggregate, nor was there evidence that health coverage in employment played a major role in the decision to leave welfare and enter the work force. But at the individual household level, of course, poor health could be the major barrier to economic status. Five to 10 percent of the population reported financial setbacks because of medical problems or suffered unmet health problems or had both difficulties because they were unable to pay for medical attention.

There were too few children with health problems in our sample for this to play a role in school performance. Parents did, however, rank health as third most important among factors holding back student performance, after "Lack of English" and "Disruption by nonrefugee children."

Secondary migration. Fifteen percent of the sample reported that they had moved from their site of original settlement in the United States. About three-quarters of these moves were from outside the current site and usually outside the state. Multivariate and bivariate analyses failed to detect a relationship between secondary migration and outcome measures. Most often reasons cited for moving were to obtain work or to rejoin other family members.

Urbanicity. Bivariate comparisons show that when compared with refugees from urban backgounds, refugees from rural areas in Southeast Asia are somewhat more likely to be on cash assistance (74 percent versus 68 percent) and to have poorer economic standing (66 percent versus 57 percent below poverty). But two variables, "Family composition" and "Arrival English," together virtually wiped out the importance of urban-rural background as a significant variable when the data were submitted to multivariate analysis. It is true that households from rural backgrounds do not achieve self-sufficiency as quickly as those from urban backgrounds, but the multivariate data tell us that a major reason for this difference is that nuclear families are more frequently found among the refugees with rural backgrounds. They are slower to achieve self-sufficiency mainly because the presence of children, particularly preschoolers, places a limit on the number of adults available for employment. Similarly, the variable "Arrival English," which is highly correlated with the attainment of self-sufficiency, shows that fluency in English is comparatively poorer among rural populations.

Programs

The Search for Bootstrappers

When we began this study, one of our funding sources expected that were we to look, we would find bootstrappers, or fiercely independent refugees in our sample who went about resettlement successfully without outside assistance. Central to the concerns of those whose duty it was to comment on the needs of refugees and immigrants, especially persons in position to influence government policy at that time, was the possibility that the level of help being provided the refugees was in excess of what was necessary and that a sizable fraction of the refugees were, in effect, welfare cheats. Those maintaining this view argued for immersion, in the belief that if plunged, sink-or-swim, into the problems of resettlement from the outset, refugees would do as well or better than they would with governmental assistance. In the end, all would be better off for it.

To answer this question, we searched the sample to identify persons who relied minimally or not at all on outside assistance, that is, households where self-sufficiency was achieved with (1) minimal or no reliance on outside financial help such as cash assistance and (2) minimal or no program involvement such as ESL classes or employment services.

The following criteria led to the identification of only twenty-nine bootstrapper households among the 1,384 sampled:

1. Currently off all forms of economic assistance
2. Past cash assistance for no more than six months
3. No program experience (ESL or employment)
4. Earned income equal to or greater than the poverty standard

Thus, only 2 percent of the households in our sample had managed to climb out of poverty after six months or less on cash assistance and without benefit of specialized refugee programs and services. The number of households that qualified on the basis of these criteria was too small for serious study, so we extended it by allowing one year of cash assistance and unlimited program involvement. Thus, our criteria for bootstrappers qualification was modified as follows:

1. Currently off all forms of cash assistance
2. Past cash assistance for no more than one year
3. Unlimited program involvement
4. Earned income equal to or greater than the poverty standard

Nine percent, or 122 of the 1,384 households, qualified using these criteria. But they are not really bootstrappers in the usual sense. Although these households may be self-sufficient, they are so only in terms of a minimally acceptable standard, that is, not on cash assistance and out of official poverty. There is a problem in deciding upon an accurate designation for these households, which, although out of poverty, could hardly be considered safely above it and by no measure approach middle-income levels. Their distinction derives from being among the first to be economically self-reliant and officially nonpoor.

Comparisons between the 122 households and the remainder of the sample revealed that they differed with respect to the following characteristics: greater proficiency in English upon arrival and a significantly smaller household size (3.7 persons versus 4.9 persons). This difference in household size is accounted for mainly by the presence of fewer preschoolers, thereby allowing opportunity for additional adults to participate in the labor force. Thus, in the main, this search for bootstrappers proved futile. We really did not find any, and those who did qualify, once the criteria were extended liberally, added nothing new to what we already knew.

Use and Impact

Almost all the refugees made use of the programs designed to assist them in their efforts at resettlement. The issue is the degree in which they were used and to what effect. The use of cash assistance and food-stamp programs has been treated in detail earlier; therefore, the discussion to follow focuses on the utilization and impact of employment and ESL programs. An exhaustive treatment and discussion of the data and findings on program impact on resettlement can be found in Caplan, Whitmore, and Bui (1985).

The category of employment services includes a broad array ranging from general orientation to the American job market and workplace practices, to assistance in locating potential jobs, to actual placement in specific jobs. The extent of assistance provided to refugees who used employment services differed widely by site and agency used. Some refugees reported receiving no more than a card to fill out or the classified section of a newspaper; others received counseling, referrals, preparation for interviews, transportation, and intercession with employers when problems arose. In general, however, the information gathered was insufficient to make discriminations concerning either the precise nature of the services received or the quality of assistance. Thus, we will focus on the use/nonuse of employment services where distinctions could be made among the types of such programs and their impact.

Job counseling and placement. Of the 4,160 adults in the sample, it was reported that 30 percent received employment services. Male refugees were more likely to use these services than women, by a margin of three to two. Chinese refugees were more likely to use them (40 percent) than Lao (30 percent) or Vietnamese (28 percent).

Employment services are difficult to analyze and evaluate because of the wide range of activities included. Our analyses show that, as a whole, refugee employment services did not make an impact on labor-force participation. Although evidence that such service did help was cited by individual respondents, for the group as a whole we were unable to establish any statistical relationship between the mere fact of having or not having such services and either being on cash assistance or finding employment. Other sources of job-related assistance appear to have been more effective. When asked "How did you get your job?" (table A-5), exactly half the refugees

TABLE A-5.   How Did You Get Your Job?
(*N* = 361)

Source	Percentage
Friends	30
Self-sought	16
Voluntary agencies	15
Sponsor	10
Schools	6
Refugee employment programs	5
Churches	4
Relatives	4
State employment services	3
Other	7

mentioned self-initiatives or personal contacts (friends and relatives), less than a third (29 percent) spoke of organizational aid (voluntary agency offices, schools, employment programs), and another 14 percent cited sponsors and local churches. The indication is that the aid provided by the informal refugee networks was most useful in obtaining employment, and organizations helped to some degree.

Vocational education. Twenty-four percent of the respondents reported having had vocational education. There was a strong tendency for those with better English skills to have had vocational education, and males again outnumbered females almost three to one (27 percent to 10 percent). Vietnamese were more likely to have had vocational education (27 percent), as compared to Chinese (22 percent) and Lao (19 percent). Except for the young and the elderly, age appeared to have little impact on the likelihood of receiving vocational education, and, as might be expected, the longer refugees were in the United States, the more likely they were to have had vocational education.

Vocational training is a more specific and concrete case and more easily identified than the miscellany of activities that fall under employment services. Yet it has some complications that need to be kept in mind as we judge its effectiveness. At first glance, such training appears to have had an impact. There is a positive and statistically significant ($p = < .01$) relationship between vocational training and being off cash assistance. Yet when we compared the employment status of those who had this training with cohort members with similar attributes (high level of English proficiency, education, etc.) but no training, the outcome was about the same. This comparison suggests that those who got into these programs might have gotten a job just about as easily without the programs. The training did, however, mean somewhat better jobs and better pay, but these differences are marginal.

English as a Second Language. Seventy-five percent of the adult refugees reported attending ESL classes. We also asked respondents which other strategies they had followed in order to develop their English. Ten percent said that they chose deliberately to live in a predominantly American area, 10 percent reported that they had a tutor, 20 percent practiced English with members of their household, and 66 percent said they picked it up by watching television or listening to the radio. This mix of learning techniques must be kept in mind when considering data on the nature of English improvement.

Those enrolled in ESL classes attended for an average of twenty-eight weeks, averaging thirteen hours per week. Of these, about half (47 percent) were taking classes at the "elementary level," 41 percent "intermediate," and 12 percent "advanced." The main providers of these classes for adults were community colleges and the public schools. Those who had "completed" ESL programs averaged 620 hours of attendance.

Respondents who attended ESL did not differ from those who did not on the basis of ethnicity or level of arrival-English proficiency. They did differ, however, from those without ESL in the following ways: (1) a higher percentage of men (61 percent) than women (46 percent), (2) more education, and (3) slightly younger, averaging thirty-three years of age versus thirty-six for those reporting no present or past ESL. These comparisons suggest that women and those with less preimmigration education, all of whom entered the country with less proficiency in English, were less likely to have ESL. Thus, there is a creaming effect noticeable among those who enter ESL. In reviewing our findings on the use of programs, it must be kept in mind that the majority of refugees arrived unable to speak any English.

As you can see in table A-6, there are substantial improvements reported in the ability of the refugees to handle English language tasks between the time of arrival and the time of our interviews. We made a strong effort to determine the factors associated with this improvement, especially the role of ESL. To determine what variable had strong correlations with improvement in English proficiency in the United States, we ran a series of stepwise regression analyses, comparing those with no English on arrival here, those with a little

English, and those with some English. These levels of proficiency were based on measures discussed in chapter 2. We did not include those refugees with higher levels of English proficiency, since the room for improvement in such cases was small, and ceiling effects would confound the problems of measuring and comparing change scores for the group. The ESL measure used in these analyses was the actual number of hours the respondent reported having attended such classes.

For the first group, those with no English on arrival, the major variables affecting improvement in English proficiency are level of education and age upon arrival in the United States: the younger and better educated were quicker to pick up English. No ESL impact was detectable.

For the second group, those with a little English on arrival, the major variables for improving their English are primarily the length of residency in the United States and age (meaning relative youth). For this group, ESL attendance did not account for changes in proficiency level.

For the third group, those with some English on arrival, length of time in the United States is the major variable, with "ESL attendance," "age," and "Southeast Asia education" adding marginal amounts to the correlation with language improvement.

There are large and significant differences for the refugees in scores between arrival and current English. But our

TABLE A-6.   English Ability for Daily Life Tasks ($N = 3,919$)

	Percentage with English Proficiency Sufficient to Perform These Tasks	
	Arrival	Current
Shop for food	32	92
Travel in city	30	81
Phone police or fire departments	18	65
Apply for aid	13	45
Explain health problems to a doctor	11	41
Read a newspaper	11	32
Hold a job as a salesperson	6	23

data on ESL exposure revealed little contributions to the acquisition of English over that gained in the welter of day-to-day living. Statistically, it contributed nothing to the multiple correlation for those who arrived with no English proficiency, it added nothing to those with little arrival English, and it contributed only marginally to those who arrived with some level of proficiency. Even though these data should not be construed as a definitive test of the effectiveness of ESL classes, they nevertheless give one reason to pause regarding its value to the refugees.

Overview of program effects. The measurement of program impact is difficult to determine empirically. Even under the best of circumstances—that is, random assignment of equivalent experimental and control groups, sustained sequencing of services over a protracted period of time, and so on—confident, verifiable assessment of outcomes is difficult to achieve, mainly because there is simply no way to constrain the effects of external events that influence recipients of these programs when conducted in the open community. The results of such research is even all the more equivocal in after-the-fact assessments such as the present study. When evaluation research can be instituted prior to the introduction of the intervention program, then necessary procedures and methodology can be adapted to the task and its adequacy monitored throughout the life of the program. But this cannot be done retroactively. The best that can be done under these circumstances is to sift through the data and, if positive results are found, attempt to reconstruct history and account for the findings, thereby laying the foundation for more ambitious quantitative studies to confirm the results; to determine the magnitude of effect; and to study the comparative advantage of program variations. Thus, we would argue that the absence of positive findings of language and employment programs and services should not be interpreted as unequivocal evidence of failure. We would argue, however, that had there been strong effects our measures would have detected them.

To summarize, ESL helps people to learn English, but not as much as other factors that influence the refugees' ability to learn the language. The role of employment counselor services is unclear. Because so many factors in the open community influence work-force participation, a different research design would be required to study the effects of counseling and placement services. The data on the effectiveness of vocational education is somewhat more conclusive: vocational education, at least moderately, facilitates employment. Those who get into such programs and who can afford to remain in them long enough land better and higher-paying jobs. They tend, however, to serve young men without families.

On the other hand, possibly it is the resourcefulness of the refugees who do not have access to service programs that makes program effects appear so weak. That is, left to their own devices, their ability to husband their own resources enables them to cope far more successfully with the adverse economic conditions. As indicated earlier, friends and relations are the main source of helpful employment information.

These findings raise a number of issues. First, there is the problem of equity of access. Those who manage to avail themselves of such services and programs are those who are already advantaged, the better-educated, young males, free of immediate family responsibilities. Conversely, those who are unable to enter them are the persons who might benefit most in terms of immediate needs.

The refugees nonetheless report that they value outside help. They rank employment and language programs very high when asked what they see as necessary to getting ahead in life, and they say that more are needed. Yet it is difficult to point to specific outcomes that would attest to their value to the attainment of economic self-sufficiency. Again, we would caution any interpretation of these results to mean that the programs are ineffectual. The problem may be one of methodology—unless a program produces a powerful and overriding effect, its outcome is difficult and often impossible to evaluate in the open community in the absence of a controlled research design.

Another matter that deserves attention here is language

proficiency among the schoolchildren. They clearly have the most problems with school subjects involving language components. Schools have made provisions for the needs of non-English-speaking students across the sites, and the refugee children attend these ESL classes. But we cannot say to what degree their needs are being met or to what extent they benefit. As with their other school experience, we can only presume that they are working hard and progressing. English skills are not being picked up at home, because the parents are so limited in this regard; adult members of nuclear households were lowest in arrival English, with most of these households having not even one person capable of survival-level English upon arrival in the United States. There may be some children who picked up English from watching TV, but that would be minimal, because in most nuclear family homes TV watching is controlled and not very extensive because the evening hours are usually preempted for homework (see chap. 4).

It emerges from the foregoing discussion that in the final consideration neither the basic demographic facts of refugee life nor the programmatic service efforts help to account for the refugees' effectiveness in using their energies and intelligence to achieve successful outcomes during early resettlement. Once we go beyond the narrow provinces of simple bivariate comparisons, few factors could be found that determine in a causal way the accomplishments of the refugees. Most important among the findings were that the level of English upon arrival in the United States has major and long-lasting consequences for economic progress and that the educational performance of schoolchildren is independent of family size and birth order. We need to look elsewhere if we wish to unravel the causal threads leading to the progress made in resettlement.

Bibliography

Aames, J. S., et al. 1977. *Indochinese refugee self-sufficiency in California: A survey and analysis of the Vietnamese, Cambodians and Lao and the agencies that serve them.* Report submitted to the State Department of Health, California.

Argyle, M. 1986. Rules for social relationships in four cultures. *Australian Journal of Psychology* 38:309–18.

Atkinson, J. 1987. Gender roles in marriage and the family: A critique and some proposals. *Journal of Family Issues* 8:5–41.

Atkinson, J. W., and Raynor, J. O. 1963. *Motivation and achievement.* New York: Halstead Press.

Azuma, H. 1984. Secondary control as a heterogeneous category. *American Psychologist* 39:970–71.

Bach, R. L., et al. 1983. The economic adjustment of Southeast Asian refugees in the U.S. *World Refugee Survey 1983.* U.S. Committee for Refugees 25th Anniversary Issue, pp. 51–55.

Bach, R. L., and Bach, J. B. 1980. Employment patterns of Southeast Asian refugees. *Monthly Labor Review* 103:31–38.

Bacon, M. K., and Ashmore, R. D. 1985. How mothers and fathers categorize descriptions of social behavior attributed to daughters and sons. *Social Cognition* 3:193–217.

Baker, D. D., and Terpstra, D. E. 1986. Locus of control and self-esteem versus demographic factors as predictors of attitudes toward women. *Basic and Applied Social Psychology* 7:163–72.

Baker, H. D. R. 1979. *Chinese family and kinship.* New York: Columbia University Press.

Banfield, E. 1970. *The unheavenly city.* Boston: Little, Brown.

Baratz, J., and Baratz, S. 1970. Early childhood intervention: The social science base of institutional racism. *Harvard Educational Review* 40:29–50.

Bar-Tal, D., and Darom, E. 1979. Pupil's attributions for success and failure. *Child Development* 50:264–67.

Bastin, J., and Benda, H. J. 1968. *A history of modern Southeast Asia.* Englewood Cliffs, N.J.: Prentice-Hall.

Battle, E. S., and Rotter, J. B. 1963. Children's feelings of personal control as related to social class and ethnic group. *Journal of Personality* 31:482–90.

Bell, D. A. 1985. The triumph of Asian-Americans. *New Republic* 193:24–31.

Bellah, R. N. 1971. Evil and the American ethos. In *Sanctions for evil,* ed. N. Sanford and C. Comstock. San Francisco: Jossey-Bass.

Bellah, R. N.; Madsen, R.; Sullivan, W. M.; Swidler, A.; and Tipton, S. M. 1985. *Habits of the heart: Individualism and commitment in American life.* Berkeley: University of California Press.

Bennett, W. J. 1987. Implications for American education. In *Japanese Education Today.* Washington, D.C.: U.S. Department of Education.

Berardo, F. M. 1980. Decade preview: Some trends and directions for family research and theory in the 1980s. *Journal of Marriage and the Family* 42:723–28.

Berger, B. 1985. *The fourth R: The repatriation of the school.* In *Challenge to American schools,* ed. J. H. Bunzel. New York: Oxford University Press.

Berkeley Planning Associates. 1982. *Study of the state administration of the refugee resettlement program.* Berkeley: author.

Bernstein, B. 1975. *Class, codes, and control,* Vol. 3. London: Routledge and Kegan Paul.

Berry, J. 1976. *Human ecology and cognitive style: Comparative studies in cultural and psychological adaptation.* New York: Sage/Halsted.

Block, J. H. 1973. Conceptions of sex role: Some cross-cultural and longitudinal perspectives. *American Psychologist* 28:512–26.

Bochner, S. 1986. Coping with unfamiliar cultures: Adjustment or culture learning? *Australian Journal of Psychology* 38:347–58.

Boissevain, J., and Grotenberg, H. 1986. Culture, structure and ethnic enterprise: The Surinamese of Amsterdam. *Ethnic and Racial Studies* 9:1–23.

Botstein, L. 1983. Nine proposals to improve our schools. *New York Times Magazine,* June 5, p. 59.

Bowman, P. J., and Howard, C. 1985. Race-related socialization, motivation, and academic achievement: A study of black youths in three-generation families. *Journal of the American Academy of Child Psychiatry* 24:134–41.

Bradley, R. H.; Caldwell, B. M.; and Elardo, R. 1977. Home environment, social status and mental test performance. *Journal of Educational Psychology* 69:697–701.

Bridgman, B., and Shipman, V. C. 1978. Preschool measures of self-esteem and achievement motivation as predictors of third-grade achievement. *Journal of Educational Psychology* 70:17–28.

Bullivant, B. 1981. *The pluralist dilemma in education.* London: George Allen and Unwin.

Bunch, M. B. 1985. California Achievement Tests, Forms C and D. In *Test critique, Vol III,* ed. D. J. Keyser and R. S. Sweetland. Kansas City: Test Corporation of America, Westport Publishers.

Burger, H. 1973. Cultural pluralism and the schools. In *Cultural challenges to education,* ed. C. Brembeck and W. Hill. Lexington, Mass.: D. C. Heath.

Buttinger, J. 1972. *A dragon defiant: A short history of Vietnam.* New York: Praeger.

Cain, G. G. 1976. The challenge by segmented labor market theories to orthodox theory: A survey. *Journal of Economic Literature* 14:1215–58.

Calleo, D. P. 1987. *Beyond American hegemony.* New York: Basic Books.

Campbell, D. T. 1975. On the conflicts between biological and social evolution and between psychology and moral tradition. *American Psychologist* 30:1103–26.

Caplan, N.; Whitmore, J.; and Bui, Q. L. 1985. *Southeast Asian refugee self-sufficiency study.* Washington, D.C.: Office of Refugee Settlement, Department of Health and Human Services.

Carnegie Forum on Education and the Economy, Task Force on Teaching as a Profession. 1986. *A nation prepared: Teachers for the 21st century.* Washington, D.C: author.

Cazden, C. B., and John, V. P. 1971. Learning in American Indian Children. In *Anthropological perspectives on education,* ed. M. L. Wax, S. Diamond, and F. O. Gearing. New York: Basic Books.

Chan, K. B. 1983. Structure and values of the Chinese family in Vietnam. In *The South East Asian environment,* ed. D. Webster. Ottawa: University of Ottawa Press.

Chiu, L. H. 1986. Locus of control in intellectual situations in American and Chinese school children. *International Journal of Psychology* 21:167–76.

Chu, H. M. 1972. Migration and mental disorder in Taiwan. In *Transcultural research in mental health,* ed. W. Lebra. Honolulu: East West Center Press.

Clark, R. 1983. *Family life and school achievement: Why poor black children succeed or fail.* Chicago: University of Chicago Press.

Coelho, G. V., and Ahmed, P. I., eds. 1980. *Uprooting and development: Dilemmas of coping with modernization.* New York: Plenum Press.

Cohen, E. G. 1982. Expectation states and interracial interaction in school settings. *Annual Review of Sociology* 8:209–35.

Cohen, G. 1981. Cultural and educational achievement. *Harvard Educational Review* 51:270–85.

Coleman, J. S., et al. 1966. *Equality of educational opportunity.* Washington, D.C.: National Center for Educational Statistics.

Covington, M. V., and Omelich, C. L. 1979. Effort: The double-edged sword in school achievement. *Journal of Education Psychology* 71:169–82.

Craft, M., ed. 1984. *Education and cultural pluralism.* London: Falmer Press.

Crandall, V. C.; Katkovsky, W.; and Crandall, V. J. 1965. Children's beliefs in their control of reinforcement in intellectual-academic achievement situations. *Child Development* 36:91–109.

DeVos, G. A. 1968. Achievement and innovation in culture and personality. In *Personality: An interdisciplinary approach,* ed. E. Norbeck, D. Price-Williams, and W. M. McCord. New York: Holt, Rinehart and Winston.

Dien, D. S. 1982. A Chinese perspective on Kohlberg's theory of moral development. *Developmental Review* 2:331–41.

Dinnerstein, L., and Reimers, D. M. 1975. *Ethnic Americans: A history of immigration and assimilation.* New York: Dodd, Mead.

Doi, T. 1973. *The anatomy of dependence.* Tokyo: Kokansha International.

Doyle, D. P. 1987. Educational turmoil in Japan, Britain, France, and at home. *Public Opinion* 10:45–47.

Duncan, G. J., and Morgan, J. N. 1980. *Five thousand American families—patterns of economic progress, 8, Analyses of the first eleven years of the panel study of income dynamics.* Ann Arbor: Institute for Social Research, University of Michigan.

Duncan, O. D. 1961. A socioeconomic index for all occupations. In *Occupations and social status,* ed. A. J. Reiss. Glencoe, Ill.: Free Press.

Dunning, B. 1982. A systematic survey of the social, psychological and economic adaptation of Vietnamese refugees representing five entry cohorts, 1975–1979. Washington, D.C.: Bureau of Social Science Research.

Duveen, G., and Lloyd, B. 1986. The significance of social identities. *British Journal of Social Psychology* 25:219–30.

Dweck, C. S., and Bempechat, J. 1983. Children's theories of intelligence: Consequences for learning. In *Learning and motivation in the classroom,* ed. S. G. Paris, G. M. Olson, and H. W. Stevenson. Hillsdale, N.J.: Erlbaum.

Dyal, J., and Dyal, R. 1981. Acculturation, stress and coping. Some implications for research and education. *Journal of Intercultural Relations* 5:301–28.

Eccles, J., et al. 1987. Parents as socializers of achievement attitudes. Unpublished. Ann Arbor: Institute for Social Research, University of Michigan.

Eccles, J. S. 1986. Gender roles and women's achievement. *Educational Researcher* 15:15–19.

Eccles, J. S. 1987. Gender roles and women's achievement-related decisions. *Psychology of Women Quarterly* 11:135–72.

Elig, T., and Frieze, I. H. 1979. Measuring causal attributions for success and failure. *Journal of Personality and Social Psychology* 37:621–34.

Ellis, A. A. 1980. *The assimilation and acculturation of Indochinese children into American culture.* Sacramento: Department of Social Services.

Erickson, F. 1987. Transformation and school success: The politics and culture of educational achievement. *Anthropology and Education Quarterly* 18:335–56.

Erickson, F. D. 1975. Gatekeeping and the melting pot: Interaction in counseling encounters. *Harvard Educational Review* 45:44–70.

Erickson, R. V., and Hoang, G. N. 1980. Health problems among Indochinese refugees. *American Journal of Public Health* 7:1003–6.

Evans, F. B., and Anderson, J. G. 1973. The psychocultural origins of achievement and achievement motivation: The Mexican-American family. *Sociology of Education* 46:396–416.

Feather, N. T. 1986. Cross-cultural studies with the Rokeach value survey: The Flinders program of research on values. *Australian Journal of Psychology* 38:269–84.

Finnan, C. R. 1982. Community influences on the occupational adaptation of Vietnamese refugees. *Anthropological Quarterly* 55:126–34.

Fordham, S., and Ogbu, J. U. 1986. Black students' school success: Coping with the "burden of acting white." *Urban Review* 18:176–206.

Foucault, M. 1979. *Discipline and punish: The birth of the prison.* New York: Random House.

Fyans, L. J.; Maehr, M. L.; Salili, F.; and Desai, K. A. 1983. A cross-cultural exploration into the meaning of achievement. *Journal of Personality and Social Psychology* 44:1000–1013.

Galbraith, R. C. 1982. Sibling spacing and intellectual development: A closer look at the confluence models. *Developmental Psychology* 18:151–73.

Gallimore, V.; Boggs, J.; and Jordan, C. 1974. *Culture, behavior and education.* Beverly Hills: Sage.

Garbarino, J. 1982. *Children and families in the social environment.* New York: Aldine.

Garza, R. T., and Herringer, L. G. 1987. Social identity: A multidimensional approach. *Journal of Social Psychology* 127:299–308.

Geertz, C. 1973. *The interpretation of cultures.* New York: Basic Books.

Gibson, M. A. 1982. Reputation and respectability: How competing cultural systems affect students' performance in school. *Anthropology and Education Quarterly* 13:3–27.

Gibson, M. A. 1987a. Punjabi immigrants in an American high school. In *Interpretive ethnography of education: At home and abroad,* ed. G. Spindler and L. Spindler. Hillsdale, N.J.: Erlbaum.

Gibson, M. A. 1987b. The school performance of immigrant minorities. *Anthropology and Education Quarterly* 18:262–75.

Gilford, D. M., and Snyder, J. 1977. *Women and minority Ph.D.'s in the 1970's: A data book.* Washington, D.C.: National Academy of Sciences, Commission on Human Resources.

Gim, W., and Litwin, T. 1980. *Indochinese refugees in America: Profiles of five communities.* Washington, D.C.: U.S. Department of State.

Glass, J.; Bengtson, V. L.; and Dunham, C. C. 1986. Attitude similarity in three-generation families: Socialization, status inheritance, or reciprocal influence? *American Sociological Review* 51:685–98.

Glazer, N., and Moynihan, D. P. 1963. *Beyond the melting pot.* Cambridge, Mass.: MIT Press.

Gorsuch, R. L. 1974. *Factor analysis.* Philadelphia: W. B. Saunders.

Gosling, L. A. P. 1979. Highlands, lowlands, and coasts. In *An introduction to Indochinese history, culture, language and life,* ed. J. K. Whitmore. Ann Arbor: University of Michigan.

Grant, B. 1979. *The Boat People: An "age" investigation.* Harmondsworth, Eng.: Penguin Books.

Grognet, A. 1981. Refugees and the English language: A crucial interface. *Journal of Refugee Resettlement* 1:43–50.

Gurin, P., et al. 1969. Internal-external control in the motivational dynamics of Negro youth. *Journal of Social Issues* 25:29–53.

Haines, D. 1983. Southeast Asian refugees in the United States: An overview. *Migration Today* 2:10–13.

Haines, D.; Rutherford, D.; and Thomas, P. 1981. Family and community among Vietnamese refugees. *International Migration Review,* 15:310–19.

Hale, J. E. 1985. *Black children: Their roots, culture, and learning styles,* 2d ed. Baltimore: Johns Hopkins University Press.

Hanh, P. T. 1979. The family in Vietnam and its social life. In *An introduction to Indochinese history, culture, language and life*, ed. J. K. Whitmore. Ann Arbor: University of Michigan.

Hansen, J. F. 1979. *Sociocultural perspectives on human learning: An introduction to educational anthropology.* Englewood Cliffs, N.J.: Prentice-Hall.

Hansen, S., and Oliver-Smith, A., eds. 1982. *Introduction, involuntary migration and resettlement: The problems and responses of dislocated people.* Boulder, Colo.: Westview Press.

Harackiewicz, J. M.; Sansone, C.; and Manderlink, G. 1985. Competence, achievement orientation, and intrinsic motivation: A process analysis. *Journal of Personality and Social Psychology* 48:493–508.

Harding, R., and Looney, J. 1977. Problems of Southeast Asian children in a refugee camp. *American Journal of Psychiatry* 134:401–11.

Harter, S. 1982. The perceived competence scale for children. *Child Development* 53:87–98.

Hawthorne, L. 1982. *Refugee, the Vietnamese experience.* New York: Oxford University Press.

Heckhausen, H. 1982. The development of achievement motivation. In *Review of child development research* 6, ed. W. W. Hartup. Chicago: University of Chicago Press.

Helmreich, R. L.; Spence, J. T.; and Gibson, R. H. 1982. Sex-role attitudes: 1972–1980. *Personality and Social Psychology Bulletin* 8:656–63.

Hess, R. D.; Chang, C. M.; and McDevitt, T. M. 1987. Cultural variations in family beliefs about children's performance in mathematics: Comparisons among People's Republic of China, Chinese-American, and Caucasian-American families. *Journal of Educational Psychology* 79: 179–88.

Hill, M. S.; Augustyniak, S.; Duncan, G. J.; Gurin, G.; Liker, J. K.; Morgan, J. N.; and Ponza, M. 1985. *Motivation and economic mobility.* Ann Arbor: Institute for Social Research, University of Michigan.

Hofstede, G. 1980. *Culture's consequences: International differences in work related values.* Beverly Hills: Sage.

Hofstede, G. 1986. Cultural differences in teaching and learning. *International Journal of Intercultural Relations* 10:301–20.

Holloway, S. D.; Kashiwagi, K.; Hess, R. D.; and Azuma, H. 1986. Causal attributions by Japanese and American mothers and children about performance in mathematics. *International Journal of Psychology* 21: 269–86.

Howard, J. A. 1987. The conceptualization and measurement of attributions. *Journal of Experimental Social Psychology* 23:32–58.

Hsia, J. 1987. *Asian Americans in higher education and at work.* Hillsdale, N.J.: Erlbaum.

Hsu, F. L. K. 1983. *Rugged individualism reconsidered: Essays in psychological anthropology.* Knoxville: University of Tennessee Press.

Imig, D. R., and Imig, G. L. 1986. Influences of family management and spousal perceptions on stressor pile-up. *Family Relations* 34:227–32.

Ishisaka, H. 1977. Audio-training tapes focused on the mental health of Indo-chinese refugees. Seattle: Department of Health, Education and Welfare, Region X, and Asian Counseling and Referral Service.

Jencks, C., et al. 1972. *Inequality: A reassessment of the effects of family and schooling in America.* New York: Basic Books.

Jencks, C., et al. 1979. *Who gets ahead? The determinants of economic success in America.* New York: Basic Books.

Jones, P. R. 1982. *Vietnamese refugees: A study of their reception and resettlement in the United Kingdom.* London: House Office.

Jung, C. G. 1978. *Psychology and the East.* Princeton, N.J.: Princeton University Press.

Katkovsky, W.; Crandall, V. C.; and Preston, A. 1964. Parent attitudes toward their personal achievements and toward the achievement behavior of their children. *Journal of Genetic Psychology* 104:67–82.

Keats, D. M. 1981. The development of values in adolescents in Malaysia and Australia. In *Perspectives in Asian cross-cultural psychology,* ed. J. L. M. Binne-Dawson, G. H. Blowers, and R. Hoosain. Lisse: Swets and Zeitlinger.

Keats, D. M. 1986. Using the cross-cultural method to study the development of values. *Australian Journal of Psychology* 38:297–308.

Kelley, K.; Cheung, F. M.; Singh, R.; Becker, M. A.; Rodriguez-Carrillo, P.; Wan, C. K.; & Eberly, C. 1986. Chronic self-destructiveness and locus of control in cross-cultural perspective. *Journal of Social Psychology* 126:573–77.

Kelly, G. P. 1977. *From Vietnam to America: A chronicle of the Vietnamese immigration to the United States.* Boulder, Colo.: Westview Press.

Kelly, G. P. 1986. Coping with America: Refugees from Vietnam, Cambodia, and Laos in the 1970s and 1980s. *Annals of the American Academy of Political and Social Sciences* 487:138–49.

Keyes, C. F. 1977. *The golden peninsula: Culture and adaptation in mainland Southeast Asia.* New York: Macmillan.

Khoa, L. X., and VanDeusen, J. 1981. Social and cultural customs: Their contribution to resettlement. *Journal of Refugee Resettlement* 1:48–51.

Kim, C., and Kim, B. C. 1977. Asian immigrants in American law: A look at the past and the challenge which remains. *American University Law Review* 26:390.

Kim, Y. Y., and Nicassio, P. M. 1980. *Survey of agencies and organizations serving Indochinese refugees.* Chicago: Travelers Aid Society of Metropolitan Chicago.

Kingston, M. H. 1978. *The woman warrior: Memories of a girlhood among ghosts.* New York: Knopf.

Kinzie, J. D., and Mason, S. 1983. Five-years' experience with Indochinese refugee psychiatric patients. *Journal of Operational Psychiatry* 14:105–11.

Kish, L. 1965. *Survey planning.* New York: John Wiley.

Klineberg, O.; Zavalloni, M.; Louis-Guerin, C.; and BenBrika, J. 1979. *Students, values, and politics: A crosscultural comparison.* New York: Free Press.

Ko, H. Y. 1986. Minuchin's structural therapy for Vietnamese Chinese families: A systems perspective. *Contemporary Family Therapy* 8:20–32.

Kochman, T. 1982. *Cross-cultural studies in cognition and mathematics.* New York: Academic Press.

Kohlberg, L. 1976. Moral stages and moral development: The cognitive-developmental approach. In *Moral development and behavior: Theory, research and social issues,* ed. T. Lickona. New York: Holt, Rinehart and Winston.

Kohn, M. L. 1976. Social class and parental values: Another confirmation of the relationship. *American Sociological Review* 41:538–45.

Kojima, H. 1984. A significant stride toward the comparative study of control. *American Psychologist* 39:972–73.

Kranichfeld, M. L. 1987. Rethinking family power. *Journal of Family Issues* 8:42–56.

Krausz, S. L. 1986. Sex roles within marriage. *Social Work* 31:457–64.

Kulka, A. 1972. Attributional determinants of achievement-related behavior. *Journal of Personality and Social Psychology* 21:166–74.

Kunstadter, P., ed. 1967. *Southeast Asian tribes, minorities, and nations.* Princeton, N.J.: Princeton University Press.

Kunz, E. F. 1973. The refugee in flight: Kinetic models and forms of displacement. *International Migration Review* 7:125–46.

Kuo, W. H., and Tsai, Y. 1986. Social networking, hardiness, and immigrant's mental health. *Journal of Health and Social Behavior* 27:133–49.

Lancy, D. F. 1983. *Cross-cultural studies in cognition and mathematics.* New York: Academic Press.

Lanphien, C. M. 1983. Refugee resettlement: Models in action. *International Migration Review* 17:22–23.

Lasch, C. 1979. *The culture of narcissism: American life in an age of diminishing expectations.* New York: Norton.

Leacock, W. B. 1969. *Teaching and learning in city schools: A comparative study.* New York: Basic Books.

Lee, D., and DeVos, G. A. 1981. *Koreans in Japan.* Berkeley: University of California Press.

Lefcourt, H.; Martin R.; and Saleh, W. 1984. Locus of control and social support: Interactive moderators of stress. *Journal of Personality and Social Psychology* 47:378–89.

Lefcourt, H. M. 1976. *Locus of control.* Hillsdale, N.J.: Erlbaum.

Leichter, H. J., ed. 1974. *The family as educator.* New York: Teachers College Press.

Lewis, O. 1968a. *La vida, A Puerto Rican family in the culture of poverty: San Juan and New York.* London: Panther Books.

Lewis, O. 1968b. *A study of slum culture: Backgrounds for la vida.* New York: Basic Books.

Liem, N. D. [n.d.] Indochinese cross-cultural adjustment and communication. Unpublished manuscript, University of Hawaii.

Light, I. 1984. Immigrant and ethnic enterprise in North America. *Ethnic and Racial Studies* 4:195–216.

Lin, K. M.; Tazuma, L.; and Masuda, M. 1979. Adaptational problems of Vietnamese refugees. *Archives of General Psychiatry* 35:955–61.

Litwin, T., and Gim, W. 1980. *Indochinese refugees in America: Profiles of five communities.* Washington, D.C.: U.S. Department of State.

Liu, W. T.; Lamanna, M.; and Murata, A. K. 1979. *Transition to nowhere.* Nashville: Charter House Publishers.

McBroom, W. H. 1987. Longitudinal change in sex role orientations: Differences between men and women. *Sex Roles* 16:439–519.

McClelland, D. C. 1961. *The achieving society.* Princeton, N.J.: Van Nostrand.

McClelland, D. C.; Atkinson, J. W.; Clark, R. A.; and Lowell, E. L. 1953. *The achievement motive.* New York: Appleton-Century-Crofts.

McClelland, D. C., and Winter, D. G. 1969. *Motivating economic achievement.* New York: Free Press.

Maccoby, M., and Terzi, K. 1981. What happened to the work ethic? In *Working changes and choices,* ed. J. O'Toole, J. Scheiber, and L. Wood. New York: Human Sciences Press.

McCubbin, H. I.; Joy, C. B.; Cauble, A. E.; Comeau, J. K.; Patterson, J. M.; and Needle, R. H. 1980. Family stress and coping: A decade review. *Journal of Marriage and the Family* 4:855–71.

McGinnes, E.; Nordholm, L. A.; Ward, C. D.; and Bhanthumnavin, D. L. 1974. Sex and cultural differences in perceived locus of control among students in five countries. *Journal of Consulting and Clinical Psychology* 42:451–55.

McInnis, K. 1981. Secondary migration among Indochinese. *Journal of Refugee Resettlement* 1:36–43.

McLean, S. A. 1983. International institutional mechanisms for refugees in U.S. immigration and refugee policy. In *Contemporary transnational migrations in historical perspective: Patterns and dilemmas in U.S. immigration and refugee policy,* ed. M. Kritz. Lexington, Mass.: Lexington Books.

Maehr, M. L. 1974. Cultural and achievement motivation. *American Psychologist* 29:887–96.

Maehr, M. L., and Nicholls, J. G. 1980. Cultural and achievement motivation: A second look. In *Studies in cross-cultural psychology,* Vol. 3, ed. N. Warren. New York: Academic Press.

Mahler, R. 1974. A comparative study of locus of control. *Psychologia* 17:135–38.

Mann, L. 1986. Cross-cultural studies of rules for determining majority and minority decision rights. *Australian Journal of Psychology* 38: 319–28.

March, R. E. 1980. Socioeconomic status of the Indochinese refugees in the United States: Progress and problems. *Social Security Bulletin* 43:11–20.

Meeks, S.; Arnkoff, D. B.; Glass, C. R.; and Notarius, C. I. 1986. Wives' employment status, hassles, communication, and relational efficacy: Intra- versus extra-relationship factors and marital adjustment. *Family Relations* 34:249–55.

Melson, G. F. 1980. *Family environment, an ecosystem approach.* Minneapolis: Burgess Publishing.

Meredith, W. H.; Cramer, S. L.; and Kohn, H. 1981. *Nebraska Indochinese refugee needs assessment.* Lincoln: University of Nebraska.

Michaelson, R. 1969. Americanization: Sacred or Profane Phenomenon? Paper presented at the American Academy of Religion. Cited in Bellah 1971.

Miller, C. L.; Eccles, J. S.; Goldsmith, R.; and Flanagan, C. A. 1987. Parent expectations for adolescent transitions: What they are and how they affect their children. Paper presented at the bienniel meeting of the Society for Research in Child Development, Baltimore.

Mirowsky, J., and Ross, C. E. 1987. Belief in innate sex roles: Sex stratification versus interpersonal influence in marriage. *Journal of Marriage and the Family* 49:527–40.

Mizokawa, D. T., and Ryckman, D. B. 1988. Attributions of academic success and failure to effort or ability: A comparison of six Asian American ethnic groups. Paper presented at the annual meeting of the American Educational Research Association, New Orleans.

Montero, D. 1979. *Vietnamese Americans: Patterns of resettlement and socioeconomic adaptation in the United States.* Boulder, Colo.: Westview Press.

Moore, S. 1977. Old and new approaches to preschool education. *Young Children* 33:69–72.

Mortimer, J. J., and Simmons, R. J. 1978. Adult socialization. In *Annual review of sociology* 4, ed. R. Turner et al. Palo Alto, Calif.: Annual Reviews.

Nakanishi, N. 1982. A report on the 'how do people spend their time survey' in 1980. Reprinted from *Studies of Broadcasting (An International Annual of Broadcasting Science)* 18:93–113.

National Commission on Excellence in Education. 1983. *A nation at risk: The imperative for educational reform.* Washington, D.C.: U.S. Department of Education.

National Research Council, Mathematical Sciences Education Board. 1987. *The under-achieving curriculum: Assessing U.S. school mathematics from an international perspective.* Washington, D.C.: author.

National Science Foundation, National Science Board Commission on Precollege Education in Mathematics, Science, and Technology. 1983. *Educating Americans for the 21st century.* Washington, D.C.: U.S. Government Printing Office.

Nguyen, L. T., and Henkin, A. B. 1982. Vietnamese refugees in the United States: Adaptation and transitional status. *Journal of Ethnic Studies* 9:101–16.

Nguyen, S. D. 1982. Psychiatric and psychosomatic problems among the Southeast Asian refugees. *Psychiatric Journal of the University of Ottawa* 7:163–72.

Nicassio, P., and Pate, J. K. 1984. An analysis of problems of resettlement of the Indochinese refugees in the United States. *Social Psychiatry* 19: 135–41.

Nicassio, P. M. 1983. Psychosocial correlates of alienation: A study of a sample of Indochinese refugees. *Journal of Cross-Cultural Psychology* 14:337–51.

Nicassio, P. M. 1985. The psychosocial adjustment of the Southeast Asian refugee: An overview of empirical findings and theoretical models. *Journal of Cross-Cultural Psychology* 16:153–73.

Nicholls, J. G. 1983. Conceptions of ability and achievement motivation: A theory and its implications for education. In *Learning and motivation in the classroom*, ed. S. G. Paris, G. M. Olson, and H. W. Stevenson. Hillsdale, N.J.: Erlbaum.

North, D. S., et al. 1982. *Kaleidoscope: The resettlement of refugees in the U.S. by the voluntary agencies.* Washington, D.C.: Office of Refugee Resettlement.

Ogbu, J. U. 1983. Minority status and schooling in plural societies. *Comparative Education Review* 27:168–90.

Ogbu, J. U. 1987. Variability in minority responses to schooling: Nonimmigrants vs. immigrants. In *Interpretive ethnography of education at home and abroad,* ed. G. Spindler and L. Spindler. Hillsdale, N.J.: Erlbaum.

Oggins, J. 1987. All in the family: Differing needs, characteristics and service considerations for Southeast Asian refugee groups. Unpublished manuscript. Ann Arbor: University of Michigan.

Olson, D. H., and McCubbin, H. I. 1982. Circumplex model of marital and family systems V: Application to family stress and crisis intervention. In *Family stress: Coping and social support,* ed. H. I. McCubbin, A. E. Cauble, and J. M. Patterson. Springfield, Ill.: C. C. Thomas.

Orfield, G. 1987. *Metropolitan Chicago high schools: Race, poverty and educational opportunity. Working paper #5.* Chicago: University of Chicago.

Orshansky, M. 1969. How poverty is measured. *Monthly Labor Review* 92:37–41.

Ouchi, W. G. 1981. *Theory Z.: How American business can meet the Japanese challenge.* Reading, Mass.: Addison-Wesley.

Padilla, A., ed. 1980. *Acculturation: Theory, models, and some new findings.* Boulder, Colo.: Westview Press.

Parsons, J. E. 1988. Sex differences in mathematics participation. In *Women in science,* ed. M. Steinkamp and M. Maehr. Greenwich, Conn.: JAI Press.

Parsons, J. E.; Adler, T.; and Kaczala, C. 1982. Socialization of achievement attitudes and beliefs: Parental influences. *Child Development* 53:310–21.

Pearl, R. 1985. Cognitive-behavioral interventions for increasing motivation. *Journal of Abnormal Child Psychology* 13:443–54.

Pearlin, L. I., et al. 1981. The stress process. *Journal of Health and Social Behavior* 22:337–56.

Pearlin, L. I., and Schooler, C. 1982. The structure of coping. In *Family stress: Coping and social support,* ed. H. I. McCubbin, A. E. Cauble, and J. M. Patterson. Springfield, Ill.: C. C. Thomas.

Perlman, R. 1976. *The economics of poverty.* New York: McGraw-Hill.

Phommasouvanh, B. 1979. Aspects of Lao family and social life. In *An introduction to Indochinese history, culture, language and life,* ed. J. K. Whitmore. Ann Arbor: University of Michigan.

Pleck, J. H. 1984. The work-family role system. In *Work and family: Changing roles of men and women,* ed. P. Voydanoff. Palo Alto, Calif.: Mayfield.

Raizen, S. 1983. *Science and mathematics in the schools: Report of a convocation.* Washington, D.C.: National Academy Press.

Ramirez, M., and Price-Williams, D. R. 1976. Achievement motivation in children of three ethnic groups in the United States. *Journal of Cross-Cultural Psychology* 7:49–60.

Reisman, D. 1962. *The culturally deprived child.* New York: Harper and Row.

Reitz, H. G., and Groff, G. K. 1974. Economic development and belief in locus of control in four countries. *Journal of Cross-Cultural Psychology* 5:344–55.

Ringer, R. J. 1978. *Looking out for number one.* New York: Fawcett.

Rodgers, J. L. 1984. Confluence effects: Not here, not now! *Developmental Psychology* 20:321–31.

Rogers, B. G. 1985. Review of California Achievement Tests, Forms C and D. In *The ninth mental measurements yearbook, Vol. 1,* ed. J. V. Mitchell, Jr. Lincoln: Buros Institute of Mental Measurements, University of Nebraska.

Rokeach, M. 1973. *The nature of human values.* New York: Free Press.

Romero, G. J., and Garza, R. T. 1986. Attributions for the occupational success/failure of ethnic minority and nonminority women. *Sex Roles* 14:445–52.

Rosen, B., and D'Andrade, R. 1959. The psychosocial origins of achievement motivation. *Sociometry* 22:185–218.

Rosen, B. C. 1956. The achievement syndrome: A psychocultural dimension of social stratification. *American Sociological Review* 21:203–11.

Rosenbaum, M., and Hadari, D. 1985. Personal efficacy, external locus of control, and perceived contingency of parental reinforcement among depressed, paranoid, and normal subjects. *Journal of Personality and Social Psychology* 49:539–47.

Rotter, J. B., and Mulry, R. C. 1965. Internal vs. external control of reinforcement and decision time. *Journal of Personality and Social Psychology* 2:598–604.

Ruble, D. N. 1980. A developmental perspective on theories of achievement motivation. In *Achievement motivation: Recent trends in theory and research,* ed. L. J. Fyans. New York: Plenum Press.

Rumbaut, R. G., and Ima, K. 1987. *The adaptation of Southeast Asian refugee youth: A comparative study.* Final report to Office of Refugee Resettlement. San Diego: San Diego State University.

Rumbaut, R. G., and Weeks, J. R. 1987. Fertility and adaptation among Indochinese refugees in the United States. Unpublished. University of California, San Diego.

Ryckman, D. B., and Mizokawa, D. T. 1988. Causal attributions of academic success and failure: Asian Americans' and white Americans' beliefs about effort and ability. Paper presented at the annual meeting of the American Educational Research Association, New Orleans.

Ryckman, D. B., and Peckham, P. 1987. Gender differences in attributions for success and failure. *Journal of Early Adolescence* 7:47–63.

Schiller, B. R. 1980. *The economics of poverty and discrimination.* Englewood Cliffs, N.J.: Prentice-Hall.

Schooler, C., and Smith, K. C. 1978. " . . . And a Japanese wife." Social structural antecedents of women's role values in Japan. *Sex Roles* 4:23–41.

Schunk, D. H., and Gunn, T. P. 1985. Modeled importance of task strategies and achievement beliefs: Effect on self-efficacy and skill development. *Journal of Early Adolescence* 5:247–58.

Schunk, D. H., and Hanson, A. R. 1985. Peer models: Influence on children's self-efficacy and achievement. *Journal of Educational Psychology* 77:313–22.

Shuval, J. T. 1980. Migration and stress. In *Handbook of stress: Theoretical and clinical aspects,* ed. L. Goldberger and S. Breznitz. New York: Free Press.

Singh, S. 1985. Perceived self-efficacy and intellectual performance of socially disadvantaged students. *Journal of Social Psychology* 125:267–68.

Skinner, B. F. 1984. The shame of American education. *American Psychologist* 39:947–54.

Skinner, K., and Hendricks, G. 1979. The shaping of ethnic self-identity among Indochinese refugees. *Journal of Ethnic Studies* 7:25–41.

Smith, H. L., and Cheung, P. P. L. 1986. Trends in the effects of family background on educational attainment in the Philippines. *American Journal of Sociology* 91:1387–1408.

Smither, R. 1982. Human migration and the acculturation of minorities. *Human Relations* 35:57–68.

Sonquist, J. A., and Morgan, J. N. 1964. *The detection of interaction effects.* Ann Arbor: Institute for Social Research, University of Michigan.

Sonquist, J. A., Baker, E. L., and Morgan, J. N. 1973. *Searching for structure,* rev. ed. Ann Arbor: Institute for Social Research, University of Michigan.

Spence, J. T. 1985. Achievement American style: The rewards and costs of individualism. *American Psychologist* 40:1285–95.

Spradley, J. P., and Phillips, M. 1972. Culture and stress: A quantitative analysis. *American Anthropologist* 74:518–29.

Starr, P. D., and Roberts, A. E. 1982. Community structure and Vietnamese refugee adaptation: The significance of context. *International Migration Review* 16:557–94.

Stein, B. N. 1979. Occupational adjustment of refugees: The Vietnamese in the United States. *International Migration Review* 13:25–45.

Steinberg, S. 1981. *The ethnic myth: Race, ethnicity and class in America.* New York: Atheneum.

Stevenson, H. W.; Lee, S. Y.; and Stigler, J. W. 1986. Mathematics achievements of Chinese, Japanese and American children. *Science* 236:693–98.

Stigler, J. W.; Lee, S.; Lucker, G. W.; and Stevenson, H. W. 1982. Curriculum and achievement in mathematics: A study of elementary school children in Japan, Taiwan, and the United States. *Journal of Educational Psychology* 74:315–22.

Stipek, K. J., and Weisz, J. R. 1981. Perceived personal control and academic achievement. *Review of Educational Research* 51:101–37.

Strand, P. 1984. Employment predictors among Indochinese refugees. *International Migration Review* 18:50–59.

Strand, P. J., and Jones, W., Jr., eds. 1985. *Indochinese refugees in America.* Durham, N.C.: Duke University Press.

Sue, D. 1973. Ethnic identity: The impact of two cultures on the psychological development of Asians in America. In *Asian-Americans: Psychological perspectives,* ed. S. Sue and N. Wagner. Ben Lomond, Calif.: Science and Behavior Books.

Sue, S., and Wagner, N., eds. 1973. *Asian-Americans: Psychological perspectives.* Ben Lomond, Calif.: Science and Behavior Books.

Taft, J.; North, D.; and Ford, D. 1979. *Refugee resettlement in the United States: Time for a new focus.* Washington, D.C.: New TransCentury Foundation.

Taft, R. 1977. Coping with unfamiliar cultures. In *Studies in cross-cultural psychology,* ed. N. Warren. London: Academic Press.

Tai, Ta Van. 1981. The status of women in traditional Vietnam: A comparison of the code of the Le dynasty (1428–1788) with the Chinese codes. *Journal of Asian History* 15:97–145.

Tangri, S. S., and Jenkins, S. R. 1986. Stability and change in role innovation and life plans. *Sex Roles* 14:647–62.

Taylor, D. M., and Dub', L. 1986. Two faces of identity: The "I" and the "we." *Journal of Social Issues* 42:81–98.

Tepper, E. L., ed. 1980. *Southeast Asian exodus: From tradition to resettlement.* Ottawa: Canada Asian Studies Association.

Thoitts, P. A. 1982. Conceptual, methodological and theoretical problems in studying support as a buffer against life stress. *Journal of Health and Social Behavior* 23:145–59.

Thomas, D. R. 1986. Culture and ethnicity: Maintaining the distinction. *Australian Journal of Psychology* 38:371–80.

Thomas, M. E., and Hughes, M. 1986. The continuing significance of race: A study of race, class, and quality of life in America, 1972–1985. *American Sociological Review* 51:830–41.

Thomas, S. B., and Bowermaster, J. 1974. *The continuity of educational development.* (ERIC Document Reproduction Service No. PS 007 571.) Alexandria, Va.: ERIC.

Thurow, L. C. 1969. *Poverty and discrimination.* Washington, D.C.: Brookings Institute.

Tienda, M., and Lii, D.-T. 1987. Minority concentration and earnings inequality: Blacks, Hispanics, and Asians compared. *American Journal of Sociology* 93:141–65.

Timmer, S. G.; Eccles, J.; and O'Brien, K. 1985. How children use time. In *Time, goods and well-being,* ed. T. F. Juster and F. P. Stafford. Ann Arbor: Survey Research Center, Institute for Social Research, University of Michigan.

Townsend, P. 1981. *The girl in the white ship.* Toronto: William Collins.

Toynbee, A. 1972. *A study of history.* New York: Oxford University Press.

Tracinski, E. 1981. *A review of the problem of limited English competence of survey respondents.* Ann Arbor: Survey Research Center, Institute for Social Research, University of Michigan.

Trautmann, M. H. 1987. Sex roles among three groups of male Southeast Asian refugees. Unpublished manuscript. Ann Arbor: University of Michigan.

Triandis, H. C. 1986. The measurement of the etic aspects of individualism and collectivism across cultures. *Australian Journal of Psychology* 38: 257–68.

Trow, M. 1963. The second transformation of American secondary education. *International Journal of Comparative Sociology* 11:144–66.

Tung, T. M. 1980. The Indochinese as patients. *Journal of Refugee Resettlement* 1:53–60.

The Twentieth Century Fund. 1983. *The report of the 20th Century Fund task force on elementary and secondary education policy.* New York: author.

U.S. Bureau of the Census. 1984. *Current population reports. Series P 60 144. Characteristics of the population below the poverty level.* Washington, D.C.: U.S. Government Printing Office.

U.S. Commission on Civil Rights. 1980. *Success of Asian Americans: Fact or fiction?* Washington, D.C.: U.S. Government Printing Office.

U.S. Commission on Civil Rights. 1988. *The economic status of Americans of Asian descent.* Washington, D.C.: U.S. Government Printing Office.

U.S. Department of Education. 1987. *Japanese education today.* Washington, D.C.: U.S. Government Printing Office.

Vandeusen, J.; Coleman, C.; Khoa, L. X.; Phan, D.; Hoeung, H. H.; Chaw, K.; Nguyen, L. T.; Pham, P.; and Bounthinh, T. 1981. Southeast social and cultural customs: Similarities and differences, Part I. *Journal of Refugee Resettlement* 1:20–39.

Vernon, P. E. 1982. *The abilities and achievements of Orientals in North America: A volume in the personality and psychopathology series.* Calgary: Academic Press.

Veroff, J.; Douvan, E.; and Kulka, R. A. 1981. *The inner American: A self-portrait from 1957 to 1976.* New York: Basic Books.

Viviani, N. 1984. *The long journey: Vietnamese migration and settlement in Australia.* Carlton, Victoria: Melbourne University Press.

Vogel, E. F. 1979. *Japan as number one: Lessons for America.* Cambridge, Mass.: Harvard University Press.

Vogt, E. Z., and Albert, E. M., eds. 1970. *People of Rimrock: A study of values in five cultures.* New York: Atheneum.

Vollmer, F. 1986. Why do men have higher expectancy than women? *Sex Roles* 14:351–62.

Waite, L. J.; Rindfuss, R. R.; and De Tray, D. 1986. Mother's expectations for children's schooling in Malaysia. *Journal of Marriage and the Family* 48:527–35.

Warner, R. L. 1986. Alternative strategies for measuring household division of labor: A comparison. *Journal of Family Issues* 7:179–95.

Weber, M. 1958. *The protestant ethic and the spirit of capitalism (1904).* New York: Charles Scribner's Sons.

Weisz, J. R.; Rothbaum, F. M.; and Blackburn, T. C. 1984. Standing out and standing in: The psychology of control in America and Japan. *American Psychologist* 39:955–69.

Whitmore, J. K. 1979. Cultural and religious patterns. In *An introduction to Indochinese history, culture, language and life,* ed. J. K. Whitmore. Ann Arbor: University of Michigan.

Whitmore, J. K. 1984. Social organization and Confucian thought in Vietnam. *Journal of Southeast Asian Studies* 15:296–306.

Whitmore, J. K. 1985. Chinese from Southeast Asia. In *Refugees in the United States,* ed. D. W. Haines. Westport, Conn.: Greenwood.

Williams, C., and Westermeyer, J. 1984. *Refugees and mental health.* New York: Hampshire.

Willson, V. L. 1985. Review of California Achievement Tests, Forms C and

D. In *The ninth mental measurements yearbook, Vol. 1,* ed. J. V. Mitchell, Jr. Lincoln: Buros Institute of Mental Measurements, University of Nebraska.

Wilson, W. J. 1987. *The truly disadvantaged: The innercity, the underclass, and public policy.* Chicago: University of Chicago Press.

Wolpert, J. 1966. Migration as an adjustment to environmental stress. *Journal of Social Issues* 22:92–102.

Wright, A. F. 1962. Values, roles, and personalities. In *The Confucian personality,* ed. A. F. Wright and D. Twitchett. Stanford: Stanford University Press.

Wright, R. 1981. Voluntary agencies and the resettlement of refugees. *International Migration Review* 15:157.

Yankelovich, D., and Immerwahr, J. 1983. *Putting the work ethic to work: A public agenda report on restoring America's competitive vitality.* New York: Public Agenda Foundation.

Yee, D. K. 1987. Participation in family decision-making: Parent and child perspective. Paper presented at the biennial meeting of the Society for Research in Child Development, Baltimore.

Yee, D. K.; Jacobs, J.; and Goldsmith, R. 1986. Sex equity in the home: Parents' influence on their children's attitudes about math. Paper presented at the annual meeting of the American Educational Research Association, San Francisco.

Yockey, J. M. 1978. Role theory and the female sex role. *Sex Roles* 4:917–27.

Zajonc, R. B. 1986. The decline and rise of Scholastic Aptitude scores: A predication derived from the confluence model. *American Psychologist* 41:862–67.

Zajonc, R. B., and Bargh, J. 1980. Birth order, family size, and decline of SAT scores. *American Psychologist* 35:662–68.

Zarb, J. M. 1981. Non-academic predictors of successful academic achievement in a normal adolescent sample. *Adolescence* 16:891–900.

Zavalloni, M. 1980. Values. In *Handbook of cross-cultural psychology 5,* ed. H. Triandis and R. W. Bristin. Newton, Mass: Allyn and Bacon.

Zigler, E. F., and Berman, W. 1983. Discerning the future of early intervention. *American Psychologist* 38:894–906.

Zinsmeister, K. 1987. Asians: Prejudice from top and bottom. *Public Opinion* 10:8–10.

Zolberg, A. R. 1983. *Contemporary transnational migrations in historical perspective: Patterns and dilemmas in U.S. immigration and refugee policy.* Lexington, Mass.: Lexington Books.

Zwingman, C. 1973. The nostalgic phenomenon and its exploitation. In *Uprooting and after,* ed. C. Zwingman and M. Pfister-Ammende. New York: Springer-Verlag.

Index